Comin' Home

Comin' Home

WALTER TOWNES

PAPERBACK: 978-1-7333603-0-2
EBOOK: 978-1-7333603-1-9

Ordering Information:

For orders and inquiries, please contact:
1-888-375-9818
www.toplinkpublishing.com
bookorder@toplinkpublishing.com

Printed in the United States of America

CONTENTS

DEDICATION

To my loving family, especially my wife Kelly, whose strength in our darkest times has been the greatest...and to my biggest fans; my children Jordyn and Jacklyn; my parents Caroline and the late John Townes; my best man Ed; my in-laws Bob and Ann Knapp; my brothers and my late sister Patricia Bailey, the ultimate fighter and the ultimate giver. To the students of the Knox School, to all the dedicated workers at the Boys' Club, who have truly saved the lives of many of our deserving youth.

ACKNOWLEDGMENTS

I sincerely want to thank all of the people who contributed not only to the birth of this novel, but also to my own personal growth and development over the years. First, let me thank my writing team of Tony Kolega and Barry Cohen, who breathed life into my story. I am compelled to give thanks to all those who believed in me from day one, beginning with Reverend John T. Meehan, my original coach, who founded the Archbishop Leadership Project in New York City. Hundreds of young brothers would not be where they are if it wasn't for him. I would also like to give special thanks to my mentors: the late great LeRoy Watkins Sr, LeRoy Watkins Jr, E. William Raynor, Kevin Clark, Armond Hill, Mike Maker, Kevin Cherry, Wally Halas, Don Lizak and the best staff on earth: Ron Rutledge, Brian Mahoney, Al Lobalbo and the great Lou Carnesecca. I can go on forever!

The beauty of this is that these are men from all backgrounds, colors, religions and philosophies. This is truly the American Dream! Let me not forget my boys like Eddie G, Glenn "Magic" Marrow, Rob Summers, Curtis Wilson, James Jones, Steve Pikell, Steve Hayn and all my great players that I coached for 25 years from D1-HS. I could never have accomplished all I have without the strength of my crew: Big Dave, Mike and the rest of the boys on 232nd Street in my old hood.

Last, but not least, let us pay tribute to the strength of the great city of Newark, which has so many Willie Joes, L.J's and Lillians that make it a testament to the continuation of the American Dream!

I would like to thank the great mayors of Newark, Cory Booker, Ras Baraka their great work has continue to produce so many more Willie Joe's in the City of Newark.

Walter "Coach" Townes

I am honored to have had the opportunity to work with such a fine gentleman as Walter Townes. Collaborating on this novel afforded me an opportunity to pull back the lens and merge my own heritage and life experience with Walter's. I was born in the great city of Newark, New Jersey. My parents grew up there. We have seen Newark rise, fall and rise up again. Cities are made of people, not buildings. This novel pays tribute to our similarities, while recognizing our differences. This is the real strength of diversity. May all of America's cities learn the lessons Newark has learned. May each of us learn what home means on the most personal level. It is my sincere hope that we have contributed to your growth with this story.

Barry Cohen

CHAPTER 1

HOME IS. . .

Six year-old Willie Joe sauntered through the apartment doorway, tossing his head with a cavalier glance around the kitchen. His mother, Bernice Cunningham, reeled around from her cooking and glared at him.

"Where have *you* been?", she snapped.

"Outside", Willie Joe answered, maintaining an attitude learned from his older brother, Carlton.

Without a moment's hesitation, Mrs. Cunningham reached over, grabbed Willie Joe by the collar and thrust his face on the table. In one well-practiced, deft move, she snatched up and wielded the wooden spoon from the stove and began beating his bottom with it. Tears welled up in Willie Joe's eyes. He was determined not to cry out. It seemed as though the beating would not end. Finally, she stopped, swung him around to face her and confronted him, her eyes glaring.

"When I ask you a question, I expect a proper answer. Is that clear?"

Willie Joe cowered, his lower lip quivering, as he sheepishly responded.

"Yes, ma'am. I was in the parking lot, playing ball."

"That's better. Now, you go and wash up for dinner. Willie Joe, you need to understand what is going on outside of these walls. The city of Newark is in flames. Brothers are rioting in the streets. You got angry cops and National Guards with tanks and guns, just waitin' to take down Black folks. I need to know where you are at all times. Is that clear now?"

"Yes ma'am."

His pride hurt; his bottom smarted; his ego hurt. Worse than that, when he first looked up from the table, he saw his older brother and the neighbor across the hall standing in the kitchen doorway, smirking. As

1

he wiped the tears from his eyes and cleared his vision, he saw his aunt and uncle observing the scene. The humiliation hurt the worst. Willie Joe felt powerless.

Returning to the table, Willie Joe squirmed in the chair, trying to find a comfortable position while his bottom continued to smart. He only ever remembered one beating worse than this one in his short life. His father had come home from the late shift at the warehouse, drunk. Willie Joe just happened to wake up and fetch a glass of water at the wrong moment. Clarence dragged him to the living room couch and proceeded to lash out at him with his belt, growling that he shouldn't be up so late. Willie Joe skulked back to his room; his father still reeking of cheap whiskey. That was Willie Joe's memory of his fourth birthday. Powerless.

Quiet throughout the dinner, Willie Joe sullenly listened to his mother and his aunt make small talk about church activities, while his father and his uncle discussed the racial unrest that swirled around them. Nobody talked about work. Why should they, when Bernice and her sister toiled as maids for well-to-do white folks in the nearby affluent suburb of West Orange. They almost never talked about it, but Willie Joe knew from the few conversations he had overheard that toiling as a maid was just a day's pay removed from slavery. He had just enough knowledge from school and from television of what Black slavery in America meant. He tried to imagine his own ancestors in chains, cowering in fear to their masters. He understood their powerlessness.

At this early age, Willie Joe had already developed a keen ability to concentrate. He tuned out his mother's and his aunt's conversation, and tuned in to his father and his uncle's discussion of the civil unrest that gripped their little world.

"Maybe I's just old school Clarence, but I prefer to think the good Reverend Dr. King speaks wisely when he preaches non-violence. It say it in the Bible, 'Vengeance is mine, thus saith the Lord', " uncle Benjamin crooned."

"And we just supposed to go out there and get our heads busted, while the White folks got all the guns? Bible says 'An eye for an eye, too'." Clarence shot his older brother-in-law a menacing glance.

Willie Joe wondered who spoke the truth. How could both men be right? To a six year-old, there is only right and wrong; black and white;

2

good and bad; old and young; rich and poor. Shades of gray just had not crept into his young life yet.

Willie Joe "changed the channel" and flipped his listening over to his mother and her sister.

"Did you bake anything for the church bazaar yet this Sunday, Agnes?" Bernice queried.

"I did, child; I did. I done baked two pies—a cherry and a rhubarb. I hear tell the Reverend Cabbagepatch will give a guest sermon this Sunday. Do you remember when he did our weddin'? Why, folks is still talkin' about it all these years later."

Willie Joe pondered how men and women could think so differently. He searched his brief existence to try and understand why. No matter. Both conversations bored him after a time. He looked up to see his brother Carlton staring off into space. Willie Joe felt better, knowing his older, more worldly brother became just as bored as he did. Carlton, after all, had twelve more years on this earth than Willie Joe, so Willie Joe figured he must know more. But he really didn't. Willie Joe just couldn't put his finger on it, but something had happened to Carlton lately. It had nothing to do with the riots either. He just seemed more distant, more withdrawn and less communicative. It seemed like the person inside of Carlton just got up and walked away one day, never to return. Maybe it had something to do with Carlton not finishing school and graduating with his class. Maybe it was that girl who hung around him all the time.

Willie Joe changed the channel in his head again. Back to mom and aunt Agnes. Both women seemed to bear the curse of so many Black females— built like beasts of burden, with broad shoulders, large breasts, thick waists and limbs like tree trunks. Destined to spend their lives performing painful manual labor. Willie Joe thought about it, as he studied the two women. Maybe it was a blessing and not a curse, after all. Maybe if these women grew up weak they would have had no means of survival—for themselves or for their families. It occurred to Willie Joe that without mothers, Black families would probably collapse. Despite the harsh discipline she had given him, deep down, Willie Joe knew that Bernice Cunningham wanted only the best for him.

The dinner ended quietly, with the whole family enjoying dessert. Clarence and uncle Benjamin retired to the living room for a smoke, trying to find some peacefulness while the war in the streets still raged on, outside the project doors. Benjamin took a long drag on his cigar; Clarence on his cigarette. Both men silently acknowledged the other. In the kitchen, meanwhile, Bernice and Aunt Agnes washed and dried the dishes, looking forward to a brief respite ahead, before the start of the next morning's work. Willie Joe followed Carlton into the tiny bedroom they shared. Carlton grabbed his jacket and dashed out the door. Willie Joe asked Carlton when he would be home.

"Don' matter none; this ain't much of a home," Carlton retorted.

"But it's *our* home," Willie Joe pleaded.

"Maybe fo' you; out there is fo' me", Carlton answered, as he swung around.

Willie Joe felt a touch of sadness as he watched his brother disappear from view. Willie Joe settled down to his books, left to do his homework alone. A short time later, he emerged, sleepy, to kiss his aunt and uncle goodbye.

"Now, you mind your folks, Willie Joe, and the good Lord will keep watchin' over you" uncle Benjamin sternly admonished."

"Yes, sir, uncle Ben", Willie Joe echoed.

He sincerely liked—not only loved, his uncle. Sometimes he even wished his dad could be more like his uncle. Secretly—and he only just now admitted this to himself—he wished his uncle *was* his dad. Uncle Ben had a quiet strength; a quiet confidence, a resolve. He didn't need anyone to tell him how good a man he was. He never seemed to need to prove anything to anyone. Ben Washington accepted his lot in life. He somehow appeared less downtrodden than all the other Black men Willie Joe had met in his six years. *Not as powerless.*

Aunt Agnes hugged Willie Joe hard, as if she didn't expect to see him again for a long time. She and Bernice were more than just sisters—they were kindred spirits. They thought alike. Willie Joe prepared for bed and kissed his parents good night. Still no Carlton. Still feeling powerless.

At least the Cunninghams lived in New Jersey. They could only imagine the horror that still occurred in the racially segregated South. The family had once visited relatives in Georgia just a few short years ago. Willie Joe was only three years old. He would never forget the stares he got when his father took him to a gas station and asked the attendant for the rest room key. The attendant, a teenage white boy, sent them around the back of the building to a door marked "Colored." Hard to believe that in mid-twentieth century America, land of the free, these things still happened. As they prepared to leave Georgia on that trip to head home, Bernice shielded Willie Joe's eyes from the sight of a rope hung over a tree, with a noose dangling from the limb. It was one of the only things his young eyes *didn't* see. Clarence prayed that the family would not get stopped by the highway patrol. Police in the South relished the sight of a Black family in fear, as they drew out the torment and the humiliation. Clarence was convinced they must don the Ku Klux Klan robes after work.

During his parents' youth, Newark, New Jersey had reached a pinnacle of prominence among America's small cities. Newark bustled with commerce and industry; families made their homes there for generations and a phenomenal infrastructure of bus and rail lines developed. Then, in the aftermath of World War II, as people—White people, began to experience an explosion of prosperity, they exited the city en masse. Sprawling suburbs stretched out, taking over farmlands. The baby boom was in full swing. As the affluent White population moved their homes out, they patronized the businesses in their new communities. Newark paid the price. Many of them kept their own businesses in Newark, commuting in to work daily. The city began to age; apartment buildings, bridges and even private homes began to crumble from neglect. City-owned housing projects rose into the skyline, gradually replacing the deteriorating slums. Projects like the one Willie Joe's family occupied were built on White guilt. Black folks remained in Newark. Despair mounted. Desperation flared.

Shortly after an outbreak of rioting and looting in the Watts section of Los Angeles, California, like a raging plague, 1967 brought riots to Newark, New Jersey and even the nearby small city of Plainfield, New Jersey. The streets were no longer safe—for anyone. Angry mobs of Black youths challenged police armed to the teeth, dressed in riot gear. Nearly every store window shattered, as the mobs pillaged and plundered. The city became polarized. In the predominantly Italian-American North Ward of Newark, Councilman Anthony Imperiale drove his army tank up and down the streets, in a macho showing of power designed to intimidate the city's Black population. Apparently, it worked. The riots never touched those neighborhoods. The Jewish business owners had a different story to tell. They emulated the Black business owners, lettering

5

their store windows with the words "Soul Brother", in an effort to fend off any attacks. Maybe the commonality of their ancestral struggle lessened the friction and the animosity. After all, the largely Christian Black population read the Jewish Bible every Sunday in church. Somehow, though, the stories of centuries old enslavement of Jews by Egyptians and Babylonians had not filtered down to 1967. Jews were still White; they must be the oppressors.

CHAPTER 2

DEAR TO OUR HEARTS

Dignity came the hardest in the Newark ghetto. Parents could work two jobs; kids could struggle to stay in school; dedicated teachers would put their heart and soul into looking after downtrodden Black children. Many came to school without breakfast in their bellies; many wore ill-fitting hand-me-down clothes; some bore the scars of abuse like war-torn soldiers. Nearly all of them dragged hopelessness wherever they went, like prisoners of old, with leg irons and a ball and chain. Willie Joe liked school. It gave him a certain peace; a kind of knowing that something better existed outside the project walls. He thirsted for knowledge; school gave it to him. His school was hardly a cocoon. Still, it provided a safe haven. The violence and drugs had not yet trickled down to the first grade. It seemed as though the older you got, the more dangerous life became in Willie Joe's world.

Willie Joe's teacher, Mrs. Abernathy, took a genuine interest in every child's welfare. Little things mattered. Did the children look washed? She knew some of them barely had running water at home. Did they appear to have slept? She knew some of them only had cots, or slept on second-hand blankets on the floor. Mrs. Abernathy paid attention to detail. One day, she quietly approached Christa, one of Willie Joe's classmates, and escorted her into the hallway. Willie Joe could see them through the window in the door, but could not quite read their lips. He knew something seemed amiss. Christa fidgeted, became agitated, then ran off and disappeared from view. Mrs. Abernathy returned. Willie Joe later learned that Christa's older sister had left their building in an ambulance the night before, and had not returned. Christa's family lived in the same building as Mrs. Abernathy. Christa never returned to class.

It bothered Willie Joe. Still, he continued to read on, burying himself deeper in his history book. Maybe Columbus had a doctor on one of his ships. Maybe a doctor like that could save Christa's sister. Willie Joe tried to imagine an America without cities, ghettos and projects—or riots and violence.

In spite of Clarence's drinking bouts and Carlton's disappearing acts, one thing the Cunningham family managed to do was go to Church together every Sunday. They attended Newark's Beulah Baptist Church on South 12th Street. Willie Joe liked Church. It went beyond having another safe haven, a sense of family—even beyond the sense of community. Willie Joe liked the choir and the music, the colorful choir robes, the pastor; but it went deeper. Church felt more like home than even home or school. When he listened to the sermons, Willie Joe felt proud, and not quite so powerless either. At six, he couldn't quite put his finger on it, but the *spirit* moved him. The Cunninghams' church, Beulah Baptist Church, a small predominantly Black congregation, seemed to beat like the heart of their community. Nothing could quite pierce it. The members made up its lifeblood; it pumped on, even through the smoke and ashes surrounding it. Then, that changed, too.

It started out like every Sunday. The Cunninghams donned their Sunday best; they gathered around their closest friends on the church steps before the pastor arrived. Willie Joe heard the organ begin to play inside. Suddenly, the peaceful scene turned to panic. Three police cars pulled up to the church. Officers in full riot gear surrounded the crowd on the steps. One policeman, a burly White man, grabbed a bullhorn, ordering the crowd to disperse. A young congregant from the church slowly made his way to the front of the group. Tension mounted; sweat beaded up on the young man's forehead. The officer with the bullhorn approached, squaring off with him, toe-to-toe. The crowd seemed to draw one collective breath. The young man, Freddie Lawrence, spoke.

"We would like to invite you to our service. All are welcome here. The Lord does not discriminate."

The officer rudely turned his back, signaled to the riot squad and as quickly as they had appeared, lights flashing, guns brandished, the police got back in their cars and left the church. Willie Joe marched into the church, wide-eyed, impressed by the sheer power of the young man's words—not to mention the courage he displayed. The rest of the congregation filed in, took their seats and listened to the pastor as he read from the Old Testament book of Isaiah.

"And ye shall beat your swords into plowshares, your spears into pruning hooks; yea, nation shall not lift up sword against nation; ye shall make war no more."

The words suddenly became very real. Willie Joe could not grasp the concept of deep-seated hatred. Why should anyone hate anyone else because of their color, their religion or their nationality? It just didn't make sense. His mind wandered back to ancient times. He imagined the slave masters of old, standing over the Israelites, as they forced them to make bricks in the hot sun. They, too, felt powerless.

Willie Joe glanced to his right, where Carlton sat hunched over. He looked as though he only pretended to follow along as the congregation read the hymns. Where did his mind drift off to? Willie Joe wished he knew. He just kept slipping further and further away. Suddenly, Carlton snapped out of his daze and darted a glance back at Willie Joe. For the first time in a long time, he flashed a smile at his admiring little brother. At one time, he had almost been a father figure, looking after Willie Joe the toddler when his parents went off to work. They had a bond then; not a strong one—more of a dutiful one, but just the same, they had one. Now, the feeling had faded. Carlton was not Carlton any more. He slept odd hours; disappeared for whole nights at a time; he hardly communicated with anyone in the family. Still, he had not lost his sense of humanity.

Clarence unfolded a few wrinkled bills from his wallet, carefully laying them in the collection plate. Bernice opened her change purse and emptied the week's tips onto the plate. Willie Joe watched in awe as Carlton withdrew a wad of bills from his pants pocket, placing several on the family fortune. He wondered where his brother could have gotten that much money. No matter. Willie Joe happily placed two quarters on the plate before passing it to the family seated next to them. Shabbily dressed, the older man placed a folded up piece of paper on the plate. It didn't look like money to Willie Joe. It looked like a note. Maybe it was a prayer. Willie Joe looked down. The man's shoes were worn right through. He could see what looked like a piece of shirt cardboard from the cleaners stuffed in the soles. Willie Joe set to wondering. If there is a

God—and he absolutely believed there was—how could he allow people to be so poor?

The shabbily dressed man reached over and took his wife's hand. She had some kind of an illness. She shook profusely. Willie Joe had never seen anything like it. Bernice gave him a nudge, as if to stop him from staring. In the next few moments, Willie Joe witnessed something he never could have even imagined. His father Clarence knelt down, oblivious to whatever passage the congregation read, tears welled up in his eyes, and he began to beseech the Lord with his own private prayer— for the shabbily dressed man and his shaking wife. As he got back up and took his seat, Bernice leaned over and kissed Clarence on the cheek. The man did not speak, but Willie Joe could read the gratefulness in his eyes. When the church service ended, Willie Joe looked around, but the couple had left in haste. He looked up at the church window. He looked away, but felt compelled to look back. He saw the outline of a bird silhouetted on the window behind the pulpit, right over the pastor's shoulder. Willie Joe thought it must be an angel. His gaze went upward to the vaulted ceiling of the small modest church. He distinctly heard the flutter of wings. The nearness of unstoppable violence rocked Willie Joe's world. If people could disrupt a religious gathering at a church, no place on earth seemed safe.

CHAPTER 3

CLOSE CALL

Willie Joe sat by the apartment window, watching the rain as it seemingly waxed the streets down below. A few random people scurried across the street like mice, holding their hats and their umbrellas; just little insignificant dots of color. The rhythm of the rain soothed Willie Joe as he listened to the drops bouncing off the project windows. It helped block out the sounds of angry neighbors arguing across the hall. Willie Joe wondered. He wondered about Clarence's drinking bouts; he wondered how long Bernice could hold the family together; he especially wondered about Carlton—where he went, whose company he chose over the family's…what he was doing during the long stretches he spent away from home.

In the next room, Willie Joe heard the chips clacking and the cards snapping as Clarence and his uncle Ben played hand after hand of cards. The room reeked of cheap whiskey. He faintly heard Bernice and Aunt Agnes practicing hymns in the bedroom. The hymns comforted Willie Joe, transporting him to another and a better place. He wondered about heaven. Did Black people have their own places in heaven? Did Black and White people get along better in heaven than on earth? Did they have guns and violence in heaven, or did everyone respect one another? He struggled with this last thought. If we were already dead when we went to heaven, no one could kill us, so they must not have guns and violence in heaven—but they could still have hatred, he reasoned.

Suddenly, Willie Joe heard a loud crash that broke his concentration and swiftly transported him back to the apartment living room. The door swung open and his brother Carlton stumbled in, falling to the floor. The next few minutes all ran into a blur. Clarence and Ben ran to

Carlton. Willie Joe stood up, terrified. The hymns continued from the other room.

"He's bleeding bad, Ben."

"I'll call for help."

"I'll get ice and some bandages."

"Willie Joe, get your mama out here now!"

The two men struggled, trying to stop the bleeding. Carlton breathed, but shallowly. Bernice and Agnes burst into the room. When they saw Carlton's bloody shirt, they screamed in panic.

"Did you call an ambulance, Clarence?"

"They on the way, Bernice. Ben took care of it."

"Call the police; you got to call the police."

"No po-lice is coming into this house, Bernice. No po-lice," Clarence asserted.

Carlton's breathing seemed regular, yet grew weaker by the moment. His eyes rolled back in his head, glazed over with a lifeless quality. He started to convulse slightly; then, ever more intensely. He broke into a sweat. Willie Joe heard the sirens, ran to the window just in time to see the ambulance parked below. He worried. They had twenty-three floors to go before they would reach the Cunningham apartment. Then he noticed for the first time ever, the black and blue marks up and down Carlton's arm.

Neighbors began appearing in the doorway, anxiously peering in to the Cunningham apartment. Then, a whole crew of emergency medical personnel marched in through the doorway, lugging stretchers, oxygen tanks and more medical equipment than Willie Joe had ever seen. Two white men, an Asian woman—probably a Filipino, one Black man and one Hispanic man gathered around Carlton. He had stopped convulsing, but lay there almost lifeless.

"Gunshot wound", the Asian woman shouted into the walkie-talkie as she slipped the blood pressure cuff around Carlton's limp arm.

"Eighty over fifty; come on. Let's not lose him", the Black man shouted, his nostrils flaring.

"Epinephrine; fifty cc's; quickly—let's go!" one of the two White men barked. The Hispanic man injected Carlton; his eyes slowly came back to life. The Filipino woman held a fresh dressing over the wound.

"Stretcher; get it ready", the other White man ordered. Without pausing a beat, the Black man and the Hispanic man rolled Carlton onto the stretcher and left the apartment as the rest of the group packed up their equipment and followed them out, one by one.

"Where you takin' him?" Clarence asked, quickly zipping up his jacket.

"Beth Israel; it's the closest hospital", the Filipino woman replied.

"Can I ride with you, please?" Clarence nearly begged.

"Okay, let's go."

As they squeezed into the elevator, tears welled up in Clarence's eyes. Carlton showed a sign of recognition. Clarence prayed. Upstairs, in the Cunningham apartment, Agnes dialed the phone nervously as Bernice buttoned her raincoat.

"Yes, I need a taxicab right away. The address it fifty-four Dayton Street— you won't send anyone to the projects? I see. Saint Lucien cab company? I'll try them. Thank you."

"Thank you sister. You'll stay here with Willie Joe? We'll call you from the hospital."

Willie Joe felt bad enough about Carlton's condition. He felt worse that he could not help in any way. Powerless again. Bernice hugged him before running out the door. Willie Joe resumed his seat at the window. He had seen so much in his six brief years. At least the rioting had stopped. Still, the city knew no peace. The Cunningham household knew no peace. Willie Joe wished he could have stopped Carlton. The drugs were bad enough, but a gunshot wound? He prayed his brother would live. He watched the ambulance pull away, sirens blaring and lights flashing. The gentle rain washed down Willie Joe's world. Maybe God cried for Carlton.

CHAPTER 4
THE HEALING BEGINS

Two weeks had passed since Carlton staggered into the Cunningham apartment, bleeding from the gunshot wound. Hospital rules forbade Willie Joe from visiting; you had to be twelve years old for admission into the intensive care and critical care units. Aunt Agnes and Uncle Ben stayed with him whenever they didn't have to work, so Bernice and Clarence could hold their daily bedside vigil at the hospital. Beth Israel Medical Center had served the community for many years. It was a Jewish hospital, but they didn't discriminate. Hurt and sick had many colors.

The healing had only begun. Carlton got stronger, but the unspoken would soon have to surface. How had he become addicted to the drugs? Who supplied him with the drugs? How did he end up in an altercation that left him with a gunshot wound? The incident had ripped a gash in the fabric of the Cunningham family, as well. More healing needed. Then, outside the hospital walls, although the rioting had ended, the healing of this once great city had not even begun yet. The racial tension, the anger, the destruction hung over it like a pall. Silent, yet deadly.

Carlton pressed the button, raising the hospital bed as the team of doctors, nurses and aides filed in. They poked here, prodded there, nodded their heads, then left his room, one by one. Clarence followed them into the hallway, as Bernice remained by Carlton's bedside.

"Excuse me, please, but what is going to be with my boy?" Clarence intoned.

"He's doing well, Mr. Cunningham", the older white-haired doctor replied, wiping his glasses on his lab coat.

"I mean, what is his condition, and how is he progressing?" Clarence asked, revealing his annoyance. The doctors often failed to communicate with patients' families.

"Mr. Cunningham, your son had massive quantities of illicit drugs in his system, along with a severe gunshot wound. You can see for yourself; he is progressing well under the circumstances. We're doing all we can for him.

He should make a full recovery in time—if he stays clean."

The embarrassment overtook Clarence. He wanted to ask Dr. Schwartz more questions, but he became overwhelmed. The gravity of the situation had begun to sink in. Before that, he must have been numb—functioning on autopilot. He kept asking himself how this could happen. Then, as he stood there in the hallway, staring into the hospital room at his wife, holding his son's hand, it finally became clear. Clarence's drinking spawned the conditions for Carlton's drug habit. Yes, his son had chosen to take the drugs, but his own addiction to alcohol gave Carlton a tacit approval, a reinforcement for his behavior. Clarence finally made the painful connection.

In spite of his own guilt, Clarence was torn between his anger at Carlton, and his love for his son. He slowly made his way back into the room and took his place by Bernice's side. Bernice suffered in silence. She refused to struggle with the questions—the why this and why that. Instead, she focused her energy and her strength on Carlton's recovery… and her role, to keep the family together.

Just then, a huge imposing figure triumphantly marched into the room. The Reverend Pearl's sheer size got him noticed wherever he went. His booming bellicose voice turned heads in church, on the street— anywhere. He removed his jacket, revealing his purple robes. Then, he gently leaned over and kissed Bernice on the cheek. Turning to Clarence, he gripped his hand with both of his own massive hands and stared into his eyes.

"We got a whole lot o' healin' to do here, so let's get started," he proclaimed, as if he was at the pulpit, delivering a powerful sermon.

Reverend Pearl took his Bible out of his jacket pocket and began what looked like a ritual. It seemed as though he sought to drive the drug demons out of Carlton. Clarence and Bernice stood by, holding hands.

The room nearly shook from his voice. He read psalms; he read hymns; he read from prophecies. All the while, Carlton slept.

Finally, the day came when the troupe of doctors and nurses returned. As they went through their head-nodding ritual, the technicians and aides began to disconnect the tubes and wires that had become extensions of Carlton's person. In a few short moments, they began to load him into a wheelchair. After that, the elevator took him to a regular room. The atmosphere was notably different. Suddenly, a great deal of weight was lifted from the Cunninghams' shoulders. It seemed as though, finally, the Carlton they knew had returned. He spoke, he sat up, he ate, he talked—he even joked. He stared down at the remaining bruises on his arm. The marks left by the hospital intravenous tubes reminded him of the needle marks he had made, injecting himself. It was time. Carlton made the first move.

"Mom and dad, I'm sorry; I didn't mean to hurt you this way. Things just —just—kinda' got out of control," Carlton stammered.

"What are we gonna' do about all this?" Clarence motioned, as he sat across from his son.

"I dunno' yet; I need some time," Carlton replied.

"You got to set a good example for your brother," Bernice asserted.

Carlton turned away. He began to realize how much he had hurt everyone around him—not just himself. He never even imagined anything like the drug deal gone bad could or would happen to him. For the first time, he began to replay the scene in his mind. He had no answers for his parents. He began to see them in a different light for the first time. The clarity that came after withdrawal. He began to realize that, in his frustration over life in the city, he had made everything all about *him*. Very selfish. It only now occurred to him how much his parents had sacrificed for his brother and for himself. He began to notice how gray his father had become. For the first time, he noticed the awful calluses on his mother's hands, the badge she earned for her years of scrubbing other people's homes clean. He ached inside, in silence.

Clarence and Bernice kissed Carlton good night, and left the hospital arm in arm. Every visit seemed to press down upon them, even though Carlton healed and regained strength. They each wondered if he would ever come back to them. They felt they had lost their grip. And they had.

CHAPTER 5

A LONG WAY TO GO

Carlton's homecoming came and went, without a lot of fanfare. Clarence and Bernice just had too much to do, working and taking care of their family. Carlton would have to get the help he needed and make the right choices on his own. Clarence had gone to a few Alcoholics Anonymous meetings, but he just could not bring himself to keep going—or to stop drinking. He did, however, learn a few important things from those meetings. He learned that he had to "Let go; let God" when it came to Carlton. He could not force or control the outcome.

Life in the Cunningham household continued on as it had before. Willie Joe celebrated his seventh birthday in style. All of his favorite people surrounded him as he blew out the candles on the cake Bernice had baked for him. Aunt Agnes and Uncle Ben; Carlton, of course; Bernice and Clarence; the Hancock twins from across the hall. He proudly looked up after he extinguished every candle with his powerful gust of wind.

"Ain't you gonna tell us whatcha wished fo'?" Uncle Ben inquired.

"Thass' a secret, Ben; bad luck. You know that. He don't hafta tell," Aunt Agnes assured Willie Joe.

Willie Joe reflected for a moment, as he locked away his wish in a secret place so no one could read his mind. Only he knew that he had wished his brother would stay off the drugs—and his father would stop drinking.

The moment had that surreal quality, almost like a dream. For a few seconds, time stopped; the voices became distant; everyone glowed, almost like a Renaissance painting—like the "Last Supper". The scene etched itself into Willie Joe's memory. He would always remember it, fondly. For once, he felt as though everyone really cared about each other. At least, that's how it looked to a seven year-old.

The undercurrent still existed in the room. Did they live in denial, or did the family just not see? They put on their party masks for the occasion. When it was over, would they go right back to doing the things that hurt the ones they loved?

Willie Joe opened his presents, one by one. As he peeled back the wrappings, his eyes grew wide with anticipation. For the first time, he had new clothes—not Carlton's hand-me-downs. He cherished the moment; he felt the love. For the first time, he felt really important.

Willie Joe opened the last box with a fervor, cutting the ribbon and tearing at the wrappings. As he tossed the tissue paper aside, he could not believe his eyes. A brand new basketball! Nothing could have thrilled him more— except, of course, if his brother were on the court playing with him. He examined it like a fine object of art, made of precious gold and jewels. This would light up his life; he was sure of it.

Willie Joe hugged each of his guests, thanking them one by one for the magical celebration they had given him. Then came the goodbyes. Holding back a tear, he kissed Aunt Agnes and Uncle Ben before they left the apartment. The Hancock twins sauntered home, across the hall. Willie Joe had followed them to their door. He returned home to find Clarence in his high-backed chair, drink in hand, as Bernice began to wash the dishes. No Carlton. Willie Joe felt a twinge, holding his breath. He bit his lip. He would not show his concern. Again, he felt powerless.

"Mom, can I go downstairs and play basketball for a while?" Willie Joe pleaded.

"Yes, you may. Just be careful, please—and don't be gone too long," Bernice replied.

Willie Joe proudly marched to the elevator, his new basketball tucked under his arm like a prize. The whole ride down, he had visions in his head of becoming the next great basketball star. He had heard of Cleo Hill, Newark's own rising star. Maybe he would become the next Cleo Hill. The elevator creaked its way down the twenty-three stories, occasionally stopping and opening. Nobody got on. No matter; Willie Joe was happy to be alone. Finally, the doors parted and he saw daylight. He wondered if the sky got brighter when you went to the White people's neighborhoods.

Somebody had enough foresight when they built the projects to at least think of the children. Although they showed the signs of wear and tear, in the courtyard, in the shadow of the four tall buildings, stood swings, a slide and two basketball backboards. The nets were long gone. Nobody around. Willie Joe began to dribble the ball, pulling from memory what he used to watch Carlton do on this same court. The blacktop had begun to crumble; the foul line's paint had faded.

Willie Joe pretended to dribble past his imaginary opponent, who guarded him closely. He went for the lay-up…and missed. Catching the ball on the rebound, he clumsily dribbled all the way to back court—and went for the long shot. To his surprise, the ball went in, effortlessly! Luck? He didn't think so. Encouraged, he continued to play against his imaginary adversaries. Willie Joe recalled watching a basketball game on television. He had seen some of the greatest players—the New York Knicks and the Philadelphia Seventy-Sixers battle it out. He pulled the memories out of his head like a film. Suddenly, they were right there. All the players he had watched graced the humble court at his projects. Why wait? Willie Joe joined in the imaginary game, dodging the players one by one. It didn't matter that he was only seven. He flew right past them and rose up for the jump. The ball seemed suspended for a moment, then hugged the rim as it circled it, then dropped in. Willie Joe triumphantly jumped for joy. He could almost hear the buzzer go off, signaling the end of the quarter. He watched the imaginary scoreboard light up, and for the first time *he felt powerful*. He had found his place.

A few more imaginary plays and Willie Joe tucked the ball under his arm and headed back to his building. Somehow the ride up in the elevator seemed to go much faster and much smoother. He arrived at the door of the Cunningham apartment. He heard voices. His parents argued. He stopped in his tracks.

"We let Carlton fall through the cracks; he just slipped right between our fingers. We gonna do the same with Willie Joe?" Bernice snapped at Clarence.

Clarence glared at her, taking another long belt of cheap whiskey from his glass.

"We both workin'. How we gonna keep an eye on him all the time?" Clarence retorted.

"You got to spend some time with him when you're not working. He needs you. Look at you, half in the bag. It's a wonder you're not sick from all you drink. I tell you, one day, it's gonna get you. You could have been down there with him, shooting some baskets—if you could stand up," Bernice admonished.

Clarence did not answer. He knew the demon in the bottle had him in its clutches.

Willie Joe slowly opened the door, cautiously looking around it before he entered the apartment.

"Go do your homework," Clarence commanded him.

"It's done, sir," Willie Joe responded weakly, fearing another outburst. He was all too familiar with Clarence's erratic blow-ups.

"Then just go to your room. Your mother and I are having a talk," Clarence ordered.

"Yes, sir," Willie Joe answered and obeyed, still fearing the unpredictable and uncontrollable wrath that came from his father's rage...rage in a bottle; that's where it came from.

Powerless again. Willie Joe strode into the room he had shared with Carlton since birth, hung up his jacket, carefully placed the basketball safely in the corner and lay on his bed. The voices resumed; he tuned them out. He returned to the basketball court in his mind. He invented new plays, new moves. He just kept scoring...and scoring...and scoring... until he fell asleep.

Willie Joe dreamt...like he never dreamt before. What was this place? From the outside, it looked like a church. He entered. The inside looked like a gymnasium. People just started to appear in groups, filling the bleachers. Nobody looked familiar. Willie Joe stood center court. Then, a team of medical people wheeled Carlton in on a hospital bed and left him there. He looked dead. None of the machines worked. Where were his parents? Another medical team wheeled in another bed. Willie Joe approached it, as his father lay there, clutching his stomach. Willie Joe backed away. He swung around to find his mother scrubbing the floor feverishly. The room went dark. Suddenly, all the people disappeared. The lights came back up. A man in uniform lead Willie Joe outside, into the sunlit world.

The smell of bacon frying and the sun streaming through the apartment window woke Willie Joe. He quickly dressed for school, grabbed his books and slid into the chair at the breakfast table. No Carlton. He secretly worried. Bernice finished cooking their breakfast and sat across from him. Clarence worked the night shift. He would not wake up for a few hours. Willie Joe looked forward to a day at school. Nobody argued there. He finished his breakfast, peered out the living room window and saw the bus ambling down the street, heading for the projects. Willie Joe kissed Bernice goodbye and headed for the elevator. The ride down always seemed longer.

CHAPTER 6

DUST TO DUST

Sometimes the peculiar reigns; sometimes the abnormal rules. For Willie Joe, most of life's mysteries just required acceptance. They kind of came together in bits and pieces, like a patchwork quilt. Time marched on; not much had changed in the Cunningham household—or in the city of Newark. Clarence drank; Carlton disappeared; Bernice worked and Willie Joe went to school. It seemed as though that patchwork quilt unraveled faster than Bernice could stitch the family together.

A year had come and gone since Willie Joe remembered first having the dream where Carlton died and his father got sick. He had it again. And then again. And then again. He didn't know much about dreams, but he knew to trust them. They represented ancient wisdom. Willie Joe remembered a rabbi from the Jewish temple visiting Beulah Baptist Church to give a guest sermon. He paid rapt attention to the man with the long gray beard. He distinctly remembered him quoting an old Hebrew proverb that read, "A dream not interpreted is like a letter not read." Willie Joe wondered about that. His dream troubled him. He wished he could ask the rabbi about it. He said his own little private prayer the next Sunday in church. It was his eighth birthday, so he was sure his prayer would carry a special meaning—like the day he heard the fluttering of wings and guessed it must be an angel.

He just couldn't bring himself to tell anyone else about his troubling dreams—or to ask for help. Then, slowly, the answers came; the truths unfolded—the knowing came. After returning home from church the following week, Willie Joe witnessed what prophesy meant, firsthand. As usual, Clarence sat in his chair, his tie loosened, with his drink in hand. Suddenly, Willie Joe saw him clench his stomach with both hands, exactly as he had done in the dream. It had begun. Then, his complexion began to change. Willie Joe could not believe his eyes. How could a Black man turn yellowish? He didn't know what it meant, but he knew it meant trouble. Bernice had gone to Aunt Agnes's; Carlton was out, as usual—it was up to him. Willie Joe had to take charge of the situation. He immediately *felt powerful.*

Clarence just moaned. He didn't move. Frightened, Willie Joe went to the phone and called the community health clinic. Nobody answered. It was Sunday. The Lord worked on Sunday. Why didn't doctors? He looked over at his father. Clarence looked worse—if that was possible. Only one thing to do. Willie Joe dialed Aunt Agnes's number. It rang. And rang. And rang. And rang.

Willie Joe looked out the living room window of the apartment. It was a gray day, overcast. Not a soul in sight. Then, he spied a taxicab pulling up to his building. He hoped and prayed it would be his mother. Sure enough, he recognized her as she emerged from the cab, clutching packages. The elevator couldn't go fast enough. He remembered how it always felt faster going up. He hoped that wasn't just his imagination. He glanced over at his father. Clarence still looked yellowish, continuing to clutch his stomach. He had never seen his father in pain. Finally, the door opened and Willie Joe rushed to his mother.

"Mom, it's dad. He's sick. I tried to call the clinic but nobody answered. Then I called Aunt Agnes's but nobody answered. What should we do?" Willie Joe blurted out.

Bernice took one look at Clarence and knew what had happened. She dialed the hospital and begged them to rush an ambulance over. She and Willie Joe followed the ambulance in a taxi. The emergency room doctor took one look at Clarence and pronounced a word Willie Joe had never heard before—"cirrhosis." The alcohol had finally destroyed his liver. The worst part—they said it was irreversible.

Bernice knew this day would come. They had no medical insurance. They would never get a liver transplant. The community clinic probably couldn't have treated this. Clarence had neglected it. He never stopped drinking and he never sought treatment. Guilt and embarrassment had stopped him. Now, it was only a matter of time—and nobody knew how much time.

After a few days in the hospital, they sent Clarence home. A few days were just not enough to dry him out. Bernice had poured every drop of liquor down the sink while he was in the hospital. He would find more, somehow. They always did, even though they knew it would destroy them in the end. Willie Joe came to understand the meaning of his recurring dream better as time went on. Nothing changed. Carlton still came and went, mysteriously.

Somehow, Willie Joe felt a sense of impending finality, as though something devastating would soon crash down on the Cunningham household. He could not put his finger on it; it just felt very close.

One day, a few weeks after Clarence came home from the hospital, it happened. Willie Joe felt like somebody had driven a knife into his heart. He came home from school as usual, before Bernice returned from work. Something didn't seem right. When he entered the living room, he saw Carlton and smiled. But, as he approached his older brother, he gasped. Carlton stood over their father, holding Clarence's hand to his face. His arm looked lifeless. Willie Joe knew it was bad. He noticed the open liquor bottle on the table beside his father's chair, empty. The glass lay on its side. Clarence's eyes were shut. His face was an ashen gray. Willie Joe knew. Carlton nodded.

Bernice stood in the front row of the church, stoic. Carlton and Willie Joe flanked her; uncle Ben and aunt Agnes on either side of the Cunningham boys. It rained furiously outside. The church slowly filled with mourners. Reverend Pearl solemnly took the pulpit. His voice rang out:

"We are here today, gathered in the sight of the Lord, to commit our brother, Clarence Cunningham, to your kingdom. I beseech you, that you accept him and bring him peace. And bring his family the peace they so deserve."

The six pallbearers wheeled the plain wooden coffin, now closed, to the front of the chapel. Willie Joe could hardly believe that this once powerful man could end up like this. He and his brother glanced up at their mother. Bernice reflected silently, as she placed a single white rose on Clarence's coffin. The organ began to play. The choir began to sing. The mourners filed out of the Beulah Baptist church, umbrellas opening all at once, in a cacophony.

The brief procession pulled into the gates of the tiny cemetery. Rivers of rain poured down the walkways. The mourners gathered under a humble canopy of reeds and leaves, shielded from the pounding storm. The Reverend Pearl read a psalm; the workmen lowered the coffin into the muddy hole in the ground. Agnes and Ben stood behind Willie Joe and Carlton, as Bernice bade Clarence a final farewell. Then, two soldiers in dress uniforms stepped up and faced the gravesite. One played a drum roll; the other played "Taps" on the trumpet. Both turned to Bernice, saluted and removed the flag that had draped the coffin. Folding it carefully, they presented it to her. In unison, they intoned,

"From a grateful nation."

Clarence never talked about his military service. His sons knew almost nothing about it. Only Bernice knew how he suffered, crawling on the ground in the mud. He served in what they referred to then as "The Colored regiment"—as if the horrors of war knew or cared for the color of a man's skin. On many nights, Bernice had awakened to hear Clarence calling out the names of the men in his company. At least, finally in death, his sons learned a newfound respect for him.

The small group of mourners lugubriously sang one last hymn, and then silently approached the waiting cars. The rain stopped. The sky brightened. A ray of sunshine and hope began to penetrate the cemetery. Bernice turned and stared out the back window of the car as it exited the cemetery gates.

"Rest in peace, my dear."

CHAPTER 7

ANOTHER NAIL IN THE COFFIN

Nothing delighted Willie Joe more than the feel of a basketball in his hands. The ball he had received as a birthday gift quickly aged with the signs of wear from the pavement—and from the grip of Willie Joe's growing hands. He proudly donned Carlton's old gym shorts and tee shirt, along with his brother's well-worn sneakers. Sitting by the apartment window, he dribbled the ball lightly, almost lovingly, the way a musician played his fine instrument. He could hardly wait for the sun to come out and dry the pavement.

Bernice scrubbed the dishes, rattling and clattering the pots and pans. Piling them high in the drain, she dried her chapped hands, turning to see Willie Joe as he dribbled the ball incessantly.

"Willie Joe, if I told you once, I told you a thousand times, not to play with that ball in the house."

"Yo, mom, I was just dribbling—"

In an instant, Bernice took two steps forward and Willie Joe released his grip on the ball, gently placing it next to the chair. Bernice's eyes widened, her hands firmly on her hips. He knew she meant business. Willie Joe straightened up.

"What did you say? We don't speak like that in this house," Bernice snapped at him.

"Yes, ma'am. I'm sorry," Willie Joe responded, eyes downcast.

"You are not on the streets, young man. And at nine years old, you're not too big for me to whup you good. You will speak properly in this house," Bernice nearly growled at him.

"Mom, may I have fifty cents for the bus? I wanna go to the park," Willie Joe pleaded.

He hadn't quite mastered the art of proper timing just yet. Bernice first gave him a cool stare, then softened as she approached him.

"And what's the matter with the basketball court right outside this building? Not good enough for you, Willie Joe?" Bernice seldom ever became sarcastic.

"No, ma'am. But there's nobody here to play with and the court downstairs is kinda' messed up. The blacktop is all broken up and the backboards are roughed up and the poles are loose, and—"

Bernice opened her bag, withdrew her change purse and counted out four quarters, handing them to Willie Joe.

"You'll need bus fare both ways. Just be back here well before dinner, Willie Joe," Bernice warned him.

"Thanks, mom!" Willie Joe replied, stuffing the change in the pocket of his shorts and grabbing his jacket from the chair.

"Aren't you forgetting something, young man?" Bernice said, her arms folded, looking down at him.

Willie Joe hugged his mother, kissed her cheek, turned and ran out the door. Bernice still worried about Willie Joe, even though she had done everything to bring him up properly. And with good reason. The streets just seemed to close in on them; the older he got, the closer temptation lurked around every corner. She could only hope and pray that he had gotten the learning and would do the right thing. Still, every day she worried. Every day somebody's child got hurt or killed. Even the rich White folks' kids began to take drugs and to fall in with the wrong crowd. But it was far worse where they lived. Newark just seethed with drugs, with guns, with car thieves, with burglaries and with attacks. The addicts would hop the fence from the projects and knock down old ladies in the neighboring garden apartments just over the city line, in Elizabeth. All for a few dollars and a quick fix. Never thinking, that was somebody's grandmother. Worst of all, Bernice kept hearing stories about Black on Black violence. This was new. Color didn't matter to an addict. He just needed his fix. Or she, for that matter. Bernice heard stories whispered among the parishioners in church, about drug-addicted pregnant daughters. She thanked God she had sons instead of daughters. One less thing to worry about.

Willie Joe boarded the bus and headed for Weequahic Park. The bus rattled up and down the streets, swinging around corners, stopping from time to time. The driver, an old Black man, played his tinny little transistor radio, oblivious to the pain and suffering of the world around him. The doors swung open; more people filed in, filling the bus. Willie Joe gripped his basketball tightly. He wondered about the story he heard in school; how Rosa Parks refused to sit at the back of the bus. He looked around, surveying the crowd. He spied an older Black woman with a purple hat adorned with fake flowers. He imagined she was Rosa Parks. It must have taken courage, he thought, to defy the accepted practice. But who gave them the authority to decide where she or anyone should sit? That was just a few short years ago. So much had changed in Willie Joe's world, in so short a time. He felt as if the earth began to spin faster and faster—like it would spin right off of its axis if the pace kept accelerating.

The bus lurched, throwing Willie Joe forward. He nearly landed on the seat in front of him. An angry looking Black teenager sneered back at him, as he apologized. The teen paid no attention to him as he adjusted the knobs on his radio. The music cranked just a little too loud. Nobody seemed to care. Willie Joe thought about a world where everyone just turned up his favorite station and tuned the other person out. He wondered what would happen to people like that after they die. Did they continue on like that, not paying attention to anyone else? Something just didn't seem right about it to Willie Joe.

The park had a special meaning for Willie Joe. When he was very young and both of his parents worked, Carlton sometimes took him there. It was the only place he ever saw grass and flowers and trees—and a pond. It transported him to another world. He once had a dream about the park. He dreamt that his whole family stood in a circle, all dressed in their Sunday best, holding hands. The Reverend Pearl led them in hymns and songs. Everyone sang; everyone laughed; everyone ate a big meal together. Then, suddenly, the sky opened up and it rained furiously. Everything blurred and the colors on everyone's clothes ran, washing off. Willie Joe was in the middle of the circle alone with Carlton. It got quiet. The sun came out. The church people all faded away-except for the Reverend Pearl.

The bus screeched to a halt, jarring Willie Joe out of his daydream. He waited impatiently, as the angry looking Black teenager with the radio pushed ahead of the crowd. Willie Joe jumped out of the bus, his basketball under his arm. The park looked inviting as he strode down the path toward the basketball courts. Then, as if he was in his dream, the atmosphere changed. The sky darkened. He heard voices. He ran.

Almost out of breath, Willie Joe began to run as fast as he could toward the sound of the voices. On the way to the basketball courts, he stopped at the playground area. Just beyond the swings and slides, a knot of people had formed around the merry-go-round. He didn't know why, but Willie Joe knew he needed to be there. He pushed his way to the front of the group. His eyes widened with terror. He dropped the ball. Carlton lay on the merry-go-round, an empty hypodermic needle sticking out of his arm. Cold and dead. Willie Joe's throat tightened.

"You know this man?" a plain-clothes policeman asked, as he tapped Willie Joe on the shoulder.

Willie Joe froze—not because his father had imbued a hatred or a fear for the police in him at an early age—but because he could not accept the reality of what he saw in front of him.

"He's my brother, sir", Willie Joe replied, his eyes still transfixed on Carlton's lifeless body.

The coroner's station wagon pulled up just moments later. Willie Joe sat on the merry-go-round where Carlton used to push him years earlier. The officer, Lieutenant Reilly, began taking notes on a small pocket-sized pad, as he interviewed Willie Joe. Willie Joe instantly recognized that this man had repeated the same scene many times over. He wondered what it must feel like when you keep showing up too late to stop terrible things from happening. Lieutenant Reilly took down the Cunningham's phone number and promised to have someone from his department call Bernice to notify her of Carlton's death. Willie Joe declined the offer of a ride home in the squad car. He knew it would upset his mother even more. He watched in silence as the Coroner's wagon pulled away with Carlton's body. He could only imagine what would happen next.

Very few people attended Carlton's funeral—just the regular church crowd. Willie Joe felt as if his family had just begun to melt away. Aunt Agnes comforted Bernice; Uncle Ben stood behind Willie Joe. Nobody said much...not even the Reverend Pearl. What could anyone say, of a life tossed away like an old newspaper.

Going home was the hardest part. As Willie Joe and Bernice entered the apartment, the stark quiet overcame them both with a flood of tears. They held each other tightly. Just the sight of Carlton's jacket sent them both into one more uncontrollable release. Willie Joe still could not accept the finality of it all—that Carlton would never walk through that door again. He stared at the apartment door. Nothing. Just a memory. That was all he left behind. Pictures in your head.

Willie Joe tried to sleep that night, but he couldn't. He kept tossing and turning. He kept seeing Carlton's lifeless body in the playground, at the park where they used to play. It seemed like there would be no more play. From that moment, he felt he had to grow up and become a man. Finally, Willie Joe fell into a deep sleep, exhausted. He began to dream. He dreamt the dream where the whole family gathered in the park again. It seemed different to him, as the drama unfolded—more meaningful. He watched the colors fade from everyone's clothes; then the people faded away. Finally, only Willie Joe and Carlton remained. Final goodbyes. Then Carlton faded away.

Willie Joe woke with a start, still trying to accept the reality that both his father and Carlton were gone from their lives. He was the man of the house now, so he had better act like one. He knew he had to look out for his mother. It was only right. She had always looked out for him.

CHAPTER 8

WHAT DREAMS ARE MADE OF

There were days in the Cunningham household when the walls just seemed to push in. It seemed as though their job was to expend all their energy just pushing back. Pushing back didn't seem to get you anywhere; it just kept the walls from closing in. Bernice felt it. Willie Joe felt it. It remained unspoken —and unspeakable.

Willie Joe had attained that awkward age—too young to go out and work; too young to have an interest in girls—and too old to play like a child. He felt stuck. He didn't know what he should be doing. Bernice continued to encourage him to do well in school, and to praise him whenever he did— which was most of the time. Still, something seemed to be missing for Willie Joe. It wasn't Clarence; he had long since accepted his father's passing. Truth be told, he wasn't there for him that much when he was alive. It wasn't even Carlton's absence; Willie Joe had long since reconciled in his own young mind that Carlton had made a choice—to make drugs his blessed sacrament. It was something else—an emptiness and a longing. Willie Joe couldn't quite put his finger on it.

Willie Joe's eleventh birthday arrived, seemingly unceremoniously— or so he thought. It felt just like any other day, but somehow just a little bit brighter. Bernice seemed to have a wry smile at the breakfast table, which only confused Willie Joe. She couldn't help but notice—and comment on, how tall he had grown. It was true. He could almost wear all of Carlton's clothes now.

"Son, you have done some serious growing. I may have to go work another job, just to buy you some new clothes," Bernice joked.

They both laughed. At that very moment, for the first time, Willie Joe noticed how much his mother had aged. For the very first time, he saw veins protruding in her hands and on her legs; he studied the dark circles under her eyes; he couldn't help but notice how much grayer her hair had become. Afraid he had stared too long, Willie Joe looked away, pretending to notice something outside the kitchen window.

Bernice studied Willie Joe proudly, drinking in her creation like an artist that had just completed her sculpture. He had the best of Clarence when she first met him—the height, the lean, muscular build…all the makings of a rising star—if she could just keep him on the straight and narrow path.

It was Sunday. They would have to hurry to make church services on time. Birthdays can wait; the Lord should not; Bernice had instilled in Willie Joe a long time ago. They quickly donned their Sunday best. These days, the church had arranged carpools for those families that did not own cars. Willie Joe and Bernice only had to walk a few blocks for the pick-up. Hattie and Thelma McWilliams, sisters, soon pulled up in their old Buick. The car glistened in the morning sun, as though someone had waxed it that very morning. The seats were spotless and white. Hattie was the choir mistress; Thelma, the organist at Beulah Baptist church. Bernice was very fond of the sisters; and they, of her.

"My, how this boy has grown," crooned Hattie.

"Handsome, too", giggled Thelma.

Willie Joe politely thanked them.

Willie Joe felt as if the congregation had shrunk over the years. Death had consumed its unfair share of the community, but something even more nefarious preyed upon them. Bernice felt it, too. As the times became more tumultuous, the fabric of the families in their community unraveled. The riots had taken a handful; the Viet Nam war took its toll; the rising tide of drugs swallowed some; gun violence and street crime crashed over them like a tidal wave.

The more the forces of evil ravaged the Newark landscape, the more families disintegrated. When they did, the church felt it first. Fewer people attended, and less often. Parents were so busy working just to maintain a home for their children, and children had been lured away by all the evil spirits. The pressures of life had overtaken them. Where did it all lead ? A new generation was on the rise; one that did not grow up with the teachings of the church. With the loss of religion in the family came the loss of morality in the home. Parents became drug-addicted, turning to gambling and prostitution. What kind of children could we expect them to raise?

Nobody felt it more than the Reverend Pearl. He prayed about it daily. He organized discussion groups. He tried to rally his flock around him. Unfortunately, only the older folks heeded his words. He scanned his Bible to find meaningful, relevant passages for his sermons. He began an outreach to the community at large. He found few takers. The other churches experienced the same decline in attendance.

One man cared. After that morning's services concluded and the last parishioner bade him goodbye, that one man approached the Reverend Pearl. They went into his study. The Reverend knew he needed to listen, as well as to preach. Everyone just called him "Coach". He ran the local Boys and Girls Club. How brilliantly simple. Form an alliance between the church and the club. Sports were relevant to children. The club was founded to nurture kids from broken homes. The club gave them another safe harbor—and another moral compass.

Coach was a simple man—or so he appeared. In truth, he was a humble man. His humility made him appear deceptively simple. The Reverend Pearl would have Coach make announcements at the conclusion of his services, inviting the youth in his congregation to attend the Boys and Girls Club. He would post his fliers on the church bulletin board. He would even mail them out to the members with the monthly church bulletins.

It wasn't long before the effort paid off. Willie Joe, on the other hand, kind of got a "jump start". After church that day, Aunt Agnes and Uncle Ben visited for lunch, and to celebrate Willie Joe's eleventh birthday. Bernice had cooked a special lunch; Aunt Agnes had baked a birthday cake. Uncle Ben had begun to take on the role of father to Willie Joe. When they had finished their celebration, Uncle Ben asked Willie Joe if he would come with him for a little side trip. Willie Joe deferred to Bernice, who encouraged him to accept the offer.

Willie Joe and Uncle Ben took the long ride down in the elevator in silence. Willie Joe recalled the many times he had taken the ride—some of them, unpleasant. He tried to block them out, but he could not. Finally, as the doors opened, Uncle Ben began to walk purposefully to their destination, known only to him. Willie Joe followed. The pace quickened. No problem. He could easily keep up. After several blocks of winding turns, Uncle Ben turned to Willie Joe.

"This here is it. You gonna like this place. I think you gonna spend a lot of time here."

The small non-descript cinder block building had a hand-painted sign that read "Newark Boys and Girls Club." They entered. The dark, tiny lobby area had no windows, and a plain tiled floor. Uncle Ben swung open a set of doors. Willie Joe's eyes widened in amazement. It might as well have been the Taj Mahal. His eyes scanned the basketball court with its hardwood floor. Two oversized but dim bulbs with wire cages around them burned overhead. A long row of open windows let a slight breeze in. Two teams of boys about Willie Joe's age practiced their game at either end of the court. A man approached.

"This here's 'Coach.' This is my nephew, Willie Joe Cunningham."

"Pleased to meet you, Mr.—" Willie Joe respectfully extended his hand.

"Coach, just call me coach. Everyone does," he replied flatly, studying Willie Joe...

"Yes, sir, I will," Willie Joe forced a smile, afraid that Coach somehow wouldn't like him.

"You'll do. We'll find a place for you ," Coach replied coolly. He showed no emotion in his face.

Coach returned to the court and blew the whistle hanging around his neck.

"Choose up sides, folks. But, before you do, we have a new player joining us today. Word has it, he's a pretty good jumper, so which ever team gets him, just may get lucky," Coach shouted.

Willie Joe looked around. Uncle Ben had taken a seat on the bleachers, joining the few parents that hung around to watch their kids play. Willie Joe felt like he had just entered the gates of heaven. This was the best birthday gift anyone could have given him.

In a short half hour, Willie Joe got to know all the regulars at the Boys Club. Malcolm towered over the rest; Jackson had the longest arms he had ever seen; Mohammed moved so fast you could hardly follow him. Then, there was Tricks, a guy Willie Joe would come to know and love well. Tricks was the clown—the goofball on and off the court. He couldn't help but like him.

Coach sauntered over to Uncle Ben. Uncle Ben stood up and the two men huddled in the corner.

"You seen' 'em; think you can work with him?" Uncle Ben scanned Coach's face while he waited for the answer.

"I've seen plenty of kids like him."

"Coach, this kid's different. Don't take my word fo' it. Jus' work with 'em. You'll see." Ben stared Coach down, determined."

"Could be the ticket we're lookin' for. We'll see what he's made of," Coach nodded.

"Listen, we got to get this kid outa here, so's he don't end up like his dad and his brother—dead. I'm countin' on him and I'm countin' on *you*," Uncle Ben gritted his teeth.

"Think he's that good, do you?" Coach asked.

"I *know* he's that good. If you work with him, he'll be that much better— good enough for the prep," Uncle Ben glared.

"Saint Anthony's? Then what? A Big East college?" Coach sneered. Somehow Ben felt he was playing him—like Coach knew all the time that he was right, but just wouldn't admit it.

"We'll see; we'll see," Coach quipped over his shoulder, as he approached center court.

A quick game, and in moments, Willie Joe had become one of them. He proved himself in fifteen minutes on the court—loyal as a pet dog to his teammates. He instinctively knew when to pass, when to shoot, when to fake out his opponent. But he still had a lot to learn. This was the first time Willie Joe ever had real teammates to play with. He was home, and that was all that mattered. He felt it, and they did, too. Coach eyed him as he walked off the court, approached Uncle Ben and embraced him. Coach knew raw talent when he saw it…and he knew how to train it. He saw star power in Willie Joe. He hoped he would reach him.

Willie Joe and Uncle Ben took the walk home, leisurely. The bond between them had just grown stronger.

CHAPTER 9

PRAYERS ANSWERED

Willie Joe lived for basketball. He couldn't get enough of the game. Every day, his obsession grew. Every day, after school, he walked to the Boys Club. Gradually, he learned the self-discipline to manage his time so well that he could leave school, spend two hours at the Boys Club, get home in time for dinner, do his homework—and practice some more… in his head. One of the first lessons he learned from Coach was how to play out the game in his head. At first, it seemed almost crazy. But, he put his trust in his new mentor and went ahead and did it. By practicing his moves in his head and anticipating his opponent's moves in his head, the next day he hit the court, he played better—and better—and still better.

"It's a mind game," Coach told him, "But it works. All the really great pro players do it."

As weird as the idea seemed, Willie Joe tried it. Again and again, he would pre-visualize his moves on the court and play them out in his mind. Each time he did it, his game became more accurate; his reflexes got faster; his timing improved.

Best of all, Willie Joe's listening skills sharpened. He soaked up every word Coach said, stored it away and called it up when he needed to use it. It was more than a game. The Boys Club and the basketball court became an owner's manual for life. Coach was a growth medium, where kids could flourish and extend themselves beyond their circumstances.

Willie Joe listened intently, as Coach called a time-out and brought the boys around him at center court.

"We have lost too many brothers overseas and at home. Viet Nam took more Black men than White men from us. Many of them came right here out of Newark. They didn't get student deferments from the

Draft Board; they got marching orders. Most of you can still remember the riots. All of us have lost loved ones to drugs and booze. Well, it ain't happenin' here! We are bigger and better than our circumstances. We will rise above them and become leaders on and off the court. Who knows what greatness is?"

Coach scanned the boys' faces. Nobody moved. Willie Joe looked up. He didn't know where the words came from, but he spoke.

"Greatness comes when people turn themselves over to a higher power than themselves, listen and follow that higher power."

"Good start, Willie Joe. Now, listen up. Any of you ever read James Baldwin? You need to do this. James Baldwin told us to 'never forget from whence you come...' Baldwin defined greatness. You still wonderin' what this has to do with basketball? Well, I'm gonna tell you. Baldwin was right. Greatness is a step beyond the basketball court; it's finishing your homework before the buzzer," Coach's voice rang out.

Willie Joe turned those words over in his mind. Out of the corner of his eye, he spied Tricks smirking. It didn't matter. Take what you need. Leave behind what you don't. If someone else finds it and can use it, they will. If they don't take it, it's their missed opportunity. Uncle Ben taught him that. He could see why his uncle and Coach remained friends; the two men thought the same way about the world.

Coach blew the whistle; that was it for today. The boys filed into the locker room. Willie Joe had just enough time for a quick shower. He didn't really feel comfortable with gang showers, but he knew better than to offend his mother with the acrid odor of the game. He quickly undressed. No sooner did he open his locker than he heard the laughter behind him. Someone had hung women's underwear in his locker. He reeled around in time to see Tricks nearly hysterical with laughter. Willie Joe took the joke in stride.

"You lose these, Tricks?" he smiled back.

The whole team began to laugh. Tricks could not stop laughing. Finally, everyone filed into the showers, still laughing. As they emerged, Coach stood there, arms folded across his chest, shaking his head.

"It's a flashy uniform, but it'll never help you go pro," he snickered.

"Now, listen up one more time. We are gettin' us a bus to go to the Princeton-Harvard game. It'll cost you just five bucks. If there's anyone who can't afford it, see me and we'll make arrangements. It's two weeks from Friday night, so it won't interfere with school. But, I do need your parents' permission. And, parents are welcome, if they want to come. So, get back to me on this one. You don't wanna miss this game," Coach's voice echoed through the locker room as the boys got dressed.

Willie Joe looked around as each of the boys took a permission slip from Coach, filing out the door.

"Son, you need to be there," Coach held Willie Joe's gaze.

"Yes, sir," Willie Joe replied, stuffing the mimeographed blue form into his jacket pocket.

The cool air of the fall night bristled on the back of Willie Joe's neck. He slung the pillowcase he used as a gym bag over his shoulder. He nodded as he passed a group of teenage girls smoking. They looked him up and down, smiling at him. They took him for much older than thirteen, noticing his height. Crossing the corner, he saw a crowd of young Hispanic men on the sidewalk outside of the drugstore. He crossed the street, not wanting to start or to stumble into any trouble. Even though he did not understand any Spanish, they sounded drunk to him. One of them called out to him; he ignored them and kept walking.

Something else began to happen to Willie Joe. His body began to change; then came the feelings. Sure, his muscles developed; he began to sprout hair in places he never had hair, but it went deeper. When he went to bed at night, he felt peculiar. When he woke up in the morning, he sometimes found he had an erection. He began to look at girls differently than he had ever looked at them before. Most of the time, he would just suppress the feelings and dismiss the changes. Still, he became curious. It seemed to preoccupy him lately. No matter; he would figure it out, sooner or later.

Willie Joe sprinted down the block and into his building. Once again, he took the long slow elevator ride up to the twenty-third floor. Bernice had just set the table and began to remove dinner from the stove. Willie Joe leaned over, kissed her on the cheek and ran to drop his bag in his room. The whole Cunningham household smelled from Bernice's cooking.

Willie Joe parked himself in his usual chair and began to reach across the table when Bernice grabbed his hand.

"Have I not taught you anything, son?" she furrowed her brow at him.

"Yes, ma'am," he responded, withdrawing his hand.

"We are good, God-fearing people in this house, and the first thing we do before we sit down to a meal is praise the Lord, thank him for what we have and ask for his forgiveness," Bernice scolded.

Willie Joe bowed his head as Bernice silently prayed. Then, she served him.

"And we don't reach across the table, young man. If you want something, you ask for it politely, and I will give it to you," Bernice warned.

"Mom, can I go with Coach and the team to see the Princeton-Harvard basketball game?" Willie Joe implored.

"It's in two weeks and it's on a Friday night, so it's not a school night," Willie Joe pleaded.

"And can Uncle Ben go with me?" he sounded almost desperate.

"I can't speak for your uncle, Willie Joe; you'll have to ask him. As for you, I'll think about it," Bernice answered.

Willie Joe searched Bernice's face, hoping to learn why she might object. No sign. He thought he might have imagined it, but it seemed to him that his mother moved more slowly, had lost some of her energy and overall, just looked tired. He noticed more fine lines on her face; her knees bruised from kneeling and scrubbing countless floors for years; and her chapped hands resembled a discarded brown paper lunch bag, wrinkled and dry.

Willie Joe finished dinner, finished his homework and lay on his bed, thinking. What would he do if anything happened to his mother? Where would he go? What would he do? After a time, his eyes grew heavy and he fell asleep, still in his clothes. He began to dream; vivid dreams, one after another. Images crashed across the screen inside of his head, in silence. None of it made sense while he experienced it. He caught glimpses of Carlton and Clarence fishing together from a shallow boat, on a river. Willie Joe had never even seen a river close-up, but there it was, plain as day. Neither of them spoke. Could they see him? Suddenly, the river swallowed up the boat. In an instant, both Clarence and Carlton rose up and stood on the surface of the water, laughing and telling stories. Willie Joe wanted to approach them; to be near them. When he tried to, they both faded until they disappeared. He sensed he did not belong where they were.

The next sequence gripped Willie Joe. He stood on the basketball court, surrounded by a team. But it wasn't the court he knew at the Boys Club. And these weren't the players he knew. He searched the crowd in the bleachers. No familiar faces anywhere. Then, he saw his mother rise up from the crowd and wave her arms. He watched her every move, but could not discern her words. He started to jump, still transfixed on his mother, but he could not move. Suddenly, he heard her scream. He dropped the ball. He could not move from the spot. She fell. She screamed again, and then fell from the top of the bleachers to the floor.

Willie Joe woke up. He could hardly breathe. Even though he knew he had dreamt it, he felt compelled to check on his mother. He opened the door to her bedroom ever so slightly and ever so quietly. Bernice slept soundly, breathing hard. Willie Joe returned to his room and got undressed. His dreams troubled him. He didn't understand them. Who could he talk to about them?

In minutes, Willie Joe fell back to sleep. This time, he dreamt peacefully, but in a way he never dreamt before. He found himself in the center of a circle, surrounded by teenage girls; some Black, some White, some Hispanic. Each one of them reached over to touch him. Their touch felt pleasant. He had never experienced a sensation like it. One by one, the girls began to undress in front of him. He felt at once embarrassed and intrigued. He got that peculiar feeling again; the one he had been having lately. The girls continued to touch him; Willie Joe became more and more aroused. Then, his loins ached.

With a start, Willie Joe woke from the dream. He looked down at his still erect penis and noticed the wet bed sheet. It seemed to him like a strange way to start the day.

CHAPTER 10

MOVIN' ON

New Jersey winters could get pretty severe. This one came on with a vengeance. So much had happened in the world, in the country and in New Jersey. It all seemed to swirl around Willie Joe and the city of Newark. A disgraced President Nixon, forced to resign after the Watergate political scandal; the finality of the Viet Nam war, with young soldiers coming home —some in boxes, some in wheelchairs; it all seemed surreal…and overwhelming at times.

Willie Joe wondered how, if we were the greatest nation in the world, we could experience such a crisis in leadership, such a loss of moral direction. He studied history, hoping to find answers. If we were so great, why did we only just abolish slavery a little over a hundred years ago? Why did the stock market crash? How could we not have seen the Great Depression coming? How could we have allowed millions of Jews, Catholics, gypsies and others to perish in Nazi death camps? Why did we have to get involved in Korea and Viet Nam? How could National Guardsman fire upon students at Kent State? None of it made any sense to Willie Joe. He found no answers in his textbooks, from his teachers or from anyone else he knew. Again, he felt powerless…but he wanted to know.

Willie Joe sat in study hall, hearing Coach's words echoing in his head, as he flipped through the pages of his books and penned an essay:

"We have lost our leaders; we must not lose their legacy. Education is your ticket to the train out of a miserable life."

He thought about Martin Luther King, the great leader who advocated non-violence—and died a violent death. It seemed to Willie Joe that not much had changed over centuries. They murdered Jesus;

41

they murdered Caesar. We never progressed morally or ethically—only technologically, Willie Joe's history teacher, Mr. Romano asserted. Indisputable words. Men like Mohammed Ali would risk their lives for a boxing title, while the crowds roared with a bloodlust—just like the crowds in the ancient Roman Coliseum. Christians and Lions; boxers and wrestlers—all the same. We might as well still live in caves, Willie Joe thought.

Suddenly, his concentration broke. He noticed the girl standing in front of him. She was only his age, but at fourteen, she had already fully developed. He could not help but notice how her breasts protruded through her tight sweater, or how her perfectly curved behind filled out her jeans. Willie Joe looked up; Lillian smiled at him.

"Did you lose this?" she asked, looking over the top of her tinted glasses.

Lillian handed him a sheet of paper filled with his own handwriting.

"I-I guess I did; thank you. I'm Willie Joe Cunningham," he managed to blurt out.

"I know. Your name is right there, on top of the page," Lillian smiled, as she took the empty chair beside him.

"I read the first page; pretty deep stuff. Mind if I read the rest?" Lillian held his gaze.

"I guess not," Willie Joe replied, handing her the pages he had labored over so tediously.

Willie Joe studied Lillian as she soaked up the words, slowly turning each page.

"Impressive. I like your style—"

"I like your style, too." Willie Joe had no idea where the words came from, since he had no experience with girls.

"I meant your writing style," Lillian answered, as she smoothed her ample lips with lip-gloss.

Willie Joe could not take his eyes off of her. Everything about Lillian mesmerized him—her looks, her voice, her scent. He just wanted to stay near her. The bell rang, signaling the end of the period.

"Will I—will I see you again?" he stammered, holding her gaze, never taking his eyes off of her.

"If you want to, I suppose," Lillian rose from her chair and tossed him a glance over her shoulder as she left the room, disappearing into the crowded hallway of the junior high school.

Willie Joe felt flushed, almost like he had a fever. He could not get over the fact that another person could affect his physical feelings and give him bodily sensations in an instant. He hoped he would see her again, often. He wondered what his mother would think of Lillian; what Uncle Ben would think; what Coach would think. He decided not to mention her to any of them, in case they did not approve. He needed to keep this private.

When the bell rang at the end of the last period, Willie Joe ran to his locker, put on Carlton's jacket—the warmest one he owned—and headed for the Boys Club. Snow had already begun to accumulate and continued to swirl around him. The cold nipped at his face. He tucked his free hand into his pocket and wrapped his makeshift gym bag around the other hand. He had forgotten his gloves. As he entered the Boys Club, the heat assaulted him. Life seemed to go from one extreme to another. His teammates welcomed him into the locker room as he undressed and put on his shorts and tee shirt.

When he reached the court, everything somehow seemed different that day. Willie Joe jumped a little higher, reached a little farther, blocked a little more accurately. He could not figure out where the energy came from. Nor could his team mates—or even Coach for that matter. He just seemed to walk, run, and jump on air. Could Lillian have done this to him? Willie Joe at first dismissed the thought. Then, as he began to see her in his mind, he began to lose focus. Now, he missed every move by just a scoche. He had let her memory distract him. During a time-out, it became clear to him. The energy of Lillian's presence fed him; the thought of her distracted him. If he could learn to feed off of the energy without *thinking* about her, it would improve his game. The reverse would sabotage it.

It took practice, but in time Willie Joe mastered the ability to control and sublimate that energy. At fourteen, he hardly understood the mysteries of libido, but he knew it ranked among the most powerful forces he had ever encountered. He had no idea what lay in wait for him.

The next night, Willie Joe and the whole team from the Boys Club boarded the bus for the Princeton-Harvard game. The snow had melted off the roadway, but the cold winds whipped across the bus. It took nearly two hours to get there. This bus ride did not resemble any Willie Joe had ever taken before. The team acted like a team, on and off the court. Coach's teachings had kicked in. Halfway through the trip, as they passed through New Brunswick, Malcolm stood up at the front of the bus and led the team in a gospel hymn. A few of the fathers had come along, and Uncle Ben, too. Their harmonies inspired everyone. Even the bus driver, a White man, joined in. Finally, they arrived. Willie Joe's excitement reached a fever pitch. He could hardly contain himself. None of the team members had ever seen any place as beautiful as the Princeton campus. For Willie Joe, the thought of drinking in the greatness that surrounded him overwhelmed him.

They entered the gym and the whole team drew a collective gasp. The floor glistened; the bright lights blazed; the air smelled so clean. Willie Joe could not help notice that nearly the entire crowd that poured in and filled the bleachers consisted of White people. Still, he and his teammates felt very much at home. In a few short minutes, the marching band came in, dressed in impeccable uniforms. They hit every note perfectly, first playing the national anthem, then the Princeton University anthem. The crowd cheered; the band filed out; then the cheerleaders and the baton twirlers took over the room. A beautiful group of girls, they leapt into formations that would impress any circus acrobat. As they fell back to the sidelines, both teams sprinted onto the court. The crowd's applause reached thunderous levels. The referee and the coaches took their positions.

Willie Joe leaned forward, transfixed on every move the Princeton team made. He watched the forward, the guard, looking for any subtle nuances he could incorporate into his own game. As the buzzer signaled each quarter, he followed each team member; every pass, every shot. They moved seamlessly, effortlessly; blocking, shooting, and scoring like a well-oiled machine. He began to appreciate the importance of how the team functioned as one. He had almost forgotten that Uncle Ben had even come along. Ben sat with Coach, behind Willie Joe. When the last quarter began, Willie Joe noticed the beads of sweat on his own forehead, as if he joined the team in the action. Then, as the last point was scored and the final buzzer rang out, he felt the adrenaline rush of the team on the court. He knew he had to do this for the rest of his life. Nothing else mattered. He just needed to know how to get there. Coach would show him the way; he knew that.

The bus ride home to Newark seemed to go so much faster than the ride down to Princeton. Willie Joe felt privileged to have seen the best of the best play. He thought, if that was college, imagine what a professional game must be like! The bus dropped the team back at the Boys Club. Willie Joe didn't even mind the cold night air. He was so pumped up from the experience, he could not even imagine going to sleep that night. He thanked Uncle Ben for coming, thanked Coach for inviting him and took the brisk walk home. He kept replaying the game in his head. He would never forget this night. He did not even notice anyone on the sidewalks or the street corners this time. He just kept wanting the game.

Surprisingly, when he arrived home, Bernice sat waiting for him.

"Did you have a good time, Willie Joe?" she asked.

"The best time I ever had in my whole life," he beamed.

"That's good, that's good; I'm glad you could go," Bernice smiled at him.

"Thanks, mom," Willie Joe glanced down at Bernice, knowing full well she looked tired and needed badly to get some rest.

"Maybe there's something we can do tomorrow, together—go to the movies or something?" Willie Joe surprised Bernice with his offer.

"We'll see; we'll see. Now, go on and get ready for bed," Bernice prodded.

Willie Joe knew he would have a hard time winding down after the week he had. He had felt one adrenaline rush after another—from meeting Lillian to playing his best game at the Boys Club, to witnessing his first college basketball game, live. Still, the week suddenly caught up with him. As his head hit the pillow, his eyes quickly grew heavy. Willie Joe dreamt. But this time it was different. He found himself on a basketball court, alone. He had no ball, but he made every jump shot. Nobody saw him make the shots, but he knew he made them. Then, after making the last shot, he turned around to face Lillian. She beckoned him. He looked around, as if he sought his mother's approval. She was nowhere to be found. He followed Lillian into a bright white room with a heart-shaped swimming pool. She undressed herself first; then, she undressed him. They floated freely, suspended in the water, locked in an embrace. Then, he awoke. It seemed so real. Willie Joe could never quite understand how he could go from dreams to reality like crossing over from one world into another, and yet, he could not connect the two experiences.

The sun streamed into the apartment window. Willie Joe headed for the bathroom. Suddenly, he felt a cold breeze, and could have sworn he saw the shower curtain rustle. He mustered up the courage to pull it back. Nobody. Somehow he felt a presence—a familiar presence. It seemed as if he knew the essence of the person, even though he saw nobody. It was Clarence; he was sure of it. He didn't dare tell his mother. She would surely think something was wrong with him. Besides, he didn't want to worry her. He thought of the many times his father had come home drunk. He dismissed the thought altogether. It didn't matter. He was gone—long gone.

CHAPTER 11

THE REACH

As much as he loved basketball and played it every day, Willie Joe welcomed the start of spring after the long, harsh New Jersey winter. He felt so much more alive when everything around him came alive. He hadn't gone to the park since the day he found Carlton's lifeless body there. It was time. After their Saturday breakfast, Willie Joe zipped up Carlton's old windbreaker, tucked his basketball under his arm, kissed Bernice and bounded out the door. He had just turned fifteen, but towered over most everybody at six-feet four. Willie Joe had achieved a certain demeanor that few boys his age had. He carried himself with confidence, coupled with a quiet serenity. But he had an undercurrent— an inner longing; an uncertainty that still pleaded for answers. And he didn't know where to look for them— let alone where to find them.

The city of Newark still had a long recovery ahead of it. Given the nice weather, Willie Joe decided to walk to the park, rather than take the bus. As he took to the footpath, the memory of finding his brother, dead, gripped him. It didn't get any easier, no matter how many years had passed. Still, he somehow instinctively knew, he needed to go there on this day. He just didn't know why.

Willie Joe passed the exact spot where he had found Carlton's lifeless body, all those years ago. He stopped in his tracks, reliving the scene in his mind. Before he could tear himself away, he reeled around, startled, when he felt the hand on his shoulder. He smiled when he recognized Lillian.

"One of my favorite places, ever since I was a kid. My mama used to take us here. What about you?" she inquired, still smiling.

Willie Joe studied her for a moment, before answering. It happened again, just like that first day he met her in school. She had him in knots—consumed by her.

"Hey, daydreamer, I was talkin' to you," Lillian retorted, her hands on her hips, striking a defiant pose.

He debated with himself, how much he should reveal to her. He decided to drop his guard and to trust her.

"It was my favorite place to come to once, too. My big brother used to take me here…until one day, when I found him here—right on this merry-go-round, with a needle in his arm, O.D'd." Willie Joe responded mechanically, still staring at the exact spot where he had found Carlton.

"So you thought you'd come back here, shoot some hoops and try to put that awful experience behind you?" Lillian looked at him over the top of her rose-colored glasses.

"Yeah, that's about right," Willie Joe returned her gaze.

"I'm sorry for your loss; I really am. But you gotta keep on keepin' on, as we say," Lillian quoted the familiar phrase that had become a part of the Black lexicon—and the Black experience.

"He must have meant a lot to you, I'm sure," Lillian answered, gripping his hand tightly.

Willie Joe just nodded. They began to walk down the path towards the basketball courts. They stopped at the ice cream vendor's cart. Willie Joe looked at Lillian, absorbing her whole presence.

"Chocolate or vanilla?" he asked, reaching in his pocket for the few folded bills he had saved up for just such a moment.

"Get one of each; we can share," Lillian urged.

He did, noticing that Lillian always seemed to know just where she was headed, and what to do next. They sat on a nearby bench, enjoying the ice cream cones—and the moment. They swapped cones—and each of their life stories. When they finished, they stood up and Willie Joe impulsively leaned over and kissed Lillian full on the lips, pulling her close to him. He had no idea what possessed him; he just followed his impulses. He nearly dropped his basketball. As he pulled her closer, her arms reached up. She pulled his neck down, as if she had caressed a giraffe. Willie Joe felt his face flush, his hands tingle—and his crotch swell. He wasn't sure what to do next. This had never happened before.

They walked around the park together in silence, holding hands, taking in the scene. Everything just felt right to Willie Joe.

Suddenly Lillian piped up.

"Let me see your stuff."

Willie Joe looked at her, puzzled.

"You came here to shoot hoops. Let's see whatcha got," she challenged him.

Willie Joe had never met anyone quite like Lillian. He would never show off; but, since she asked, he would grant her wish. They made their way back to the basketball courts. The sight of the neglected courts pained Willie Joe. No one seemed to care. The foul line had long since faded; the blacktop had broken up; only torn threads—fragments of the nets, remained. The backboard looked worn.

Willie Joe went into his head and imagined himself on the sparkling, pristine Princeton court where he and the Boys Club team witnessed his first college game. He dribbled and went for the lay-up. Lillian beamed with excitement as he effortlessly executed a perfect jump and dunked the ball into the hoop. It barely touched the rim, dropping in. He took another hard dribble into his shot, touching nothing but the bottom of the net. Lillian applauded.

Willie Joe held the moment in his head, wanting the magical day to last longer. He knew he had to head home. Why couldn't every day go like this one? Lillian clasped his hand, and then reached up and pulled Willie Joe down to face her. This time, she kissed him—long and hard. He returned the embrace. He knew he would see her again, soon and often.

As they went their separate ways to head home, Willie Joe wondered if he deserved Lillian's love. He almost felt unworthy. Of all the boys in his school, he wondered why she chose him. She—the most beautiful, together and smartest girl he knew. He needed to let it in.

That night, at the dinner table, Willie Joe remained quiet, listening to the conversations around the table. Bernice had invited the sisters, Thelma and Hattie to dinner, so they could discuss preparations for tomorrow's Easter observances at the Beulah Baptist Church. As usual, Aunt Agnes and Uncle Ben also came to dinner. Uncle Ben studied Willie Joe. He sensed the quiet unrest. After dinner, the two men retired to the living room as the ladies did the dishes and made their plans for the church festivities.

"You getting' on okay with Coach?" Uncle Ben asked.

"Just fine, Uncle Ben; just fine," Willie Joe responded.

Uncle Ben had taken Clarence's old chair. It just seemed fitting.

"I've learned a lot from him; an awful lot. I'm just not sure where I'm going yet with my game," Willie Joe offered.

"Me an' Coach; maybe we got to have a talk about that," Uncle Ben suggested.

"We got to think about getting' you in the right school, so's everything will work out—but you got time yet. Mo' important, you got to make Varsity at yo' own school next year. Now, that's important," Uncle Ben counseled.

Even though it was foremost on his mind, and he needed advice, Willie Joe resisted the urge to discuss girls—particularly Lillian, with Uncle Ben. Maybe some other time, when they were alone.

That night, Willie Joe could hardly sleep—or even think about sleeping. Lillian dominated his every thought. He had to have her in his life. He felt sure of it. The fleeting moments of the day just kept replaying in his head— how she clasped his hand; how she kissed him; how she responded to his kisses. He had no idea where things would go between them. He wished he could have some assurances. When he was away from her, he felt an aching in the pit of his stomach. Finally, he gave in to sleep...and to his dreams.

This time, he dreamt of a huge celebration—in a church with basketball courts. Everyone important to him was there—his mother, his aunt and uncle, his deceased father and brother, his pastor, his favorite teachers, Coach and the whole team from the Boys Club—and of course, Lillian. Reverend Pearl handed Willie Joe a shiny gold basketball. He took a jumper, made the shot and everyone cheered. As the ball hit the floor, it shattered into thousands of pieces. The fragments of gold ascended into the air. Each of them turned into gold coins and showered down upon the crowd. Lillian embraced him.

CHAPTER 12

THE GAME OF LIFE

Playing on the freshman team at the high school just seemed to come natural to Willie Joe. He sharpened his skills; he observed every move his teammates made, from the court and from the bench. He studied basketball with the same intensity he studied history. And they won game after game. Maybe it came too easy. Willie Joe wondered about that, too. Both Coach and Uncle Ben had imbued him with the need to keep challenging himself. He recalled a conversation they had a few weeks ago at the Boys Club.

"Bein' a basketball player, it's a lot like bein' a chess player. If you was to play the best—the world-class champions, your game would get better every time. If you play against fish, you ain't gonna get no better," Coach furrowed his brow as he lectured Willie Joe.

"If you sharpen your game, we're gonna get you into one of the best schools. If you play college ball—and you play it well, one day a scout is gonna pick you up and you will go pro, son; I know you will," Uncle Ben nodded his head to Coach—as though the words were meant for him as much as they were for Willie Joe. Indeed, they were.

Coach returned the gesture, knowingly.

Willie Joe snapped out of his daze, noticing Lillian standing over him, the same way she always did—the same way she did that day they first met.

"Hey stranger, where you been?" she smiled at him provocatively.

"On the court; studying; in church—you know," Willie Joe replied.

"I mean, I haven't heard from you," Lillian challenged him.

"Oh, yeah. I'm sorry. I didn't mean anything by it; I've just been real busy.

Forgive me?" Willie Joe pleaded, sincerely.

"I'll let you make it up to me. We can do dinner and a movie this weekend," Lillian suggested. In her case, it was more like she instructed.

"That's cool; we can do that. I'll meet you at your house—"

"Saturday at 6 PM will be just fine," Lillian smiled and turned, sauntering down the school hallway.

Willie Joe watched her swing her hips. Something inside him stirred. She turned her head and waved back at him, over her shoulder. He knew she would. He returned the salute. He could not take his eyes off of her. So smart, so beautiful and so together. And she was sweet on him. He held the moment in his hand, turning it over in his mind.

The bell rang as Willie Joe slid into his chair for the last class of the day. He couldn't wait to get home, grab his gear and hit the court at the Boys Club. As much focus as he had learned to develop from basketball, somehow Lillian derailed it. He had only to see her, and he could not get her off of his mind.

When he arrived home, Willie Joe found Uncle Ben waiting for him. Just Uncle Ben; no aunt Agnes.

"What's up, Uncle Ben?" he queried.

"Oh, I just thought I would take the walk with you on over to the Boys Club, catch up with Coach and look in on your game a bit," Uncle Ben responded.

"Sure, sure; that'd be great," Willie Joe replied, dashing into his room to grab his makeshift gym bag.

"You won't be needin' that," Uncle Ben pointed to the bag.

"Why not?" Willie Joe looked puzzled.

"'Cause now you got this," Uncle Ben reached behind Clarence's chair and produced a real gym bag.

"It's got your school colors," Willie Joe.

"Thanks!" he threw an arm around Uncle Ben's neck.

Willie Joe kissed Bernice goodbye and they were in the elevator, arriving in the street in minutes.

As they rounded the corner leaving the projects, Uncle Ben stopped Willie Joe and confronted him. He reached into his jacket pocket, retrieved a small packet and slid it into Willie Joe's hand. It was a pack of condoms.

"You gonna need this, boy; I know you are. Use 'em wisely," Uncle Ben counseled Willie Joe.

They walked in silence, and Willie Joe wondered how Uncle Ben knew the things he knew. Maybe it was just plain experience. He remembered something he read in school, written by Mark Twain. His mother made him write it, and she hung it on the wall. It read like this:

"When I was fourteen, my old man was the dumbest person I ever met. By the time I was twenty-one, I was amazed at how much the old man had learned in seven years."

He never forgot those words. Uncle Ben had peasant wisdom; an innate knowing of the important things in life. He took on the role of a guardian angel in Willie Joe's life.

Arriving at the Boys Club, both Willie Joe and Uncle Ben knew something was in the air. They both could feel it. As soon as he got suited up and on the court, Willie Joe searched out his teammates. Nothing different there. He took his place on the bleachers. It was Coach that seemed to be on edge. Willie Joe studied him—the same way a wild animal studies its prey. Coach circled him when they took a time-out.

"If you' gonna try out for the Varsity team at your school, we got serious business ahead to get you ready. If you really want this, you got to give it all you got—"

No sooner than Coach had delivered those words to Willie Joe, the door to the gym swung open. Lillian strode in and took a seat on the bleachers. Willie Joe lost his concentration, following her.

"That's what I mean, Willie Joe; you got to choose, if you really want this."

Willie Joe's mind froze abruptly with that thought. Why couldn't he have a girlfriend and still play basketball? It didn't make sense to him. Still, he was not about to decide his entire future at that moment. He looked up. Coach blew the whistle; they resumed play…and Lillian remained, fixed on Willie Joe. As he went for a jump, he saw Coach staring her down from the sidelines. No matter. Willie Joe's energy level rose, and he made the shot— and the next one—and the last one.

When he emerged from the locker room, Willie Joe instinctively went to do the right thing. He put his arm around Lillian, walking her first to meet Uncle Ben, then to introduce her to Coach.

"Coach, I would like you to meet, Miss Lillian—"

To Willie Joe's surprise, Coach just glared at both of them, turned away and huddled with the rest of the team. They all listened and laughed as Tricks cracked jokes and related his favorite pranks. Willie Joe thanked Uncle Ben again for the gym bag, and asked if he wanted to walk back to the Cunningham apartment with him.

"No, no; I'll be on my way. You see this fine young lady home, Willie Joe," Uncle Ben suggested.

"Yes, sir, I will," Willie Joe replied, as he and Lillian left the gym, arm in arm.

The weekend rolled around quickly, as it always did. Willie Joe knew he would have to explain his whereabouts to Bernice. He knew he had to tell her the truth. He just had to figure out how to tell his mother he was going on a date.

"Mom, I won't be having dinner with you tonight. I am taking one of the girls from school out for dinner and a movie," he almost blurted it out.

Much to his surprise, Bernice seemed elated.

"Why, Willie Joe, that's wonderful. When do I get to meet this young lady?" Bernice inquired.

"Oh, I'm sure you will meet her soon, very soon," Willie Joe made sure to placate any touch of doubt Bernice might have harbored.

"Well, you just have a wonderful time, be careful and don't be home too late. It's still not safe around here late at night," Bernice cautioned.

"Okay, mom. Don't you worry now, "Willie Joe leaned down and kissed Bernice on the cheek.

Lillian lived within walking distance, on a tree-lined block of older two and three-family homes. Her family had the top floor apartment. Willie Joe climbed the stairs. As he passed the second floor of the walkup, he heard voices. Outside, behind the house, he heard the deep bark of a German Shepherd. He cringed for just a second, recalling a time when he came face-to-face with a fierce dog that had broken its leash and blocked his path. Willie Joe was much smaller and feared for his life at the time. He stopped in his tracks until the dog stopped barking. The steps creaked. He knocked on Lillian's apartment door.

"That you, Willie Joe?" Lillian queried from behind the door.

"Yes, it is," he replied, as he heard the sound of the lock turning and the chain removed.

The door swung open. Lillian stood there in her bathrobe. Willie Joe caught the scent of her perfume.

"Are you okay? I mean, you're not sick or—"

Lillian grabbed his hand, pulled him in and closed the door behind him. She reached her arms up around his neck, leaning him down to her for a long, sensuous kiss.

"No, I'm not sick, silly; come on in."

She looked him up and down. He caught the aroma of cooking wafting its way to the door from the kitchen.

"Aren't we going out? I thought you said we were doing dinner and a move," Willie Joe looked at Lillian, puzzled.

"I did say dinner and a movie; I didn't say where. I'm making you dinner, and the folks at the TV station have provided us with our choice of movies... if that's okay with you, that is."

Willie Joe smiled. Lillian was always full of surprises.

"And in case you're wondering, my folks took the weekend away, to visit family out of town, so you'll just have to meet them another time."

Lillian motioned for Willie Joe to take a seat at the kitchen table. Ever obedient, he slid into the chair. As she served them both the meal, Willie Joe studied Lillian. She moved like a cat, gracefully, but purposefully. She took the seat across from him. He instinctively bowed his head, ready to pray, as he had always done at home. Lillian studied him. She admired his unspoiled naivety. Not like the other boys she knew—certainly the older ones she had dated.

Pork chops; collared greens and sweet potatoes; Lillian knew how to prepare a meal. No dessert, he mused, watching her clear the dishes from the table and place them in the sink. Then, she took him by the hand and led him into the living room. They flipped the channels, searching for a movie. Not much worth watching. Nothing but old war movies and nineteen-forties comedies. Lillian got up from the couch, turned off the television and pressed the power button on the stereo. Newark's own Jazz 88 came on. A velvet-throated deejay gave the time and the temperature, introduced the next record and Willie Joe heard the sweet sultry sounds of an alto sax with a gentle bass underpinning.

Lillian strode back over to the couch, curled up next to Willie Joe, and then climbed up on his lap. He did whatever came naturally. Inside of about two minutes, his hands began to caress her back, her thighs and then her breasts. Lillian returned the favor, deeply massaging his neck and shoulders, slipping her tongue into his mouth and then gently working her fingers over his crotch.

Willie Joe began to feel sensations he had never felt before. He practically had a full erection when Lillian straddled him. She moved up and down against him. He could feel her heat up like a furnace. Willie Joe began to sweat profusely. Lillian stood up, taking his hand and pulled him up from the couch. He followed her to her bedroom. A lone candle burned, flickering. He saw their shadows cast on the wall, larger than life. Lillian opened her robe and let it drop to the floor. She had nothing but underwear on. Willie Joe had never seen a naked woman before. It was almost too much, too soon. Still, he drank in the sight of this masterful work of art. Was this really happening? It felt like a dream to him.

In her usual fashion, Lillian commanded him.

"Get undressed."

Willie Joe pulled his sweater over his head, kicked off his sneakers and began to unbuckle his belt when Lillian unzipped his fly and yanked his blue jeans off. In a moment, he stood in front of her in just his under shorts. She grabbed the waistband and slid them down. He stepped out of them. Lillian pulled Willie Joe on top of her. He felt his penis throbbing, almost in pain. He looked down at her.

"You've, uh, done this before?"

She nodded.

"You?"

He couldn't lie to her. His awkwardness showed. He shook his head.

"No matter. Just take it easy and I'll help you," Lillian crooned.

Willie Joe reached over to where he had dropped his jeans, rifling the pockets. He withdrew the packet of condoms Uncle Ben had given him. He began to fumble with them. Lillian reached down and slid the sheath over his erect penis. Willie Joe mounted her, ever so gently. He began to rock.

"Lubricated or not?" Lillian asked.

"I, uh, don't know," Willie Joe was glad for the darkness in the room. His clumsiness wouldn't show as much.

"Use your fingers; I'm not ready yet—and you're a bit large," Lillian advised.

Slowly, he stimulated her until she felt ready. Then, mounting her, he anxiously began pumping furiously. He felt almost ready to climax. He tried with all his might to hold back. Then, he reached underneath and lifted Lillian's buttocks, penetrating her with the full length of his penis. She began to cry out. Willie Joe got scared, thinking he had somehow hurt her.

"No, no; don't stop, baby. Give it to me, please," she cried out.

Lillian raised her legs, crossed them and locked them behind Willie Joe's back. With one final thrust, he felt himself slam inside of her and both of them climaxed. Sweat poured off of both of their bodies. He rolled off of her and slipped the condom off. Full. He walked to the bathroom, tied it off and flushed it, embarrassed and afraid that anyone might find it.

Returning to the bedroom, Willie Joe found Lillian sprawled out on the bed, naked. The sight of her body thrilled him. She was perfect, all over. He still had trouble placing himself in the scene that just occurred. Still, he felt powerful. He lay down beside her.

"You were incredible, you know," she said, planting a kiss on his forehead.

"You're pretty amazing yourself," he responded, pulling her closer to him.

The neighbors argued. The dog outside barked. They fell asleep briefly. An hour later, Willie Joe awoke with a start, looked at the clock and sat up.

"I hate to go, but I'm going to have to leave soon. You know my mother is all alone. I can't leave her for too long," Willie Joe said.

Big man of the world. If you come home too late, she'll ground you, he thought. Reasons and excuses. Life was made up of both. Willie Joe had to walk between two worlds. He was pretty much an adult now, but he was still his mother's child. Difficult to reconcile. He stood up and began to get dressed.

"Thank you for dinner—and dessert," he grinned, bending down and kissing Lillian.

"You delight and amaze me, Mr. Cunningham," she answered.

"I'll walk you to the door."

Lillian slipped into her robe, took Willie Joe's arm and walked him to the door.

"Sweet dreams, Miss Lillian," he whispered, as he pulled her against him one more time.

He felt her erect nipples; she felt his erect penis. Jazz 88 played on as Willie Joe bounded down each flight of steps to the ground floor of Lillian's house. The street lights glowed. Willie Joe walked with a purposeful gait.

Arriving home, the projects seemed dismal. He took the elevator to the twenty-third floor as he had always done, but it felt different this time. He was no longer Willie Joe the little boy, walking in somebody else's shadow. For the first time, he felt like a grown man. Bernice sat in her chair, reading. He bent down and give her a quick kiss. Willie Joe suddenly realized his mother might detect Lillian's scent—or the acrid smell of intercourse on him. For the first time, he knew he had to deceive her.

"Did you have a good time?" Bernice asked.

"Oh yes; we had a very good time—both of us did. I'm really tired. I'm going to get ready for bed. We have to get up early for church," Willie Joe deftly covered his tracks—and his true intentions. He didn't look back at his mother, who eyed him suspiciously. Willie Joe quickly took a shower, hoping Bernice would not think anything was amiss. He should have known better.

CHAPTER 13

RUDE AWAKENING

Willie Joe continued his steady brand of devotion to the things he loved—basketball, his studies, Lillian and his mother—in that order. As his life's journey began to accelerate, he began to make life-changing choices, day by day—choices he could not make earlier on... Still, he took his cues from the influential leaders and mentors in his life. Only now, he discarded the things that didn't fit into his plan—a plan that seemed to magically take on a life of its own as it developed. He really didn't know who orchestrated it. He just kept following it.

Willie Joe had more dates with Lillian—and more intimate encounters, whenever they could find the time and the place to be alone. Teenagers, unlike adults, couldn't take motel rooms. As time went on, Willie Joe became more expert at conning his way into "borrowing" friends' houses for an hour or two. Lillian's independent streak seemed to rub off on him. After most of their late Saturday night dates, he could barely drag himself out of bed to accompany his mother to church. When he did, he sat there bleary-eyed, paying less and less attention to Reverend Pearl's reading of Scriptures—and still less attention to his sermons. He wanted to take charge of his life. Right or wrong, he wanted to make his own choices. At his age, most kids did. They simply forgot that they had to take the consequences for those decisions.

He still had his life ahead of him, so what was the hurry? He felt pressured to choose at every step. Uncle Ben and Coach kept telling him how critical his choice of college would be. He still had two more years of high school. He didn't see the need to set a career path in stone so early on. He continued to resist the idea that he had to give up Lillian in order to have a career in basketball. After church, he returned home with Bernice, grabbed his gym bag and headed for the Boys Club to practice.

The whole team had arrived. Everyone suited up and hit the court. It seemed like a free-for-all, compared to the more structured practice at the high school. Pass, dribble, shoot; pass, dribble and shoot. Willie Joe began to feel he had mastered all the moves he needed—until Tricks took him down before he could complete his jumper. Had he lost his concentration, or did he need a lot more practice? He began to doubt himself. Coach called a time-out. The team members headed for the bleachers. Coach called to Willie Joe.

"Cunningham—my office!"

Coach didn't have an office. He referred to a corner of the Boys Club locker room as "his office." Willie Joe obediently complied. Coach began to circle him, nostrils flaring, like a predator that had trapped his quarry.

"I'm gonna tell you this, just once, Willie Joe. You got what it takes, but you' gonna blow it. That pussy will kill your game. You got to focus on the prize. I been watchin' you; you're losin' it. That's all I'm gonna say. It's up to you."

Willie Joe listened, nodded and returned to the court. Coach blew the whistle and practice resumed. Pass, jump, guard, shoot. It had become a routine, ingrained in him. When practice ended, Willie Joe hit the showers, playing the scenes of his life in his head like a slide show. He wanted to make some sense of it all. His life didn't seem to have a discernible pattern he could follow. Clarence's death, Carlton's death, life in the projects, the backdrop of the riots that burned Newark to the ground—even basketball and sex with Lillian didn't paint a clear picture for him. He felt like he had drifted from one place to another, from one experience to another. He still wondered who was in charge of his life.

As Willie Joe slung his gym bag out of the locker and walked back out to the court, he spied Uncle Ben talking to Coach. He waited on the sidelines, but could overhear their conversation. It became heated.

"He's got to get into a good school—the ones the scouts pay attention to. Don't matter how good he is if they don't find him, he'll never go pro. The boy's got good grades. We got to get him into St. John's or Syracuse;

maybe even Seton Hall or Rutgers. I heard Rutgers is out there recruiting right now. We got to go for the best," Uncle Ben asserted.

"Ben, we go back a long way. You know I want what's best fo' him, but that ain't it. Those Catholic schools especially; they come in, they make noise, they recruit our boys, but when it come time to cough up the scholarship money, somehow it don't materialize. We can get him into Howard or Easton—maybe even Princeton," Coach countered.

"We gonna work on it. Together, we gonna figure it out, Coach," Uncle Ben replied, shaking Coach's hand and approaching Willie Joe.

Uncle Ben put his arm around Willie Joe, flashing him a smile. The crow's feet around his eyes deepened. He and Coach just didn't agree on the best path for Willie Joe's future. No matter. They would work it out, as he promised.

"Come on with me; I'll buy you lunch," Uncle Ben offered.

"Sure, sure; that sounds good," Willie Joe answered.

As they opened the door to the deli, the smell of freshly cooked corned beef and pickles wafted its way over to them. Willie Joe had never smelled anything like it. The waiter greeted Uncle Ben; he was a regular at the Jewish deli for years. Morris seated them by the window. Seymour, the owner, spied Uncle Ben and stopped by the table.

"This your boy, Ben?" Morris asked.

"My nephew. Willie Joe Cunningham, meet Seymour Kartzman. Seymour, meet the next pro basketball star to come out of Newark. Willie Joe, Mr. Kartzman here graduated from your same school, Weequahic High, thirty years ago," Uncle Ben informed Willie Joe.

Seymour shook Willie Joe's hand and gave him a knowing wink and nod —as if to say, "Stick with your uncle; he'll steer you right." Another gold vested waiter passed their table with a tray piled high. Willie Joe had never seen that much food on one plate. More customers filed in. Uncle Ben and Willie Joe studied the menu. Morris returned to take their order.

"Whatever you want, son; whatever you want. I highly recommend either the corned beef or the pastrami. I'll take the pastrami with a Doctor Brown's cream soda," Uncle Ben instructed Morris.

"I'll try the same, please," Willie Joe nodded to Morris. Unaccustomed to a deli menu, he followed Uncle Ben's lead.

"Son, it's real important we keep things on track fo' you; you understand, right?" Uncle Ben seldom preached to Willie Joe, but he could feel it coming.

"You know we are real proud of you; you been keepin' yo' grades up; you been helpin' the freshman team winnin' this season. We just got to keep the momentum goin'. You know, soon we got to look at some schools fo' you. Now, you know me and Coach go back a long way. You know I think the world of him. That's why I trusted him to work with you on yo' game. But, Coach and me—well, we got different ideas about what school gonna be best fo' you. Coach wants you to go to Howard University or one of the other Black colleges. I would like to see you go to St. John's or Syracuse—some place where the scouts are gonna see you play," Uncle Ben confided, taking a long sip of his cream soda.

Morris the waiter proudly strode over to their table, carefully placing the plates in front of each of them. Willie Joe's eyes popped as he looked at the steaming deli sandwiches. Morris replaced the pickle bucket with a fresh one, and then disappeared into the kitchen behind the swinging doors and the clattering dishes.

Uncle Ben continued as Willie Joe began to attack his sandwich with a ravenous hunger.

"There's one mo' thing you got to know about. That's women. I know you just learnin' and feelin' your way, and you need to do that. But you got to be careful here. A woman can derail yo' career faster than any one or any thing you'll ever see. If yo' serious about goin' pro, you got to keep yo' mind on yo' game. Don' let no woman get you off the track or you'll be workin' like your daddy and me; railroads and factories, " Uncle Ben counseled.

Willie Joe knew Uncle Ben meant well. He just got tired of everyone lecturing him. Still, he took it all in. Somehow, at not quite sixteen, he had a hard time seeing life as a zero-sum game—one where you either win or lose —and somebody else has to lose for you to win. Surely, there had to be a win-win equation—a way he could have it all.

"All I'm sayin', son, is, don't be thinkin' with your Johnson," Uncle Ben offered, as he picked up the check. Willie Joe swung his gym bag out of the restaurant booth and followed Uncle Ben to the cash register, then waved to Seymour as they left.

Willie Joe noticed that Uncle Ben seemed to drag his leg as he walked. He suggested they take the bus to the projects. Uncle Ben agreed. The ride was brief. When they arrived in the Cunningham apartment, Aunt Agnes and Bernice greeted them.

"You spoiled that boy's appetite for dinner, didn't you, Ben?" Aunt Agnes scolded.

"I guess you could say that," Uncle Ben admitted.

"Then we'll just hold dinner a little later," Bernice suggested.

As many years as had passed since Clarence and Carlton's deaths, the dinner table at the Cunningham household still seemed incomplete. Willie Joe could not help but notice how his mother struggled with the usual household tasks she had performed so routinely, for so many years. In spite of it, her spirit carried her. Willie Joe wondered how any one person could endure as much as Bernice had, and just keep going. Still, it took a toll on her. She just seemed somehow diminished—she had become a shadow of her former self.

After the late dinner, Aunt Agnes and Uncle Ben left hurriedly. Willie Joe offered to help Bernice with the dishes, much to her surprise. In the past, she would not even have accepted his offer. Her fatigue made her accept, graciously. As Bernice washed and Willie Joe dried the dishes, the inevitable happened.

"Willie Joe, you know I have always wanted the best in life for you— even if we couldn't give it to you," Bernice began.

"Yes, momma, I know that. I never doubted it," Willie Joe answered.

"But we have come to a point where I can no longer protect you from the evil in this world," Bernice took him by surprise.

"Evil? I'm not sure I understand what—"

"Willie Joe, there is evil all around you; there always has been. Just don't let it into your heart," Bernice warned him.

"I'm not sure I understand, momma," Willie Joe countered.

"Son, I know you've got a girlfriend, and I'm sure she is important to you. But you've got to keep your focus on your studies. Don't let *any* woman slow you down. School is important. Please promise me you will do that, Willie Joe," Bernice pleaded with him.

"I promise. I'm sorry I haven't brought Lillian around to meet you yet. I will, momma," Willie Joe replied.

That night, Willie Joe tossed and turned restlessly. He could not give up Lillian. He had to find a way to have it all—school, basketball and a woman who cared about him and made him feel special. He felt as if everyone had judged him harshly—like he and Lillian were Adam and Eve in the Garden of Eden. His mother had even hinted at the idea that he might become evil. Had he sinned so badly, biting into forbidden fruit? Had he turned his back on doing the right thing? He didn't think so.

CHAPTER 14

LIFE IS FULL OF SURPRISES

From the moment he woke up that morning, Willie Joe rehearsed his every move on the court. From the shower to breakfast to the walk to school, he mentally visualized the court, the players, the coach, the referee and the imaginary fans in the bleachers. Today might just be one of the most important days of his life. Willie Joe would try out for the high school varsity basketball team. It wasn't so much that he would learn a lot more. After all, Coach at the Boys Club taught him more than any high school coach could. He was a retired pro; he had seen and done it all. He groomed more players that went pro than any high school coach in the state. Really, it came down to visibility more than anything else. Playing on the varsity team would place Willie Joe right in the cross hairs of all the major college scouts.

Even during his classes, lunch and study hall, Willie Joe continued to play out his mental game of basketball, just as Coach had instructed him to do— until he caught the scent of Lillian's perfume. That always broke his concentration.

"Three o'clock in the gym; I know. I'll be waiting outside...unless you don't want me to," Lillian offered, coyly.

"Sure I do. I just got to keep my mind on my game; that's all," Willie Joe replied, sincerely.

"Am I that distracting?" Lillian flashed him a smile.

She knew she was. Everything about her captivated his attention, nearly mesmerizing him. Still, he knew he had to maintain his focus. Those try-outs meant everything to him now. He could hardly wait for three o'clock to roll around. Finally, the eighth period bell rang and Willie Joe sprinted to his locker, dropped off his books and grabbed his gym bag. His locker could not have been closer to the gym if he had picked the location himself. Willie Joe wondered—first in, first out? No. Coach's words just kept going through his head. Uncle Ben's face flashed in front of him. So much rode on his performance today. He had to take Lillian's energy and use it without letting it consume him. He entered the gym locker room. Dead quiet.

Minutes later, a line of varsity hopefuls filed out of the gym locker room, waiting for their instructions. Twenty-four students showed up to try out, every member of the freshman team among them. Willie Joe saw faces he did not even recognize from a casual passing in the halls or the lunchroom. The bleachers began to fill with the scouts; college coaches watching for the rising stars they would later recruit. Those same stars might populate a future professional basketball team one day soon. It could happen. Last year, Rutgers had made it to the Final Four in the prestigious NCAA competition. And Rutgers sent none other than Tom Young, Head Coach. Willie Joe recognized each of the scouts from seeing their pictures in the newspaper. Seton Hall's Bill Rafferty and Saint John's Lou Carnesseca sat at the top row of the bleachers. Coach was right. This could be the most important afternoon of his life. The tension in the room mounted. Only five of today's hopefuls would make next season's starting line-up, with just three more in reserve. Willie Joe calculated his odds of making the team. Just then, the whistle blew.

In seconds, the first two players sprang into action. They were good, but not good enough. Willie Joe watched them intently, as they passed, guarded, dribbled, jumped, shot and scored. He studied the competition. He observed the coach with his clipboard, making notes. The assistant coach called the next pair of hopefuls. As he shouted out names, Willie Joe watched his freshman teammates take to the floor. He scanned the bleachers. In minutes, the second pair completed its moves and the whistle blew. They had both missed their shots. The coach called for a brief time-out. Willie Joe stood up to stretch. He noticed Lillian through the glass, standing outside of the gym. She waved. He returned the gesture.

The whistle blew again. Willie Joe heard his name, and bounded onto the court. Everything went like clockwork. He felt like a gear in a well-oiled machine. They passed; he jumped; he made the shot. It couldn't have gone better. The entire sequence passed so quickly, he could hardly believe it. Willie Joe returned to the bleachers. Lillian waited patiently for him. Willie Joe watched the coach and the two assistant coaches as the three men scribbled wildly on their clipboards. All of the aspiring players filed back into the locker room to shower and change back into their street clothes.

The tension in the room rose to a fever pitch. Everyone waited anxiously as the head coach, Al Jackson, read the names of the newly selected Weequahic High varsity basketball team. Willie Joe leaped for joy as he heard his name called out. The applause in the background barely registered as he left the gym. He leaned down and Lillian kissed him He couldn't wait to get home and share the news with his mother.

The excitement overcame Willie Joe as he nearly ran home, waited for the creaky old elevator to reach the twenty-third floor and pushed the door of the Cunningham apartment open. A deadly silence greeted him.

"Momma? Mom, are you home? I've got great news for you!" Willie Joe called out.

No response. He cautiously looked around for a note. No note. He began to worry. Did she miss the bus home? It had begun to get dark outside. Willie Joe approached his mother's room, peering around the doorway. He gasped. She lay in bed, covered with blankets up to the neck. In all her years, Bernice Cunningham had never missed a day of work on account of illness. Willie Joe froze in his tracks. He had never even seen his mother sick. She always took care of everyone else. He thought she always would. Finally, he approached her.

"Momma, what's the matter?" Willie Joe leaned over her, whispering to her.

"I'm sorry son; I'm sick. I just couldn't get out of bed today. I could hardly move. I felt like I just ran out of energy," Bernice replied in hushed tones.

"Did you call the doctor?" Willie Joe began to tremble as he felt her cold forehead.

"No, I thought I would just lay it out and see how I felt by morning. If I don't feel better after a good night's sleep, then I'll make an appointment to go and see him," Bernice assured Willie Joe.

"How about if I bring you some soup? You can have it right here in bed," Willie Joe offered.

"No, no. Let me go and get you your dinner; that's what I need to do. Maybe I'll feel better if I get myself busy," Bernice suggested.

But she could not raise herself. She tried to stand up, but she felt too weak and dizzy. Willie Joe felt a panic grip him inside. He would not let her see it. He just let her rest.

"Don't worry about me, momma. I'll get my dinner ready myself," Willie Joe assured her.

He wanted to blurt out his good news, but at that moment, it didn't seem so important. Bernice didn't ask how the try-outs went. She just drifted off to sleep.

Willie Joe tried to sleep, but the restlessness overcame him. What if something happened to his mother? The thought of her mortality had never even occurred to him. Finally, he dropped off to sleep. He began to dream one disturbing dream after another. He stood in a field, naked. Lillian approached him. Suddenly, his penis turned into a snake and attacked her repeatedly. She lay dead. His mother stood over him, shaking her head. He woke up with a start. In a few minutes, he fell back to sleep. He worried about his mother.

When he awoke, Willie Joe checked in on Bernice, first thing. She seemed more alert and rested, but still didn't have her usual energy level. She assured Willie Joe she would see the doctor as soon as possible. He got dressed and left for school. Still, he worried. What would become of him if anything happened to his mother? A sixteen year-old couldn't live alone in the projects. All day, his thoughts kept reverting back to the sight of his mother, weak, sick and alone in bed. Finally, after his last class, Willie Joe went straight home, rather than stopping at the Boys' Club. He dreaded the thought of what he might find.

The minutes raced by as Willie Joe waited once again for the elevator to deposit him at his floor. He ran down the hallway and into the Cunningham apartment. Bernice had begun to prepare for dinner. He felt a huge sense of relief just seeing his mother dressed and up and around. Still, she admitted that she did not quite feel like herself.

"Willie Joe, sit down. I need to talk to you. I did go to the doctor today. He wants me to go to the hospital, but just to have some tests. He can't really tell me anything until we get the tests done. Now, I don't want you worrying. Everything will work out; you know that. It always does," Bernice said with resolve.

The doctor had scheduled Bernice's tests over the weekend, so Willie Joe accompanied her to Beth Israel Medical Center. He didn't like hospitals. As they entered, Willie Joe flashed back to the time when Carlton lay in this very hospital. Then, he recalled Clarence's time in the hospital. He felt uneasy. Bernice paid the cab driver and held onto his arm as they traversed the vestibule and made their way to the Admissions Desk.

"Bernice Cunningham, for Oncology exams," she stated, weakly.

The phrase stunned Willie Joe. Bernice had never mentioned that the doctor suspected cancer.

"Take the fourth floor, go to the right when you come out of the elevator, then go right again. You'll see it," Mrs. Marrotta advised, pointing the way.

"Momma, why didn't you tell me? I had no idea the doctor said anything about cancer," Willie Joe queried.

"I didn't need to worry you, son. I'm just glad you're here with me. Let's just get this over and done with. Maybe it won't be anything at all," Bernice replied.

Willie Joe panicked inside, fearing the worst. What would he do if Bernice was really sick? He couldn't imagine his life without her. Thoughts raced through his head. Could he have been a better son to her? Didn't she deserve better than this? What would he do now? Would he have to trash all of his career plans to take care of her? As they rounded the corner, the shock of seeing the word "Oncology" gripped him. Bernice held his arm tightly. They approached the nurse's station.

"Bernice Cunningham, for testing," Willie Joe and Bernice blurted out mechanically, in unison.

Willie Joe waited in a small anteroom while Bernice undressed, donned a hospital gown and followed the technician into the exam room. He nervously flipped through one magazine after another, looking for something to distract his attention from the gloom that hung over him. Nothing worked. The news magazines bored him; the sports magazines flashed new car ads. He picked up a discarded newspaper. He tried to concentrate on a report of President Gerald Ford's latest speech to government workers, asking them for patience during a slow economy. No raises. Even their usual cost-of-living increase cut to the bone. He scanned the front page of the daily paper. New Jersey's governor continued to lose popularity; property taxes continued to rise; a huge pile-up accident put a half dozen people in the hospital.

69

The high heat in the tiny room just added to the stuffiness. Willie Joe stood up and began pacing up and down the corridor. The quiet disturbed him. Finally, Bernice emerged, dressed again and ready to return home. Willie Joe offered his arm. The two silently made their way back to the elevator. Bernice found a pay phone and called for a cab. Still not a word between them. Willie Joe didn't know what to say.

Finally, in the taxi, Bernice turned to Willie Joe and confronted him.

"We won't have any test results for a few days. Doctor wants me to stay home and not go back to work until we know what's what," Bernice stated, flatly.

Willie Joe couldn't hold himself back any longer.

"Maybe some good news will help. I made the varsity team, mom," Willie Joe blurted out.

"I'm proud of you, son; I really am proud. That's good, that's good," Bernice forced a smile as she took Willie Joe's hand and gave it a weak squeeze.

Willie Joe couldn't help noticing that he had to help Bernice out of the taxi and hold onto her the whole time they made their way into their building. She just had no energy left.

The beginning of the week flashed by, blurring into a jumble of meaningless activities. A pall continued to hang over the Cunningham household. Willie Joe just didn't know what to do. Once again, he felt powerless. Bernice spent most of the day in bed, in and out of sleep. Willie Joe knew he had to just be there for her. Finally, the telephone rang. He took the dreaded call.

"Is this the Cunningham residence? Is Bernice Cunningham at home? This is Doctor Wildman's office," the voice on the other end sent shock waves through Willie Joe.

"This is her son, Willie Joe. I will see if she is awake. Please hold on," Willie Joe rested the phone on the kitchen counter and quietly peeked in to Bernice's room.

He debated with himself whether to wake his mother, take the call himself or just take a message. Finally, he decided to wake her.

"Momma, it's the doctor's office. I think they have your test results," Willie Joe urged her to take the call. He helped her to the phone.

"Yes, this is Bernice Cunningham. He wants me to come to the office? You can't tell me anything now, on the phone? I see. Yes, I'll come tomorrow morning. Nine-thirty is fine," Bernice replied, conflicted with a sense of relief and terror, both at the same time. She looked forward to ending the wait, yet the fear of the possible outcome overcame her.

Willie Joe took the morning off from school to accompany Bernice to Dr. Wildman's office. It was in a professional building right near the hospital. He had come to hate the sight of the hospital. After filling out the medical questionnaires, Bernice and Willie Joe studied the faces of the other patients and their family members. Hopeless faces. Willie Joe had never seen that many sick people before. How could we build bombs, launch rockets and satellites, but not cure cancer, Willie Joe wondered? He could not fathom it. Suddenly, basketball seemed to pale in importance. Finally, the receptionist called out his mother's name.

Willie Joe and Bernice sat across the desk from Dr. Wildman. He looked as though he had done this countless times. They held their breath waiting, as he studied Bernice's chart. Then, he stood up and placed her films on the light box, motioning for them to join him.

"This, I don't like. I'm afraid I don't have any good news at all for you," he asserted, matter-of-factly.

They rejoined him at the desk.

"Mrs. Cunningham, my diagnosis is pancreatic cancer," he stated, flatly.

"What kind of cure rate is there? You must have some treatment program," Willie Joe pleaded.

"Wrong on both counts. I'm sorry to have to tell you this. There is no cure; there are no approved treatments. The few experimental treatments have not produced any results. There is nothing I can do for you, Mrs. Cunningham. I recommend you put your affairs in order. I'm sorry," Dr. Wildman completed his statement.

"I understand. I understand," Bernice nodded.

Willie Joe and Bernice both felt the same gnawing in the pit of their stomachs as they left. They were devastated, like somebody had dropped a bomb right in their midst. They felt paralyzed. They simply did not know what to do. Nothing else mattered. Bernice hoped she could find the strength to pray for a miracle—if there were any miracles left. Willie Joe felt embittered. What had his mother ever done wrong in her life, to have to face an incurable disease? Why didn't we have a cure? What good were doctors if they couldn't help us when we needed them most? Was this some cruel joke? Everything began to whirl around in Willie Joe's head. None of it made sense. He couldn't accept it. Maybe the doctor was wrong. Maybe there were more tests.

As each day passed, Bernice grew weaker. Willie Joe found it painful to look at her, wasting away. She insisted he go to school.

"I'll be here when you come home from practice," she urged.

Then, finally, it happened. Willie Joe arrived home as he had every day since the dreaded diagnosis, ready to prepare dinner for himself and Bernice. He called out to her. She did not answer. He ran into her room. Her breath was shallow. He felt her arm. Her pulse was weak. He fought back a tear.

"Momma? It's me, Willie Joe."

Bernice opened her eyes and forced a smile.

"I know, I know. I'm sorry, Willie Joe. I'm sorry to do this to you. I just can't hang on. Please, just promise me you'll finish school?" she begged him, weakly.

"I promise, momma; I promise," he choked back his tears, not wanting her to see him cry.

In a rush, Willie Joe had a flood of thoughts of everything he had ever done wrong. He wished he had brought Lillian to meet his mother. He wished he hadn't deceived his mother when he began sleeping with Lillian. Too late for all that. Was this his payback for lying? He took Bernice's hand. It was frigid. He leaned over her. Not a breath. Gone.

After calling Aunt Agnes and Uncle Ben, Willie Joe called the Wiggins Funeral Home. They had always handled the Cunningham family funerals— and most of the members of Newark's Black community. Spending the night alone proved difficult for Willie Joe. He had never been alone in his entire life. He wondered what the next chapter of his life would look like. In spite of the draining experience, he still had difficulty falling asleep. His thoughts tortured him. What good did it serve to live a model life like his mother had, when it ends in tragedy like this? How could God allow someone as healthy as Bernice to die of a horrible and incurable disease? How could he get on with his life and career plans? No justice.

Waiting for the funeral proved even more trying for Willie Joe. The Jewish people had the right idea. They bury quickly. Finally, Willie Joe found himself in the front row of the Beulah Baptist Church with Aunt

Agnes and Uncle Ben at his side. The Reverend Pearl's booming voice resonated to a full congregation.

"God has created nothing more perfect than a mother, and no mother more perfect than our dear sister, Bernice Cunningham. Join me not in mourning her passing, but in celebrating the life of a totally dear and devoted woman. Everything she did, she did for her family. She labored and toiled as a domestic worker; but, everything she did, she did her best. Live as this woman did, and you shall be rewarded in heaven. Amen."

"Amen," the entire congregation responded.

When the funeral service concluded, each and every member of the congregation came up and personally paid their respects to Willie Joe, Aunt Agnes and Uncle Ben. Reverend Pearl placed his arm on Willie Joe's shoulder after the last person filed out. Willie Joe just stared down at his mother's casket, trying to wrap his mind around the idea that this is how her life ended.

"Our doors will always be open to you, son. You will find all the love and the guidance you need here. Just ask for it, and you shall receive it," Reverend Pearl nodded to Willie Joe.

Somehow, he just couldn't let those words in. Willie Joe could not see beyond what lay in front of him. The finality of death trumped any thought of an afterlife. In fact, he had lost any feeling of spirituality. He was just plain numb.

The funeral procession made its way to the cemetery, where Bernice's body was laid to rest next to Clarence's. Willie Joe remembered that day so clearly, when he first learned of his father's valor as a soldier. He wondered if there was peace in heaven. There was very little on earth

Just after the funeral, Willie Joe had the week off from school for spring vacation. Uncle Ben called him, asking him to meet him at the bus stop. When he arrived, Willie Joe boarded the bus and sat quietly, waiting for Uncle Ben to speak.

"Willie Joe, I want you to meet a good friend of the family. His name is Danny Oppenheim, and he's a lawyer here in Newark. He and one of his two sons have a practice together, over on Academy Street. Let me tell you how I met Mr. Oppenheim. When I was just finishing up my days as a trainman, I met this new, young conductor. One day we was havin' lunch together over at Newark Penn Station. Well, he tells me his story. You see, he went all the way through law school just like his brother did. When he finished, he went to his father and told him he really didn't want to practice law. His daddy said, 'Well, what do you want to do?' He answered, 'What I always wanted to do; I love trains.' Well, Mr. Oppenheim told him to go ahead and do what he loves. So, somewhere, riding these rails, we got a train conductor with a law degree. Any way, he introduced me to his father, and he has been a friend as well as a lawyer to us ever since then."

The bus stopped and Willie Joe and Uncle Ben got off at the corner of Broad and Market Streets, taking the walk over to Academy Street. The Oppenheim law firm had occupied the same offices for years, in an older professional building. As they entered the office suite, Willie Joe had a surprise. Aunt Agnes greeted him. This puzzled him. Usually, Uncle Ben took him on these excursions by himself. He leaned over and kissed his Aunt, who still showed signs of distress over the painful loss of her sister.

The secretary ushered them into Mr. Oppenheim's office as he finished his phone call. He stood up for the introductions. A kindly man, aging gracefully, he loved his clients as much as he loved his work.

"So, do you know why you're here, Willie Joe?" he asked.

"No, sir, I don't. I mean, my uncle said he wanted me to meet a friend of the family. That's all I know," Willie Joe answered.

"Well, there's a bit more to it than that, Willie Joe. Your aunt and uncle have asked me to file a petition to the court to become your legal guardians. How do you feel about that?" Mr. Oppenheim queried. Willie Joe looked at Uncle Ben, then at Aunt Agnes, then at Mr. Oppenheim. He didn't know what to say. Overcome, he finally spoke.

"I always knew you would be there for me, but I never expected this. Are you sure you want to do this?" Willie Joe asked.

"Most certainly, we do. We do" his aunt and uncle chimed in, one after the other.

"Then it's settled. I've already drawn up the necessary papers. All we need is to have all of you sign them, and I'll file them tomorrow morning," Mr. Oppenheim smiled, indicating where to sign.

Willie Joe could hardly believe it. Of course, he would have to move in with Aunt Agnes and Uncle Ben. Maybe this signaled the beginning of brighter days for him. He hoped so.

CHAPTER 15

MOVIN' ON

Uncle Ben and Aunt Agnes lived in a small upstairs apartment in a three family house, much like the one Lillian lived in. Mapes Avenue had held up well, a tree-lined street. Number 63 must have been the prestige address in the home's younger day. Yellow brick, it had seen many families come and go. Sam Cohen, the real estate developer, owned it and lived there before he built himself a custom home in the nearby suburb of West Orange. His son and his daughter each occupied a floor with their young families before moving out of Newark. With Uncle Ben's railroad pension, veterans pension and Aunt Agnes's small Social Security check, they had moved out of the projects when Uncle Ben retired.

Willie Joe occupied a tiny room with a folding couch that opened into a bed. The room looked more like a closet than a bedroom, but it was fine for him. He didn't spend much time in it. The few important items he treasured adorned the room—a photo of the whole Cunningham family taken on a Christmas eve; Carlton's jacket and Clarence's medals, neatly framed. The folded flag presented to Bernice by the honor guard at Clarence's funeral lay on the shelf in Willie Joe's closet.

His entire sophomore year of high school just seemed to melt away. He lived for the basketball games. For the first time in his life, Willie Joe began to see the rest of New Jersey, as the team traveled to other schools. He had never seen all the farms out in Hunterdon County until they played against the North Hunterdon Regional High School. These kids rode five to ten miles each to get to school. Willie Joe couldn't believe the campus. Their high school looked like a college, sprawling out all over two acres. They had a football field, a track; even the air smelled cleaner. It must have been. Years earlier, the State had built a tuberculosis sanitarium in the tiny borough of Glen Gardner, believing it was the cleanest air spot in New Jersey. Not a factory in sight, either.

Willie Joe's encounters with Lillian became ever more intense—and secretive. He could not possibly bring her to Uncle Ben and Aunt Agnes's apartment. They borrowed friends' houses, sneaked into church basements, even janitors' closets. They took their chances, anywhere they could. They nearly threw all caution aside, risking getting caught. Then, one day, Lillian took Willie Joe by surprise.

They had just finished a passionate encounter. As he began to get dressed, Lillian grabbed his arm and pulled him close to her. As he leaned over her, her eyes widened and she implored him.

"Do you love me, Willie Joe Cunningham?"

He was taken aback—so taken by surprise, he didn't answer. She sat up.

The long, silent pause made the moment more uncomfortable.

"You don't, do you? You been sleeping with me all this time, but you don't really mean it, do you?" Lillian sounded more hurt than angry.

Willie Joe sat on the edge of the bed, took her hand and looked into Lillian's eyes.

"I would never hurt you; you know that. You just took me by surprise; I thought you knew how I felt. I didn't think—"

"You didn't think you needed to tell me? That's where you're wrong. You always got to tell a woman you love her. I need to hear that—even if you think I know," Lillian's tone had turned almost bitter.

Willie Joe pulled her against his chest, embracing her.

"Lillian, you know I never had a woman before you. I don't know that much about women. I'm still learning. Don't give up on me so fast, you hear?" Willie Joe leaned down and planted a kiss on her cheek.

He remembered one night when he and Uncle Ben sat on the porch the three families shared at the house. Uncle Ben rocked in the wooden Adirondack chair; Willie Joe sat on the stone steps. Uncle Ben warned him not to ever tell a woman he loved her unless he meant it—especially "'just to get in her drawers.' They find out quick, and they will cut you to the quick," he admonished. Willie Joe never forgot those words.

"Of course I love you. I guess I'm just not that good at showin' it," he replied sincerely.

"You're forgiven, Mr. Cunningham. But you owe me," Lillian responded as she buttoned her blouse.

Willie Joe wasn't real sure just what he owed her, but he accepted her conciliatory answer, as she had accepted his. He wondered if this signaled cracks beginning to form in the foundation of their relationship. He knew a woman demanded a certain amount of a man's attention, but he wasn't prepared to give up basketball, college or a career just to have a woman's affection. He debated with himself whether this signified selfishness or simply dedication to his life's goals and remaining faithful to himself. No matter. He felt powerful and in charge of his life, at least for now.

Still, he had seen so many of his neighbors and his classmates mess up their whole lives for a few moments of passion. He realized how little stood between him and the end of his dreams. One tiny membrane; what if the condom broke and Lillian became pregnant? What would happen to all his dreams and plans then? He thought about this silently as he walked her home. Maybe he needed to rethink the relationship. Maybe they needed to think about some extra protection. He didn't even know how to have that conversation without upsetting her. He decided to wait.

When he arrived home, Aunt Agnes busied herself preparing for the next day's festivities at the church. Willie Joe had not set foot in Beulah Baptist Church since his mother's funeral. He just couldn't bring himself to. He wasn't sure why. Did he feel unworthy? Did he think he had sinned so badly? Or, did he just no longer find any comfort there? He didn't want to disappoint Aunt Agnes and Uncle Ben, so he contrived a story about a mandatory early Sunday morning basketball practice for an upcoming game. The lie fit. Even better, it worked. Nobody questioned him. He guessed the Lord liked basketball enough to let him slide.

CHAPTER 16

MIND OF THE MAN

Ever since grade school, history had taken the lead as Willie Joe's favorite subject. Then, in high school, English Literature became a close second. Through his readings, Willie Joe discovered the rest of the world. Historical writings seemed to fill the gaps; the missing pieces of the puzzle no one had imparted to him while growing up. He had always wondered whether great men and women of color had walked the earth for generations. He wondered what achievements and contributions they had made—and what had happened to them, and to their legacies. Finally, at last, in his junior year of high school, he began to learn about them.

Willie Joe became completely absorbed during study hall, spending more and more time in the school library. He read about the great Egyptian Pharaohs, about Alexander's generals, the Moors of Africa that migrated to Spain. He read about biologists and chemists, physicians and authors; suddenly he began to feel connected to a great long string of Black energy and consciousness. All the dots seemed to connect and form a pattern. Willie Joe's life became just a little more meaningful.

The bell rang; Willie Joe re-shelved the reference books he had been poring over, nodded to Miss Phelps the librarian and then entered the throngs of students in the hall. They resembled a school of fish, all streaming together in one direction. He often thought of them as molecules, like the ones he had read about in science class, randomly bumping and colliding through life. Did any of them have a purpose? He spied Lillian and came up behind her. It must have been the first time he ever surprised her. She always appeared to him when he least expected it. He approached her just before she entered their classroom. Still a little unsure of himself, he tapped her on the shoulder. She spun around. Seeing him, she reached her arm up around his neck, holding her books in her other arm. He always felt like a giraffe when she did that. Willie Joe leaned down to give her a quick peck on the cheek. Lillian surprised him and turned toward him, locking his lips. Willie Joe embarrassed easily—especially when the teacher brushed past them to enter the classroom.

They took their seats. Willie Joe noticed how nearly everyone sat in the same place every time, even though they did not have assigned seats in most of their classes. We remain creatures of habit, he thought. Weequahic High School had a long tradition, serving the hard working families of Newark. Its academic record remained strong; its sports teams excelled. While the school didn't have the funding of its nearby suburban counterparts, it still attracted dedicated teachers. The scourge of the riots had scarred the school to some extent. The rise of youth gangs left a pall over it. Weequahic held its own in competition against its Newark rivals at Central and Barringer High Schools. Its teams almost always beat the North Ward.

"Mr. Webster, today I am challenging you to tell me why James Baldwin made an impact on both Black America and on White America," Mrs. Morgan's voice rang out as she paced back and forth in front of the blackboard.

"Mr. Webster, I am speaking to you," she stopped, held her gaze and placed her hands on her hips.

Willie Joe nudged Tricks.

"She's talking to you, bro'."

"I don't answer to no slave name," Tricks scowled.

Willie Joe could smell the alcohol on his friend's breath.

"I can't cover for you this time, bro'. If she gets wind of your breath, your toast," Willie Joe whispered.

"Amos, I'll give you one last chance to tell me what you know about James Baldwin," Mrs. Morgan stepped forward toward him.

"I don't know nobody by that name, Missy—nobody named Baldywin and nobody named no Amos Webster. Folks calls me 'Tricks'," he retorted.

"Then I suggest you pick yourself up, go to the library and find out about James Baldwin, 'Mr. 'Tricks,' " Mrs. Morgan's eyes flashed as she pointed to the door.

Tricks slung his jacket over his back, nearly clocking Willie Joe with it as he rose from his chair. Willie Joe felt something hard in the pocket. Suspicions confirmed: a bottle. Tricks had a nasty drinking habit. Willie Joe feared he would get thrown off the Boys Club and the High School basketball teams if he didn't get a grip on it. Worse yet, he could get thrown out of school. Kids really believed they were adults in young bodies. If they were, they would have better control; they would know there's a time and a place for everything. Tricks was a case of arrested development. Stuck in early adolescence. Most alcoholics were just that.

"Mr. Cunningham, I'm sure you know that life after high school will probably mean more than just basketball. So, tell me what you know about James Baldwin," Izza Morgan smiled wryly at Willie Joe.

"Yes, ma'am. James Baldwin wrote *Go Tell it on the Mountain*. He said 'Know from whence you came. If you know where you came from, there are no limitations to where you can go.'"

"Very good, Mr. Cunningham; very good indeed. I am very impressed. Now, let's take it a step further. Give me some comparison, some connection or some parallel to someone else in literature, with James Baldwin's observations on life," Mrs. Morgan replied as she began to write Willie Joe's quotation on the board.

"William Shakespeare's Julius Caesar; there was a line that read 'And he scorned the base degrees from which he ascended,'" Willie Joe replied.

"And exactly what does that mean, Mr. Cunningham?"

"Julius Caesar looked down on his humble beginnings, while James Baldwin said to know one's self, you really need to return to your roots. Goin' home is important," Willie Joe responded.

"Well done, Mr. Cunningham, well done indeed. 'A' for the day," Mrs. Morgan then wrote Willie Joe's quotation from "Julius Caesar" on the board, next to his James Baldwin citation.

"Does anyone else here have a clue what they read, or do we need to go back to reading Doctor Seuss in this class?" Mrs. Morgan's anger made her look like she had caught fire.

Lillian raised her hand.

"Ah, a light in the darkness. Ms. Jefferson, what do you have to contribute to our discussion today?" Mrs. Morgan seemed relieved to see a spark of hope that she had reached more than one student in the class.

"Would it be okay if I give you another Shakespearian reference, Mrs.

Morgan?" Lillian asked.

"I would be delighted. Please proceed," Mrs. Morgan waved her hand.

Lillian stood up.

"Would it be okay if I acted it out, since Shakespeare wrote plays?" Lillian inquired.

"Be my guest," Mrs. Morgan stepped aside and motioned to Lillian, as if she had cleared the stage for her.

Lillian tapped Willie Joe on the shoulder.

"Let's go. I need you for this one," Lillian whispered to him.

The class began to applaud.

To everyone's surprise, Lillian lay across Mrs. Morgan's desk. Willie Joe began pacing in front of the desk, then turned and looked over her, gesturing broadly.

"Put out the light; and then, put out the light. If I do quench thee, thou flaming minister, I can again thy former light relume. But once put out thy light—"

"My lord…why gnaw you so your nether lip?"

Willie Joe and Lillian mesmerized the class as they portrayed Othello and Desdemona. Mrs. Morgan applauded.

"Well done, well done, both of you. Now, explain why you chose this piece," she implored.

"Othello needed to return home in a sense, too. He had an internal struggle. He knew he needed to listen to the voices in his head, but he chose the wrong one to listen to. He listened to Iago instead of listening to Desdemona, his lover. He believed that she was untrue to him, based on Iago's deception. Still, he struggled with his decision after he killed her. Going home for Othello meant he had to kill himself to be at peace. I realize it's metaphorical, but there is a parallel to James Baldwin," Lillian asserted.

"A distant one, but I'll give you an 'A' for reading the material, for your performance—and for justifying your interpretation…even if I don't necessarily agree with it. Well done, Ms. Jefferson," Mrs. Morgan nodded.

Lillian and Willie Joe returned to their seats, just as the bell rang.

"Not so fast. Your assignment for next week: Shakespeare's 'The Merchant of Venice'. Prepare a brief essay giving me Shakespeare's commentary on prejudice," Mrs. Morgan commanded the class like an officer ordering his troops. She even dressed in paramilitary outfits from time to time.

Willie Joe and Lillian left the room, arm in arm. As they passed Mrs. Morgan, she looked up from her desk and remarked,

"Romeo and Juliet will follow."

They laughed as they left the room and joined the throngs of students in the hall.

"Where you off to?" Lillian asked.

"My locker. I gotta switch up some books and all," Willie Joe answered.

"See you later?" Lillian clasped his hand in hers.

"See you later," Willie Joe gave her a hug.

Just then, Tara Jackson slowly brushed by, blowing a kiss at Willie Joe. Lillian's nostrils flared like a wild animal in heat. Tara and Lillian had a lasting rivalry. Nobody knew what started it. Nobody else cared. Still, Lillian had no reason to be jealous of Tara; she just felt threatened by her. Tara came from a good family. Her father had practiced medicine in Newark for years. The girls grew up together. Everyone in the city knew Dr. Jackson. He had served on the Newark Board of Education. Tara had more boyfriends than any girl in school, so what did she want with Willie Joe? Nothing. She just seemed to enjoy getting Lillian riled up. Lillian studied Willie Joe to see if he took the bait. He didn't even react; he seemed oblivious to Tara's gesture. Lillian and Willie Joe each went their separate ways.

Willie Joe opened his locker. Switching his books, he noticed the brown envelope he had gotten from the guidance office, with all of the college applications. He needed to take them home and begin to work on them. He had reached that critical point where he had to make the decisions that would affect his future. He felt like Othello, with everyone whispering in his ear. Which voices would he listen to? Uncle Ben's? Coach's? He would have to choose, soon enough.

Just then, a noise distracted him. Willie Joe turned around, just in time to see Tricks slammed into a row of lockers. He dropped his books and ran towards the site of the commotion. Mr. Cavett, the custodian, had Tricks by the collar.

"Boy, you goin' home. You in a bad way, son. If you was my son, I'd be givin' you a beatin'," he growled, as he stared down at Tricks.

"What are *you* lookin' at?" Mr. Cavett snarled at Willie Joe.

"Let him go. I'll take care of him. He's my friend," Willie Joe slowly stepped between the two.

"Damn kids don't have no respect for nobody," Mr. Cavett mumbled as he sauntered away.

"Tricks, we got to get you some help. Come on. It's me, Willie Joe, your bro'. I'll take care of you," Willie Joe eased Tricks under his arm, picked up his own books and walked him down to the nurse's office.

"Let him sleep it off. Don't call the principal; just get him some help, okay?" Willie Joe begged the school nurse. Martha Washington—yes, that was her real name—had seen drunk and drug addicted teens before, many times. She knew the drill. As soon as Willie Joe left her office, she had Tricks on a cot and started dialing the hospital's detox unit, matter-of-factly. It might take a week, but at least they would dry him out. Ms. Washington shook her head as the paramedics took Tricks out on a stretcher. If they had already fallen this far by age seventeen, what would happen to these kids when they got older? She knew. They found her own son in an alleyway, frozen to death last winter. A Viet Nam veteran, he ended up homeless, like so many others. Thank you for your service. It made no sense. Every time she looked at another student, she saw her son. Bottles, needles—it didn't make a difference. Each one chose his or her weapon of choice to fight a private war. Why couldn't they cope, when other kids did? She found no answers. But she never stopped looking for them. After the paramedics took Tricks out, she reached in her desk drawer and withdrew her only weapon in this terrible war on our youth—her Bible.

CHAPTER 17

LEAVIN' HOME

Friday rolled around. It just sort of crept up on Willie Joe. This Friday marked the only day in November with no game and no varsity practice scheduled. The three o'clock bell rang and Willie Joe sprinted through the halls to his locker. Willie Joe slipped the brown envelope the guidance counselor had given him into his loose-leaf notebook. He headed for the school library, the only place he would have the peace and quiet he needed for the task he had put off these last few weeks.

Willie Joe felt pulled in so many directions. Coach urged him to apply to the best academic colleges; Uncle Ben pressed him to apply to the high-profile universities the professional team scouts monitored; his high school team coach just whispered a few words to the guidance counselor—and then, there was Lillian. Lillian never suggested what schools Willie Joe should apply to; she simply mentioned where she would apply, dropping broad hints about how they could see each other if they attended nearby schools—and how the relationship would probably end right then and there if they went their separate ways for four years.

An unseasonably cold wind swept through Newark that afternoon. Willie Joe looked out the library windows. He thought he saw snow flurries. No matter. He studied the college applications. He felt as if he had embarked on a Christmas shopping journey. "We'll get Syracuse, Saint John's and Duke for Uncle Ben; we'll pick up Rutgers, Howard and Easton for Coach." Uncle Ben's words ran through Willie Joe's head.

"Easton? Ain't nobody never even heard of Easton. Why on God's green earth would you even think of goin' there?" Because your dear friend Coach recommended it, Willie Joe heard the dialog replaying in his head. Uncle Ben disagreed vehemently with Coach on this point, but he would never challenge his friend openly. He knew that ultimately, Willie Joe's future depended upon two people—Coach, and himself. Willie Joe often wondered how the two men became such close friends. He had never asked either one.

His eyes grew heavy as he began to handwrite an essay for each application. He had decided to pen his essay on the challenge and responsibility of facing death. He quoted the Bible, citing that "I am my brother's keeper". After all, who would dispute the word of God? He continued on, drawing upon his readings in both History and English classes. He drew the proverbial line in the sand, throwing down the gauntlet for each man and woman to decide whether they will rise to the occasion when his or her own and their brethren's lives are on the line. He used Shakespeare's Hamlet as the model for failure—inaction and indecision never work. Neither does the action of a man with no moral compass, like Shakespeare's Mac Beth. In the end, he wrote, every day is judgment day and every day is a championship challenge.

Willie Joe sat back. The library clock read four-thirty. He needed to get home. The last thing he wanted to do was worry Aunt Agnes. She had begun to show the same signs of wear that his mother had in her later days, before her sudden illness and death. He suspected Uncle Ben's health may have begun to deteriorate. He just wore it better. Willie Joe grabbed his books and his jacket, heading for the door. As he headed down the stairs, he noticed a figure behind the staircase, hunched over. He approached carefully. Mr. Cavett, the custodian that had roughed up Tricks, clutched his chest. Willie Joe saw the spot on his uniform. Blood dripped slowly. Willie Joe swung Mr. Cavett's arm over his shoulder and eased him onto the steps.

"Who did this to you, Mr. Cavett?"

Mr. Cavett didn't reply. He shook his head. Willie Joe opened the man's shirt and examined the wound. Superficial, but bleeding profusely, nonetheless. Willie Joe pulled his sweater off, removed his T-shirt and pressed it over the wound. The direct pressure seemed to slow the bleeding. What to do now. The school nurse had left; the principal's offices were all locked up. Willie Joe ran to the phone booth on the other side of the building. Somebody had disabled the phone. He sprinted back to where he had left Mr. Cavett. He could not find him. No blood trail. Willie Joe canvassed the dark hallways until he saw a light. Mr. Cavett had used his keys to open the nurse's office. Willie Joe found the man bandaging himself up.

"Don't say nothing to nobody, you hear?"

"If that's how you want it."

"Here's your T-shirt; I'm sorry I bled all over it. You're okay, kid. I can take care of myself."

Willie Joe zipped up his jacket and left the building. The biting night air woke him up. He passed the newsstand and caught a glimpse of the headlines. The Knicks-Celtics game had gotten more play than President-elect Carter's speech on the economy. He rounded the corner to his aunt and uncle's house. As he entered, Aunt Agnes spied the bloody T-shirt and panicked. In his haste, he had forgotten to conceal or dispose of the shirt.

"Lordy be, what happened? Are you all right, Willie Joe?"

"Yes, I'm fine. I had to help out a friend. It's okay. He's fine now."

"We got us a dinner guest, so go and wash up. We're almost ready," Aunt Agnes prodded him.

"No practice and no date tonight? You mean we got the great William Joseph Cunningham all to ourselves tonight?" Uncle Ben joked.

Willie Joe emerged from his tiny bedroom and answered the knock at the door. Coach entered, offering a rose to Aunt Agnes.

"We sure is glad to see you, my old friend," Uncle Ben motioned Coach to take a seat at the dinner table. "After you taste Agnes's fine pork chops, chitlins with rice and peas and her home-made shoo-fly pie, we got to discuss this boy's future," Uncle Ben asserted.

"Don't be worryin' none about this fine young man, Ben. He'll do just fine. We gonna get him into a good school; you'll see. Everything's gonna work out," Coach assured Uncle Ben.

"That's just what I mean, Coach. We got to get him in the right school so's he can go pro," Uncle Ben countered, becoming agitated.

"Just leave it to me; I'll do right by him. That's why you done brought him to me, Ben," Coach assuaged him.

"Now, just enjoy your dinner, gentlemen; just enjoy this fine and bountiful feast the Lord has bestowed upon us," Aunt Agnes chided.

After dinner, Coach motioned to Willie Joe to step outside.

"We gonna get some air, Willie Joe and me."

They stood on the porch.

"Son, when they in church Sunday morning, you gonna come with me for a ride. We be visitin' an old friend of mine. I'll pick you up at nine o'clock in the mornin'. Just be ready," Coach nodded to Willie Joe.

They walked back up to the third floor. Coach bade them goodbye and winked at Willie Joe as he left the apartment.

"Whatch you two cookin' up there, Willie Joe?" Uncle Ben asked as he cleaned his eyeglasses on his sweater.

"Nothing; nothing at all. We're just getting our game plan ready," Willie Joe responded.

"Well, we gonna turn in early. When you get to be our age, you got to get your rest," Uncle Ben said, clamping a hand over Willie Joe's shoulder.

Willie Joe spent the better part of Saturday doing his homework. He read selections from Frederick Douglass's *Diary of a Slave*, Thomas Payne's *Common Sense* and Shakespeare's "Romeo and Juliet." He hadn't made any plans for the evening. As much as he enjoyed Lillian's company—and their passionate encounters, he began to wonder how he might enjoy the company of other women. It seemed strange. He had missed the whole dating scene. They had just become a couple seemingly overnight. He didn't want to stop seeing her. He just didn't want to fall into a rut. Relationships could get strange. People stayed together because they became comfortable. Had he missed something by not dating other girls? He decided not to call her. He knew she would not like that. He would tell her he needed some time with his family; that's all.

For the first time, Willie Joe decided to go out by himself. He took a walk to the bowling alley. He had never bowled in his entire life. He just wanted to watch. He bought a coke, took a seat by himself and watched a family of five play. The father took the youngest child by the hand and helped her roll the ball down the alley. She rolled a perfect gutter ball. No matter. She screeched for joy. Willie Joe watched each family member step up. He watched the father help the mother to get her stance just right before she rolled her first ever strike. They embraced. The kids cheered. Willie Joe felt that empty feeling creep back up on him. This is what he had missed. His family had never done anything together when he was growing up. As sad as he felt for himself, he felt just as much happiness for this family. Voices behind him at the next table suddenly snapped him out of his musings.

"I come up behind him like this, see—and I grabbed him. Then I cut him good," the first voice laughed.

"You cut Cavett? Did he bleed?" the second voice became excited.

"Shit yeah, he bled—like a stuck pig," the first voice answered, flatly. "And I'd do it again."

Willie Joe knew he couldn't turn around, but he had to find out who stabbed Mr. Cavett. He tried hard to place the voice. Then it came to him.

"Leroy, let's go pick up them chicks you said was waitin' on us."

Leroy Watson. That's who stabbed Mr. Cavett, the school custodian. Leroy Watson would probably end up in prison if he kept following the path he had chosen. Willie Joe waited until Leroy and his friends left before he stood up. What good was knowing something if you weren't going to do anything about it? Willie Joe pondered his options. He could make an anonymous call to the police. He could leave a note in the principal's office. He could tell Martha Washington, the school nurse. What if Leroy and his friends came after him? He decided not to do anything.

Sunday morning at nine o'clock Coach pulled up in front of Aunt Agnes and Uncle Ben's house and honked the horn once. Willie Joe grabbed his warm-up jacket and bounded down the steps. Coach's old rattle trap Chevy still ran, but it could wake up the whole city of Newark, it made so much noise. Willie Joe got in.

"Coffee?"

Coach handed him a container of piping hot coffee. It felt good against Willie Joe's hand that brisk morning. Coach fiddled with the radio to catch a few game scores, and then turned it off.

"Where are we headed?" Willie Joe earnestly inquired.

"To Easton, my boy, to Easton. I want you to meet the head coach at the University. School's closed for Thanksgiving break, but since we's old friends, he's gonna meet us on campus, so's you can see the place. How's that sound?" Coach cleared his throat, then took a belt of his coffee.

"That sounds great. I've never seen any college except when you arranged that road trip for us to see the Princeton game," Willie Joe replied. "Coach, I've been meaning to ask you this. How did you and my Uncle Ben meet and become friends? You don't mind me asking, do you? I just wondered," Willie Joe sat wide-eyed, waiting anxiously to hear the answer.

"In a foxhole in Korea, son; in a foxhole. You see, your uncle saved my ass. He and your daddy was both war heroes, you know," Coach confided, then slowly sipped his coffee.

"No, I didn't know. I only found out about my father's military service at his funeral. I always loved and respected my uncle. I didn't need a reason. Now, I guess I have one," Willie Joe offered.

Interstate Route 78 stretched a long way into the horizon. Luckily for them, they were traveling with the bright sun behind them. They passed through little towns with picturesque names that Willie Joe had never even heard of: Millington, Liberty Corner, Readington, Whitehouse Station. Finally, they saw signs for Phillipsburg and Easton. Suddenly, the road came to an abrupt end. They exited onto US Route 22 West, passing a small diner. In a few short minutes, they were over the bridge and into Pennsylvania, entering Easton. In no time, they entered the gates of the campus. No guard on duty at the shack. They proceeded straight to the gym.

They parked and entered the building.

"Check out this here swimming pool, Willie Joe, Coach opened the door.

Instantly, the smell of chlorine wafted over to them. The full Olympic size pool beckoned them. Two students practiced their laps. Coach closed the door and proceeded to a small row of offices outside a gymnasium. A burly middle-aged White man got up to greet them.

"Phil, meet my protégé here, Willie Joe Cunningham. He's like family to me," Coach stepped back.

The man surveyed Willie Joe's height and build like an engineer.

"So, you're Willie Joe Cunningham. Coach here has told me a lot about your game," Phil smiled.

"Yes, sir. I hope he had a few good things to say along the way. I really do appreciate you're coming out to see us on your day off like this—"

"Son, for Coach, I would do almost anything. Now, no guarantees here, but I do want you to at least apply for admission. I'll make sure our Financial Aid Officer sees your application before it goes to the Admissions office. You get me your varsity game schedule and I'll make it my business to come and watch you play," Phil assured Willie Joe.

"I do thank you, sir. I really want to thank you," Willie Joe could hardly contain himself.

"We gonna take a stroll around the campus and then leave. We'll be in touch. Thanks, Phil," Coach waved and escorted Willie Joe out of the office.

They passed the gym, peeking into the basketball courts. Willie Joe felt a rush as he watched a group of students practicing.

"Beats the city of Newark for atmosphere, doesn't it?" Coach chuckled.

CHAPTER 18

ASCENT

The winter of '77-'78 roared and growled its way through the mid-Atlantic and the Northeast. Nearly every day, the citizens of greater Newark found themselves either digging out with snow shovels or ducking to safety from the extremely high winds. Life went on, as it always does, in spite of the weather. America found itself once again engaged with the players of a different kind of team in the Middle East. The culture clash between East and West never resulted in any wins. Every newscast on radio and television, every newspaper headline, every news magazine cover profiled the dreaded Ayatollah Khomeini. How do you play a game when you don't know the rules? A high stakes game, at that. Willie Joe imagined himself on a basketball court, playing for his own life. He envisioned our American soldiers on the court, bleeding. It made no sense. But it did make for a good essay in history class. It earned him an "A" from Ms. Rogers.

Ms. Mary Rogers had arrived in Newark this year from her home city of Washington, D.C. She had replaced one of the most revered and respected teachers the Newark school system had ever known. Dr. Franklin had the distinction and claim of being the first Black teacher in Newark with a doctorate degree. After thirty-five years, he decided to hang up his gloves— not to retire to a golf course, but to travel the world and see the historic sites he had taught so many hundreds of students about. Ms. Mary Rogers had big shoes to fill, indeed. But her style worked. She challenged the students to make history relevant. She always said, "I'm not your real teacher; history is." So be it. She imparted a certain perspective to the students, inspiring them to make history work for them.

"Who can tell me how a current event you read about over the weekend repeats a lesson we should have learned about from an earlier era?" Ms. Rogers voice rang out.

After a moment of silence, she scanned the faces, seeking a sign of recognition.

"I knew we had a light in the darkness. Mr. Cunningham, please enlighten your classmates."

Willie Joe stood up.

"May I use the blackboard, please, Ms. Rogers?" Willie Joe asked.

"Most certainly; please do."

Willie Joe approached the front of the room, took up the chalk and began to write: "Napoleon Bonaparte; James Earl Carter." Then he turned and spoke.

"Iran will go down in history as Jimmy Carter's Waterloo."

"Very impressive, Mr. Cunningham; very impressive. Anyone else?" Ms. Rogers surveyed the room, hopeful that someone else had paid enough attention to her assignments—and the world around them, to engage in critical thinking.

No response. Ms. Rogers placed her hands on her hips, defiantly.

"The only way you are going to make something of your lives is through education. If you want more out of your life later, you need to pay attention *now*. Life is not going to wait for you. If you want a better life than your parents had, education is the pathway. Now, how many of you plan to go on to college?" Ms. Rogers frowned as a few hands went up, gingerly.

"If you have no enthusiasm for life, no passion for anything, you will not succeed at anything you attempt. I have seen too many of your generation end up on the scrap heap. I have seen their vitality sucked out of them by drug dealers and pimps. The great legislator from Colorado, Wellington Webb, told an audience of students a few years ago, 'It's time for Black people to stop being the three P's: pimps, porters and prostitutes.' Well, if you're not willing to settle for that kind of a life, you better get on board now because this train is pulling out of the station—whether you're on it or not," Ms. Rogers tossed the book she had held onto the desk, as if to punctuate her sentence.

Nobody moved. The room grew silent.

"I will say one more thing to you, in closing. If you think the world owes you anything, think again. I don't care if you're Black, White, Puerto Rican or Chinese-American, each of us has to earn his or her own way in this world. And if you think you'll get an athletic scholarship, think again. The second word there is still scholarship. You've got to have the grades. If you think you can get to college just by memorizing what's in your textbook, think again. Because if and when you do get there, they are going to expect you to *think*. So, here is your assignment: Each of you will write a five page paper— with research to back up what you say—on who the best ruler was in history, and why. Someone will be chosen from among you to present your findings to the whole junior and senior classes at the next assembly. You have one week to complete this. Good luck."

As if she had timed it, the bell rang...on cue. The class filed out of the room. Ms. Rogers smiled at Willie Joe. Before he could leave, she looked up at him, smiled and said, "I'm expecting great things from you."

Willie Joe headed for the staircase. The throng of students enveloped him. When he reached the bottom, he had a sinking feeling. He stood exactly where he had founded the bleeding Mr. Cavett. He knew who stabbed him, and he did nothing about it. The guilt ate away at him. No one else knew that he knew. Just then he noticed Leroy Watson in the crowd. The knot of students moved toward him. Just then, Willie Joe saw Leroy grab a female student and press her against the row of lockers. Willie Joe took three long strides toward them. Nobody else even stopped; they just kept moving. At the very moment Willie Joe broke through the crowd and stood over Leroy, Watson brandished a knife. In one deft move, Willie Joe grabbed the knife from Leroy's hand and swung him around to face him. He saw fear in Leroy's eyes. Willie Joe stepped on the knife. The girl turned around. It was Lillian. Leroy disappeared into the crowded hallway. Lillian embraced Willie Joe and the two of them walked down the hallway, arm in arm.

Practice after practice, game after game, Willie Joe applied the same intensity to his playing skills. He observed the pros on television, watching their every move. He listened intently to everything his coaches told him. And both his Boys Club and his high school teams went on a winning streak. One day, when they arrived for practice in the high school gym, the team read a note on the door, directing them to a nearby classroom. When they arrived they opened the door to a darkened room.

The coach beckoned them to take seats as he clicked on a film projector. The film consisted of interviews on camera with former Green Bay Packers football players. Confusion reigned throughout the room. Why does he want us to watch a film about football players, they all wondered. When the film concluded, the coach flipped on the lights.

"Every one of the former pro players you saw in that film became a success in life after they ended their football careers. No coincidence. Every one of those players took their direction from the greatest coach that ever lived, in any sport—Vince Lombardi. Become a success on the field—or the court, in your case—and apply the same success principles in life, and you will continue to succeed, wherever you go, whatever you do. Not every professional athlete followed the Lombardi method. You need to know that many guys went pro and then ended up broke just a few years after they left the field or the court. This is a young man's career. If you do make it as a pro, you won't play for long. You've got to think about what you'll do when your game is over. That's it for today," the coach confided, as he looked the team up and down.

As Willie Joe headed home, thoughts buzzed through his head. Which school would he end up in? Would he ever go pro? What would he do after basketball? Would he ever have the family life he had missed out on as a child? He stomped the snow off of his wet sneakers on the porch before heading up the steps to Aunt Agnes and Uncle Ben's apartment.

Once inside, it seemed unusually quiet. No TV, no radio playing. Uncle Ben emerged from the bedroom. Beads of sweat populated his brow. He quickly withdrew his handkerchief and mopped his brow.

"She's not feeling well, your aunt. Don' quite know what's wrong. She don't want to go to the doctor, neither. She just say she don't feel right," Uncle Ben seemed bewildered.

"Do you want me to talk to her?" Willie Joe asked, concerned.

"Naw, jus' let her rest a bit. She awready got dinner all made up fo' us. Les' just eat and we'll check in on her later. Oh, by the way, you got some college mail there on the kitchen counter. Go and check it out an' see whatcha got before we eat, son," Uncle Ben urged him.

Willie Joe sorted through the envelopes. He anxiously slit each one open and read it. Uncle Ben stood by, waiting. Willie Joe looked up, pointing to the envelopes.

"St. John's is a no; Georgetown is a no; Syracuse has not decided yet; Kentucky did not respond; Rutgers is a yes and Easton is a yes," Willie Joe observed Uncle Ben's disapproving look.

"What ever happened to 'equal opportunity'? I bet if we had the money and you was White, you could go to any school you want," Uncle Ben scowled.

"We'll see. The game's not over yet, Uncle Ben," Willie Joe smiled as he clasped Uncle Ben's shoulder.

"Remember when you were fighting in the war, just because you won or lost a battle didn't mean it was time to walk away," Willie Joe offered.

"That's wise; that's righteous, son. You got a good head on your shoulders," Uncle Ben seemed placated—at least for the moment, by Willie Joe's words. Even though Willie Joe knew how much Uncle Ben had his heart set on getting him into the "right school", he felt the agitation at the moment probably resulted more from Aunt Agnes's condition than from the rejected college applications.

The two men shared a quiet dinner as Aunt Agnes slept. Willie Joe thought about his his past, his present and his future. He wondered how much control we really had over the events in our lives. He wondered whether his mother's way would serve him better. Bernice had learned to cope the way most of those close to an alcoholic did—by learning to 'let go, let God.' Maybe we just can't control the outcome of everything that happens in our lives, he thought.

After dinner, Uncle Ben checked in on Aunt Agnes, who rested comfortably. He retired to his easy chair. Willie Joe took the college letters into his tiny room and placed them in his book bag. He thought about his history essay. He thought about how he had saved Lillian from Leroy Watson. He felt exonerated from his earlier failure after Leroy had attacked Mr. Cavett. He knew he did right. At the time, he didn't even know it was Lillian that Leroy had grabbed. When he looked at the clock, Willie Joe noticed the hour had grown late. He needed to rest.

As he fell into a deep sleep, Willie Joe succumbed to a dream. Nothing made any sense while it happened. All of the action in the dream seemed to swirl around him, rather than to involve him. He found himself on a college campus, surrounded by all unfamiliar people. He didn't know or recognize anyone. When he went to the gym, he stood on the basketball court in street clothes. The uniformed team played around him. They never passed the ball to him. In the classroom, the professors didn't hear him speak. He could never find the right books. He ran out of breath trying to find the right buildings and the right rooms. He arrived late to nearly every class, and nobody would give him the assignments. Finally, he went to the college library. The books spoke to him. Suddenly, he felt a hand on his shoulder. It roused him from his sleep. It was Uncle Ben.

"Son, it's your aunt. I can't wait no more. We got to get her over to the hospital. She's been in pain. Please call us a taxi and come with me," Uncle Ben implored Willie Joe.

"Done. Consider it done. I'm on it," Willie Joe sprang up and went straight to the telephone.

They bundled Aunt Agnes up as much as they could against the harsh, cold night winds. The clear night air stung their faces as they approached the waiting cab. They eased Aunt Agnes into the back seat of the spacious Checker cab. Uncle Ben slid in next to her on the other side. Willie Joe scrunched into the front passenger seat. The cabbie, a Haitian, sped off. Willie Joe studied his hack's license. Jean Delacroix screeched around the corners, reaching the emergency room in record time. He understood the gravity of the situation. Uncle Ben slipped him a ten-dollar bill. Delacroix refused to keep the change as a tip. Instead, he stared Uncle Ben directly in the eye and said, "A votre sante". They emerged from the cab, approached the Emergency Room doors and the cab sped off. The automatic doors swung open and they entered. Aunt Agnes's breathing had become shallow; her gait unsteady. A nurse's aide quickly brought a wheelchair and took her to an empty bed. Uncle Ben and Willie Joe paced nervously while they waited for a doctor. A Filipino resident introduced himself and began to check Aunt Agnes's vital signs, noting them on a clipboard. He summoned a nurse. The nurse summoned the nurse's aide and they placed Aunt Agnes back into the wheelchair. It would be a long night.

CHAPTER 19

GROWING PAINS

Uncle Ben and Willie Joe visited Aunt Agnes one more time in the hospital, following all the tests. She didn't look too bad, but she just had no energy. Uncle Ben paced the floor in the corridor outside her room, nervously waiting for the doctor. Time passed. No doctor arrived. Willie Joe approached the nurse's station. The nurse, a young Chinese-American girl, looked up at him and smiled. At least she had empathy. The world had seemingly become a cold place during Willie Joe's lifetime.

"How may I help you?"

"The lady in Room 206—she's my aunt. Can we get any update on her condition? My uncle's real upset, and—"

"I'll ring Doctor Weissman. He's her attending physician. If he's on the floor, he should be able to tell you something," nurse Wong assured him.

"Thank you. That would really mean a lot to us," Willie Joe answered, heading back to Uncle Ben.

When he arrived at the room, Doctor Weissman had already checked in and had reviewed Aunt Agnes's chart. He smiled at her and motioned to Uncle Ben to accompany him out into the hallway. Willie Joe remained by Aunt Agnes's side. He had that sinking feeling he got every time he entered the hospital. He could almost see the spirits of his mother, his father and his brother hovering over his aunt. He sat in the chair by the bedside. He must have dozed off. He could have sworn he saw his mother standing over him. He felt a cold rush, then looked up as Uncle Ben made his way across the room. Uncle Ben leaned over Aunt Agnes, gently kissing her forehead. She smiled and closed her eyes.

"We gonna go now, honey. I'll see you in the morning. You just rest now, you hear. Is there anything you need before we leave? " Uncle Ben tried to soothe her. Aunt Agnes shook her head, then closed her eyes.

The two men slowly walked down the long corridor. Willie Joe broke the silence.

"What did he say to you, the doctor?"

"He say he don' rightly know what it is. He didn't find nothin' in all the tests they did. He say he's gonna send her to the convalescent center over in Orange, where she can rest—but she don't need no hospital," Uncle Ben's voice cracked. He tried to hold back and conceal how upset he was, but Willie Joe knew. He decided not to respond.

Every day, Uncle Ben rode the bus from Newark to nearby Orange. Every day he sat with Aunt Agnes. Her spirits lifted, but she just didn't seem to regain any energy. On the weekends, Willie Joe accompanied him. Uncle Ben brought her flowers, a box of chocolates, skeins of yarn and knitting needles, magazines—anything he could think of to keep her occupied.

The long winter finally came to an end. Uncle Ben's absence from home made it easier for Willie Joe to receive guests—not girlfriends, but the constant visitors from the colleges and universities that courted him. Word got around fast that Newark had another rising star on its basketball courts. It seemed like that's all that mattered to these schools—to win a Big East Conference Championship; to make it to the Final Four of the NCAA. Willie Joe hardly knew the politics behind it all, but he began to learn the machinery that ran these schools.

One Sunday morning, Willie Joe opened the door to none other than the head coach from Syracuse himself. He could hardly believe it. He recognized the man from televised games. He had seen him standing on the sidelines. Willie Joe offered him a cup of coffee.

"Mr. Cunningham, we have reviewed both your transcripts and your game. We sent a scout to watch you play. Provided you maintain your grades throughout your senior year, we are prepared to make you a generous offer. We would like to have you join our starting line-up during your freshman year. To that end, I am authorized to offer you a full scholarship, including housing. Are you prepared to accept our offer?" The man sat back in his chair, folded his hands and waited, silently.

Willie Joe could hardly believe it.

"Well, sir, that is a most generous offer. In all honesty, I haven't made up my mind yet. I couldn't really give you an answer just yet, but—"

"What will it take for you to be an Orangeman?"

"I promise I will give it very careful thought. I just can't tell you now. I have to evaluate my other offers, sir."

"You do drive a hard bargain, Mr. Cunningham. Here's my number. I'll call you by the end of the week."

After he watched the man get into his car, Willie Joe's head spun. So this is how they play the game.

They seemed to come in pairs. The following week, Willie Joe received visits from coaches at Boston, NC State, St. Bonaventure. Each one seemed intent on outdoing the others' offers. One of them hinted at procuring girls; another promised to supply tutors to take his tests. After a while, they began to have a reverse effect on him. They seemed ready to resort to almost anything for their recruitment efforts. They just rubbed him the wrong way. Willie Joe hoped he could find a few schools with some integrity. He couldn't tell Uncle Ben about any of these offers. He decided to confide in Coach.

"I tol' you they was bad news. We call 'em 'handout schools'. Now, we got to take a look at the schools where you gonna get in on your own merit. You still got choices. We gonna talk to my friends at Rutgers, Seton Hall, Princeton and Easton. We gonna make the right choice for you."

Willie Joe and Coach set up appointments during his spring break to visit each school. Coach picked him up in his rattletrap Chevy while Uncle Ben visited Aunt Agnes at the convalescent center. The interviews went well, which just added to Willie Joe's confusion. Princeton might be a "reach"; Rutgers and Seton Hall would both provide a great experience, yet something attracted Willie Joe to that obscure little low-profile campus in Easton. They decided to schedule another visit there.

This time, when they arrived in Easton, the campus activity roared at full tilt. Everywhere they looked, co-eds traversed the grounds, from building to building. The soccer team practiced outside the gym. Cheerleaders practiced their routines in the parking lot. Music blared from the student center. They entered the gym. As before, Coach and Willie Joe peered through the doors into the Olympic-sized pool. A team of female students performed laps. They made their way into coach Phil

Warshaw's office. Another man stood behind him. Burly and white, with a bull neck, he scanned the stat sheets on Phil's desk.

"Coach; Willie Joe. Meet our Assistant Coach, Chamber Higgins— our very own version of the fighting Irish. He makes Notre Dame cringe. I wanted you folks to meet Mr. Higgins. He's the one empowered to make the offer to you."

"Phil's told me a lot about your game, Willie Joe. I would like to come and see you play myself. Your friend and mentor Coach only sends us the best. Now, I'm going to tell you right now, we don't play any of those games the big schools engage in. If you're looking for cars and girls, we don't do that here. We want serious students who are serious about their games, their college careers and the rest of their lives. From what I've been told, you seem to fit the bill. We can offer you a full scholarship. You may have to work on campus part-time to subsidize part of your housing costs. I'm sure you'll want to think carefully before you decide. We're not in a hurry. We want you to make the best decision. Any questions?"

"No, sir. I do want to thank you gentlemen. I promise you I will give this a lot of thought. I do have a good feeling about you people," Willie Joe offered, sincerely.

"And we have a good feeling about you, Mr. Cunningham. That's the way it should be. We like to win, but we like to win fairly and squarely. We'll wait to hear from you," Mr. Higgins extended a firm handshake."

Coach and Willie Joe enjoyed the long ride back from Easton. The road opened up before them. Cars flew by. Willie Joe had never seen so many hi-marque luxury cars before. He felt cheated in a way, unable to share his good news with his parents or his brother. He dreaded facing Uncle Ben. He didn't want to disappoint him with his choice of schools, but he knew he probably would. He leaned toward choosing Easton, even before hearing what Rutgers and Seton Hall had to say. Maybe it had something to do with getting out of the gravitational pull of the Newark orbit. He wanted that badly. Coach had always wanted that for him, too. He felt the time had come to leave Newark behind. Perhaps it had.

CHAPTER 20

DRESS REHEARSAL

Someone once said that this life amounted to nothing more than a dress rehearsal for the next one. Willie Joe wondered about that. After the hottest summer on record in Newark, he welcomed the beginnings of fall—and his senior year of high school. With Aunt Agnes still at the convalescent center, and Uncle Ben making his daily pilgrimage there, Willie Joe spent more time by himself. He saw less and less of Lillian, too. He began to take on some of the household chores, like the food shopping, on Saturday mornings. After that, he would take the later bus to Orange and visit Aunt Agnes, returning home with Uncle Ben.

On an unusually cool September Saturday morning, Willie Joe arrived at the supermarket on Frelinghuysen Avenue. The supermarket, a small stand-alone building, had in its earlier life, served as a men's wear shop. Right down the street from the roller rink, it stirred memories. He could almost see his brother Carlton leading him by the hand. The glint of the sunlight on broken glass beer bottles across the parking lot woke him from his momentary daze. No sooner than he entered the supermarket, picked up a basket and began to shop, he stood face to face with the imposing figure of the Reverend Pearl.

"Well, well, it has been a long time indeed, Willie Joe. I almost didn't recognize you. You have certainly grown to become a fine young man. We miss you over at Beulah Baptist church. I paid a visit to your aunt just the other day. Fine folks, your aunt and uncle; they certainly have done right by you. So, what are your plans, young man? I suppose you'll be leaving our fair city soon?" the Reverend Pearl boomed in his bombastic, yet sonorous voice. Everything he said sounded like a sermon delivered from the pulpit. Willie Joe imagined him pontificating as he selected oranges and apples. He probably even proclaimed scripture aloud in his sleep, Willie Joe mused to himself.

"Yes, sir, I probably will be leaving town about this time next year, if all goes well. Thanks for asking, and I do appreciate you looking in on Aunt Agnes. Well, it was nice seeing you, as well, Reverend," Willie Joe wanted to break away. Guilt pangs tugged at his gut. He had completely pulled away from the church. He knew his mother would not approve. He quickly nodded —almost bowed to Reverend Pearl, and whisked away, hastily filling his basket with the items on his grocery list.

Later that day, he joined Uncle Ben at the convalescent center. Aunt Agnes had fallen asleep.

"I almost forgot to tell you. Yo' young lady called, and she don't sound too happy, Willie Joe. You maybe better call her when we get home. We got to look after our ladies," Uncle Ben lectured him.

They took the last bus home, riding in silence. Willie Joe knew Aunt Agnes might never come home. He knew Uncle Ben wouldn't approve of his choice of colleges. He knew the time had come to leave Newark behind. He thought of James Baldwin's words; he thought of Shakespeare's Julius Caesar's words. He could always come home. The world waited for him. College waited for him. His basketball career waited for him. And he had to say goodbye to Lillian, painful as it might be. He had to be his own man, make his own choices—and live with them, good, bad, right or wrong. He knew that.

Senior year flew by at breakneck speed. Willie Joe no longer played on the Boys' Club team. He needed to devote full attention to his studies and his to his varsity team's season, in order to maintain the scholarship offer from Easton. With great difficulty, he had turned down all of the other offers. He had visited the Rutgers and Seton Hall campuses; he had watched their teams play, with great interest, thanks to Coach, who drove him to the games. Still, Easton had a lure, a magnetic pull that seemed to draw him to the campus of this obscure little school. Willie Joe had his doubts about trusting any of the White coaches, but he decided to put his fears aside and trust Chamber Higgins—mostly on Coach's say-so. That would have to be enough.

Weequahic High had a winning season, thanks in large part to Willie Joe's efforts. His game kept improving. Still, he knew he had more to learn. He felt sure he would learn it when he got to Easton.

He observed the downtrodden look in Uncle Ben's eyes when he finally confided in him about this choice to go to Easton. He had never seen that look before. True to form, Uncle Ben accepted his choice. His words stuck with Willie Joe.

"Son, it's not about approval, it's about acceptance. I accept your decision, whether I agree with it or not. I want the best fo' you, and I hope it turns out that way."

Willie Joe felt the pure love this man had for him. What more could he ask for?

The break-up with Lillian was not so easy. He decided to meet her on neutral ground. She sensed it; she could feel the tension. Willie Joe met her in the park, where they had shared ice cream cones—and their first kiss. Lillian spoke first.

"I know why we're here, Willie Joe, so let me make it easier for you. I'm going to Boston; you're going to Easton. We're not going to see each other and that's the end of it," Lillian looked him square in the eye. She did make it easier for him.

"And don't tell me we can write letters, or that you'll come visit me on break. That's just not going to work for me. You know that."

"You're right, Lillian; I do know that. And I will miss you. You played a very important part in my life, and—"

"Don't say it. I know. I was part of your 'growing up plan,'" Lillian shot back. Willie Joe could see the hurt and the anger in her eyes. He had never seen her like this.

"I will always care for you deeply. Nobody will ever take your place. I meant everything I ever said to you, but we do have to go our separate ways now. We each have a calling, a destiny and a path to follow. I know you will do great things in your life," Willie Joe held her hands tightly. Lillian's face dropped. When she raised her head, the tears streamed silently down her face.

"Come on; I'll take you home," Willie Joe offered. Lillian pulled away and ran off. He followed her. Out of breath, he stood by her side at the bus stop.

"Lillian, come on. Please don't make this any harder than it already is. Do you think this is easy for me? You were my first love. That means a lot to me, but it's over now," Willie Joe put his hand on her shoulder. She turned to him.

"I had been with boys before, but I didn't love them. I really loved you. I never knew if you really loved me. You keep everything inside. So many times, I wondered how you really felt. I think I know now. I'm not saying you used me intentionally, but I never felt you loved me back the same way I loved you, and that hurts. It really cuts deep," Lillian gazed into his eyes.

"I could never hurt you; really, I couldn't. You have to know that. I guess I still have a lot to learn about women," Willie Joe wiped Lillian's tears away with his hands.

"Goodbye, my Mr. Cunningham. We'll meet again some day," Lillian composed herself, turned and ascended the steps into the bus. Willie Joe waited for the next bus, feeling the gnawing in the pit of his stomach. They say time heals all wounds; he hoped they were right.

When he arrived home, Willie Joe took one look at Uncle Ben's face and he knew. Aunt Agnes had taken a turn for the worse. Still no diagnosis, no help, no comfort. He knew he would leave his uncle at the worst time. Did he need to worry? A war hero could certainly take care of himself. Maybe his mother's way would prove right. For the first time in years, Willie Joe decided to pray. He didn't tell Uncle Ben. He just went into his room, closed the door and dropped to his knees. He prayed that God would spare Aunt Agnes; that God would protect Uncle Ben; and that He would forgive him and guide Willie Joe onto the right path. For the first time, he felt peace and solace.

That night, Willie Joe dreamt one dream after another. In one dream, he and Coach drove off, leaving Newark behind. No sooner did they leave the city than Willie Joe turned around just in time to see it burst into flames and explode. Willie Joe wanted to turn back. Coach laughed and said he could never return home. Everything about the dream seemed to fly in the face of reality. Coach would never say that. If Newark survived the riots fifteen years ago, the city would always be there. Willie Joe was sure of it. Still, the dream disturbed him. Newark would always be home. He knew he would come back some day. He just needed to see what lay outside the city—what awaited him. He knew Newark held his past, but not his future. He worried about his aunt and uncle. What would become of them? Who would take care of them in their waning years? He felt responsible for them, yet he knew he needed to move on.

Shafts of daylight filled Willie Joe's tiny room. He stood up, stretched and looked out the window. Wind blown snow swirled around the house, covering the steps and the sidewalk. The city's trucks had begun sanding and salting the street a few hours ago. Willie Joe quickly got dressed and grabbed the old garden shovel at the bottom of the stairs. He pulled on his gloves and stepped out into the cold. The flakes began to pile up on his jacket and his wool ski cap. He shoveled the steps and the sidewalk, but they became quickly covered by the time he had finished.

Snow or no snow, Willie Joe knew he had mid-term exams today. He had to ace them. He remained focused on maintaining his grades and keeping his scholarship to Easton, which was tied to his grade point average. Nothing else mattered, except keeping up his game. Uncle Ben met him in the kitchen, where they shared a breakfast of hot oatmeal. Uncle Ben smiled at him.

"Willie Joe, you know you mean everything to me and your aunt. We know you will succeed. We just want you to make us proud. I wish your folks could see you now—see how you turned out. Nobody's perfect; we all make mistakes, but you are a fine young man, and we are mighty proud of you. I got something fo' you. I been waiting until the time was right," Uncle Ben said, as he reached into the pocket of his bathrobe. He withdrew a pocket-sized Bible.

"Keep this with you, always. I had it in my flack jacket in the foxhole in Korea, when I saved Coach's life. It's yours now. May the Lord watch over you and protect you, as he did fo' me," Uncle Ben pressed the well-worn book into Willie Joe's hand.

"Thank you," were the only words that would come out. Willie Joe felt overwhelmed. No single gesture could have had more meaning than this simple one. He didn't know how to begin to give back to this man, whom he had always admired, and who gave so much to him.

"I've got to get going; we've got mid-terms today," Willie Joe smiled, and then embraced Uncle Ben before he bounded down the steps. Mapes Avenue looked like a winter wonderland…and it felt like home.

CHAPTER 21

ONWARD AND UPWARD

It seemed like Willie Joe had just taken his midterms, yet final exams were just around the corner. He still had guilt pangs every time he passed Lillian in the hallway at school. He remained focused, and everything just went along smoothly. The varsity team closed out a winning season; his grants and financial aid letters of confirmation arrived in the mail from Easton; he continued to practice at the Boys' Club throughout the spring.

Aunt Agnes remained at the convalescent center. No amount of physical therapy could really help her condition. Uncle Ben faithfully visited her every day. Willie Joe continued to join him there on weekends. They read her favorite passages from Willie Joe's well-worn Bible, and kept her spirits up. He couldn't help but notice how much she reminded him of his mother. Sisters are often like that— they keep one another's memory alive.

Newark came alive in the spring. The city began to see real estate investors coming in. New office buildings sprang up. The railroad rider ship became robust. People began to give Newark a chance again. Even though nearly everyone speculated about corruption in city government, at least the crime rate had gone down. When people feel safe, great things can happen.

Finally, the big day arrived—graduation. A certain pride overtook everyone in the school. The marching band donned its uniforms, the students their caps and gowns and the gym swelled with parents and family members. For many, they would see the first child ever go on to college. For many of the students, they would leave Newark for the first time in their lives. The graduates lined up, men on one side of the gym in their blue caps and gowns, women on the other side of the gym, in their white caps and gowns. The pomp and circumstance was monumental. The Reverend Pearl gave the benediction. Principal Young introduced the Valedictorian and then the Salutatorian. The student speeches hit the mark—a few memories, but mostly tributes to the departed—young lives cut down in their prime by drugs and violence. Willie Joe spotted Mr. Cavett, the custodian, who smiled directly at him. Willie Joe nodded to him. He had never seen him out of uniform— certainly not in a jacket and tie.

Willie Joe scanned the crowd as Principal Young introduced the next speaker. Suddenly, he felt overcome as he spotted Uncle Ben slowly bringing Aunt Agnes forward in a wheelchair. She waved to him, beaming with pride. Next, the keynote speaker stepped up. Willie Joe recognized him. A retired Black basketball player—only the second Black coach to win a World Championship with the Golden State Warriors…and a native of Newark. He cut an imposing figure as he took the stage. The room went absolutely quiet.

"Many are called, but few are chosen. It is not *that* we are chosen; it is what *we* choose that matters. When you leave these halls, and if you leave this city, what you do for others will follow you. What you do for yourself will not be remembered. Do not ever forget your humble homes and your modest beginnings. What makes you great is what you carry inside of you. Whether you carry it to the ball field, to the office building, to the factory or anywhere else does not matter. Never forget—it's not about what happens to you—it's about what you *do* about it. Always be who you are, and never stop giving to the rest of the world. You are gifted and you are blessed. Never sell yourself short."

The thunderous applause filled the gym. Then came the awards. Kids tend to zone out during these long ceremonies. The mind wanders. Willie Joe was no different. He thought about his parents and his brother. He wished he could have shared this moment with them. Suddenly, Willie Joe woke up with a start.

"And the Outstanding Student Athlete Award goes to William Joseph Cunningham, for his all around playing on our winning basketball team," his varsity coach's voice rang out. Willie Joe could hardly believe it as he stepped forward to accept the trophy. He held it, examined it and then thrust it into the air before returning to his place in the line. The moment seemed surreal—just like the many moments when the buzzer rang, after he had scored the winning shot. Victory kept getting sweeter for Willie Joe.

When the festivities ended, Willie Joe made his way over to Aunt Agnes and Uncle Ben, thanking them profusely for being there. Aunt Agnes wiped the tears from her eyes as Willie Joe bent down to kiss her. She reminded him so much of his mother, it became painful. Pain and joy intertwined; isn't that how life always went? Fragments of those now forgotten dreams came rushing into Willie Joe's head.

"Now, you go on and spend some time with yo' friends, Willie Joe. You earned it. I'll take that trophy home fo' you if you like, and keep it safe," Uncle Ben assured him.

Aunt Agnes and Uncle Ben made their way to the back of the gym, the trophy resting on her lap. Willie Joe felt a tap on his shoulder. The next face he saw was Coach's.

"It won't be long befo' you be leavin' town, Willie Joe. You done good; you're on the right path—out of Newark and on to a great career. I feel it," Coach placed his hand on his shoulder.

Willie Joe felt his face flush.

"Because of you, Coach; because of you," Willie Joe's gratitude oozed from ever pore.

"No, sir. Because you paid attention, listened and learned, "Coach replied, as he began to walk away.

"I'll see you soon; I promise—" Willie Joe stopped in his tracks as he reeled around to face Lillian.

"Come on. Let's go somewhere," she urged, smiling.

Willie Joe felt relieved, knowing they still could treat one another respectfully. Friendship never dies. They ducked out of the gym, took off the caps and gowns and ran to the bus stop. Willie Joe took Lillian to the delicatessen where Uncle Ben had brought him the day he became his guardian. Mr. Kartzmann recognized him and sent Morris the waiter over to their table. After ordering, Willie Joe took Lillian's hands and held them in his own.

"I'm sorry I hurt you. I didn't mean to; you have to believe me. You deserve the best, and I want that for you," Willie Joe confided.

"I never doubted your sincerity, Willie Joe. I guess I just thought it would be forever, you and me. You aren't ready for that; I understand.

There's a bigger world out there than this one, and we both have to see it. We both have to make our mark on it. You need to find out who you really are. I know you, Willie Joe—better than you know yourself. I never knew your mother, but I know she would be proud of you. Listen, we've got to think about the next generation. We owe them something. We've got to make this a better place for them. We maybe can't fix the whole world, but we can come back here and make Newark a better place for the kids to live and grow up in. We have to *stand for something*. Will you commit to that, Willie Joe?" Lillian pleaded with him.

Willie Joe had never really thought about what kind of an impact he could have on anyone else's life He came from the projects; he overcame, and it always seemed enough to just focus on where he was going with his own future. Lillian had just thrown his world into a tailspin. He needed to think about that.

"I can't think that far ahead yet, I really can't. We only just graduated from high school today," Willie Joe felt challenged and confronted.

"If we don't, who will? Willie Joe, you are so much more than just a great athlete. You're a wonderful human being. And giving back is both your right and your obligation. You need to commit to it," Lillian implored him. He looked up as Morris the waiter stood by, ready to take their order.

"Okay. I will some day figure out a way to help the kids in Newark," he struggled to get the words out.

"You don't sound committed, but I'll accept that—and I'll hold you to it," Lillian smiled as she set her glasses aside on the table in front of them.

Great things always come from people who stretch themselves beyond their comfort zones, beyond the small world of self. Those that listen for the beat of the global village and join the dance, make it rain. Nothing trumps that.

CHAPTER 22

WELCOME TO COLLEGE

Willie Joe took a summer job at the supermarket on Frelinghuysen Avenue, where he had his chance meeting months before with the Reverend Pearl. At least it was a cool refuge from the brutal New Jersey summer heat. Even with the generous financial aid package from Easton, he still needed to earn additional money. He liked the store, his co-workers, the customers—even the work was pleasant enough. It gave him time to think while he stacked the crates and emptied the produce. He thought about his family, his game, his college years ahead—and the promise of a career. Secretly, he couldn't wait to leave Newark, even though it was the only home he had ever known.

Finally, the day came. Willie Joe bade his supermarket co-workers goodbye, collected his last paycheck, went home and began to pack his clothes into the well-worn duffel bag Uncle Ben had given him the night before. He felt proud, knowing he used the very same duffel bag his uncle carried with him through the war. After a bus ride up to wish Aunt Agnes goodbye at the convalescent center, he carefully loaded up his gym bag with the last minute items—toiletry items. He stopped for a minute, glancing around the tiny room. He slipped the frame with his father's medals and the flag presented by the honor guard at his funeral, into the duffel bag. He couldn't leave them behind. One last look, and he bounded down the steps just as he heard the horn sound.

Coach stood outside his old rattletrap Chevy with the trunk open, motioning for Willie Joe to deposit his bags. The trunk slammed, and in a moment, they sped off for Easton. Coach handed Willie Joe a container of coffee. The two men shared their drinks in silence. Willie Joe saw Newark disappear into the rearview mirror. He thought of James

Baldwin's words. You can always go home. He felt guilty about leaving Uncle Ben and Aunt Agnes. Still, he knew his destiny waited for him. Not the least bit homesick, the excitement of beginning the next chapter of his life nearly overwhelmed him.

Finally, they crossed the bridge into Pennsylvania. Just a few short miles left to go. The sun nearly blinded the two men as they entered the gates of the campus. Stopping at the gate, the security guard directed them to Radcliff Hall, Willie Joe's assigned dormitory. Coach pulled up to the parking area, opened the trunk and confronted Willie Joe in that inimitable way of his.

"You ain't never comin' back. You know that, don't you?"

"I'll come back; you'll see," Willie Joe grinned.

Coach stared him down, dead serious.

"Show 'em your stuff, Willie Joe—just show 'em your stuff," Coach nodded as Willie Joe slung the duffel bag over his shoulder and headed toward the dormitory entrance.

Willie Joe ascended the steps to the third floor, passing a few laughing co-eds in the stair well. A girl with long blond hair turned and smiled at him over her shoulder as she floated down the steps, still laughing. When he reached the third floor, he saw rows of open doors with students scurrying about, opening suitcases and steamer trunks. He saw only White faces. He finally found his assigned room. He knocked on the tightly closed door. It opened slowly, half cautiously, revealing a well-groomed, innocent looking White boy. Evan Bixby looked up at Willie Joe as if he had come face to face with a giraffe. Willie Joe towered over him.

"I think this is my room," Willie Joe said, weakly.

"Three of the four of us assigned are here, so yeah, maybe. There's supposed to be a William Joseph Cunningham joining us—"

"That would be me," Willie Joe smiled.

"The other guys are checking out the campus. Come on in," Evan welcomed him warmly.

"That's your bed, next to mine. Where's the rest of your gear? Are they shipping it for you?" Evan studied Willie Joe's duffel bag and his gym bag.

"This is it; it's all I've got," Willie Joe replied, surveying the room. He felt the culture clash instantly. Still, he felt that he and Evan would become fast friends.

"Come on into the living room. I'll introduce you to my folks. Where are yours?" Evan inquired.

"They both passed on. I live with my Uncle. My aunt's in a nursing home now," Willie Joe responded.

"Mom, dad, come meet our other roommate," Evan called out.

A middle-aged White couple emerged from the couch, slightly in shock— as if they had never seen a Black man before.

"Willie Joe Cunningham. You must be Mr. And Mrs. Bixby. I'm from Newark, New Jersey. Where do you folks hail from?" Willie Joe felt almost playful, sensing their discomfort.

"We're not too far from Newark. We live in Glen Ridge. Have you ever heard of Glen Ridge, Willie Joe?" Mr. Bixby asked, adjusting his turtleneck sweater.

"Certainly. We beat 'em in basketball last year when we won the title," Willie Joe couldn't hold back his smile.

"I'm sure you and Evan and the other boys will get along just fine, Willie Joe," Mrs. Bixby drawled. Willie Joe picked up her Southern accent immediately.

"I'm sure we will. And I'm sure we'll learn a lot from each other," Willie Joe smiled again.

Just then, Alex and Craig appeared in the doorway. The other two roommates that shared the suite came from small towns in Maryland and Pennsylvania. More culture clash. They had probably never seen a city like Newark—maybe never even seen any urban blight before. Just the same, they welcomed Willie Joe warmly and sincerely. Young people haven't had the time to develop deep-seated prejudice yet.

"We're going to leave you boys now, and let you all get acquainted," Mrs. Bixby drawled.

After the Bixbys left, Evan gave Willie Joe a quick run-down on the dorm set-up.

"Here's the skinny on Radcliff Hall: it was the first co-ed dorm Easton experimented with. We don't have to sign in our guests. The apartments alternate, men and women. We don't have any curfews either. So, we just set up our own signal system. If you've got a woman in the room, leave a pillow outside the door, so we know not to disturb you. Are you cool with that?" Evan smiled. Alex and Craig nodded as Alex went over to the radio and began flipping the dial. Finally, he cranked up an Eagles tune. More culture clash for Willie Joe. He grew up on the Motown sound. But it started to feel like home.

Willie Joe excused himself and began to unpack his few belongings, placing them carefully into the open dresser drawers. He surveyed the room; record albums, stereos, tape decks—these kids had everything. He peered out the window, just in time to see the blond who had smiled at him on the stairway returning to the building. Willie Joe knew these distractions would make it difficult to study and to stay focused on his game.

Just then, they heard a knock on the door. A pizza delivery man dressed in white stood with an armload of boxes.

"Somebody order these pies?" he asked.

Alex, Craig, Evan and Willie Joe all looked at one another quizzically.

"No one here. Try down the hall," Alex held back a chuckle.

As the pizza man began knocking on doors, Alex called after him.

"Hey, if no one buys 'em, come back and we'll see if we can work something out."

Willie Joe got wise to the caper. An old college trick. Order a bunch of pizzas; tell them nobody here ordered them; then, make a half-price deal when they have to unload them. Willie Joe shook his head, laughing at Alex.

After traversing the whole floor, the pizza man returned, both annoyed and embarrassed.

"Okay, I tell you what. Take all of them, half price."

"But they're cold. Anyway, I don't like pepperoni. Any of you guys like pepperoni?"

All four of them shook their heads.

"Okay, so take the other two for half price. I'll throw these in. You can give 'em to someone else. I can't bring 'em back or my boss will kill me."

Alex reached into his pocket.

"Hey I only have five bucks. Any of you guys got any money?"

They all shook their heads. The pizza man grabbed the five dollar bill from Alex and handed him all four boxes.

Alex closed the door. They all laughed, placing the first pie in the oven. Evan went across the hall and knocked on the door. Grace, the longhaired blond appeared. Her roommate Sandy followed her. And the first of many parties began. Grace never took her eyes off of Willie Joe as they chowed down on the pizza. Evan never took his eyes off of Sandy. The smell of the pizza wafted across the hall and the other two girls from the suite sauntered in. Alex cranked up the music. It doesn't get much better than this, thought Willie Joe.

CHAPTER 23

THE LONG ROAD AHEAD

Evan's alarm clock buzzed, waking Willie Joe. Evan, an English major, called himself a "news junkie", and had his sights on a journalism career. While Evan hit the shower, Willie Joe listened intently to the radio newscaster. The network news came on first, followed by the local news. The network newscaster's mellifluous tones cut through the ambient morning air as the shafts of sunlight penetrated the blinds.

"Although campus protests have declined nationwide, a new survey reports, racial tensions account for the undercurrent of unrest. Recent Supreme Court cases have become deadlocked in the wake of President Reagan's efforts to cut college grants. National Student Association President Alan Slater contends that the cuts are racist, discriminating against poorer minority students that need the financial aid the most. The Reverend Jessie Jackson plans to organize a nationwide march on Washington, in an effort to restore the cuts. In other news, *Playboy* magazine publisher Hugh Hefner won a freedom of speech battle in the courts yesterday. The justices' decision —"

Willie Joe flipped off the radio. He perused his schedule for the first day of classes. Typical enough, he thought—History of Western Civilization, English Composition, Introduction to Philosophy, The Cultural Revolution and Introduction to Psychology. Fifteen credits toward the one hundred twenty-four he needed for graduation. Better to start slow, get into the study groove and work his way up, he thought.

As he started out the door with Evan behind him, Willie Joe noticed Grace leaving. She flashed him a smile, then gave that characteristic toss of her head, swishing her long blond hair like a thoroughbred. Sandy followed; Evan timidly watched her, transfixed. Alex and Craig had just awakened. Willie Joe could hear them scurrying around the suite as he and Evan headed for the stairwell. A handicapped student slowly made his way down the steps, on two crutches. They passed him by in a flurry.

Freshman year was full of surprises. Willie Joe listened intently to his history instructor, Professor Auschlander. He and Evan attended this one class together. Willie Joe could hardly believe his ears as this man pontificated, droning on endlessly. He asserted that all of the great contributions to the world came from the West—and nearly all from the Caucasian Anglo-Saxon culture. He seemed oblivious to anyone and anything from anywhere else. Willie Joe at first found Dr. Auschlander offensive. In time, he just figured it amounted to ignorance. One day's lesson showed his true colors. Dr. Aushlander surveyed the room. Willie Joe was the only Black student of the thirty registered for that section of the course. The professor sat on the edge of his desk and launched into a diatribe.

"Take Black people in America, for example. Do you know what the difference between White people and Black people is, fundamentally? It has to do with their attitude. You see, Blacks allow work to work them, while White people work work," he elaborated.

Willie Joe stared at him, almost in disbelief. As they left class, Evan stopped him in the hallway.

"He's probably a closet Nazi. Don't let it get to you. See you back at the ranch later."

At the close of the first week, Willie Joe had purchased an armload of books. As excited as he was, he wondered how he would ever have enough time to read them all, attend classes, go to basketball practice and work his part-time job. When he arrived at the gym for his first day of practice, Chamber Higgins pulled him aside.

"I'm expecting great things from you, you know that. Remember, you're not in Newark any more. You have to start all over again. They're watching every move you make, every shot you take. I know you won't disappoint me. Order your Easton shirts from the bookstore and get your practice gear from Binky the equipment manager."

In a matter of a few short weeks, Willie Joe proved himself—both in the classroom and on the court, he gave them something to watch. Faculty, staff, administrators and students became enamored of him. He felt like some kind of a novelty act. People began to seek him out. Still, he felt as if they saw him as some sort of a token—someone placed in their midst to meet an Affirmative Action quota. He had overheard enough conversations in the student center cafeteria from people who thought that way. But, they never mentioned his name or expressed it to his face. One day, he had just changed into his white food service uniform and reported for work at the cafeteria. An obese man, dressed like a professor in a tweed jacket with elbow patches, thumped on the glass display case and called to Willie Joe.

"Hey, can I get some service here? Don't you have any pie left?"

Willie Joe promptly filled in the empty slots under the warming lights with the single-serve pies. The man muttered, grabbed one and moved down the line toward the cashier. Willie Joe recognized him. His philosophy professor, who had congratulated him at last night's scrimmage, didn't seem to recognize him. It became very clear. Just the change from a basketball uniform to a cafeteria worker's uniform resulted in completely different treatment from the same person. How very revealing. Willie Joe mused about the incident as he washed the dishes in the stainless steel sink. His psychology professor would probably have a field day with this one. He thought about using the incident for a paper he had to write. He figured Evan would probably love to use this one for a journalism assignment, too. It was a beautiful world—with a few ugly people in it, thought Willie Joe.

As much as Willie Joe felt he had made the right choice coming to Easton, at times he felt as if he just didn't fit in. His roommates accepted him completely, but the race issue kept surfacing at every turn. Even though Easton had a small student population, at most Willie counted about fifteen Black students. Beyond that, a few cafeteria workers, maintenance workers, a security guard and one low level administrator comprised the entire Black population on campus. Willie Joe made a conscious effort to seek out the other Black students. Much to his surprise, they considered him the token because of his athletic scholarship. Worse than that, when he tried to get to know the few Black female students, they treated him with condescension.

Willie Joe had tried to strike up a conversation in the lobby of the campus library with Tanya Freeman, a girl who reminded him a lot of Lillian. She seemed to rebuff him at every turn. Finally, he extended his arm across the doorway and confronted her.

"Did I offend you in some way? If I did, I'm not aware of it, and I apologize in advance."

"No, you didn't. It's just that we come from very different worlds, Willie Joe. I grew up in Yardley, Pennsylvania, a small Bucks County suburb. Most of my friends growing up were White. My parents both have advanced degrees and professional jobs. That's a far cry from Newark. We just don't have anything in common, that's all."

If she slapped him in the face, it couldn't have felt worse. They went their separate ways. He never spoke to her again.

Friday night rolled around and the dormitory rocked. It was party time in Radcliff Hall. Students congregated in the hallways, in their suites, in the stairwells. Music blasted from one end of the building to another. Still, nearly everyone respected one another. Willie Joe returned from basketball practice to find Evan, Alex and Craig stacking six-packs of beer in their refrigerator. Before long, every room in their suite filled to capacity with students. The beer went fast and furious. Willie Joe shouted over the music, to Evan.

"I can't drink; I'm in training."

He plopped down in a chair. A minute later, Grace dropped into his lap. He could smell the beer on her breath. She turned to face Willie Joe, and slung her arm around his shoulder. Not drunk enough to do anything stupid; just loose enough to have a good time, Willie Joe mused to himself. She took him by surprise. Grace planted a kiss on his cheek, unbuttoned his shirt, slipped her hand inside and began to stroke his chest gently at first, then more vigorously. Willie Joe looked around to see if anyone was watching. Evan gave him the thumbs up and motioned toward their bedroom. Grace noticed the gesture, got up and went to the other side of the room to join a conversation. To say the least, Willie Joe became confused. What game was she playing?

The next evening, Alex, Craig, Evan and Willie Joe took it down a notch. They played some quiet music and just shared some conversation. The inevitable subject of pussy chasing came up. Evan listened quietly as Alex and Craig described their conquests and their exploits in detail. Willie Joe surmised that Evan was most likely a virgin at that point. Willie Joe gave only the sketchiest of details. The guys wanted to know if sex was different with Black women than it was with White women. Willie Joe confessed that he couldn't really answer that question, since he had only slept with Black women. But, he decided to open up and confide in his roommates.

"Look, you guys saw what happened with Grace last night. What's the deal here? She does this approach-avoidance thing. She comes on to me and then backs off. What's the deal with that?"

Alex took a stab, assuming the role of the elder statesman.

"She digs you, but she's afraid you'll think she's a whore if she puts out too fast. She's still stuck in that high school mode of taking baby steps toward sex. Give her time. You'll see. She'll come around."

Then Craig weighed in on the conversation.

"Au contraire, mon frere. She's a cock teaser. I've been watching her from day one. She like to know she can get a rise out of you, but as soon as it looks like anything's gonna happen, she backs off."

Evan surprised the group as he spoke up.

"If I may. I don't claim to know everything about women, but I know this. They're more careful than guys are. They don't shit where they eat. When I was in junior high, the smartest girl in the class wrote something in my yearbook. This is what Donna wrote: 'Don't fall in love by the garden gate; love is blind but the neighbors ain't.' I never forgot that. Grace here just doesn't want everyone else knowing her business. She's discreet about it. She likes you Willie Joe, but she's not going to let anything happen right under her nose. She'll sooner go out with—and go to bed with, someone across campus or at another school. That's my unadulterated opinion."

The room fell silent. Secretly, Willie Joe ached for her. He had never even thought about having a White woman before. He kept his thoughts to himself. But he dreamt about it. In his dreams, he saw himself in bed with a woman. In the dark room, he could not discern her race. Confusion reigned. He knew it would work itself out.

The dormitory had only one pay phone on each floor. Often, they were tied up for hours. Students were courteous enough to try and track down a fellow student if an incoming call sounded urgent. One Sunday morning, Willie Joe heard a knock at the door. He bounded out of bed to see a student knocking on one door after another, asking if anyone knew a Willie Joe Cunningham. He ran after him, calling.

"That's me. I'm Willie Joe Cunningham."

The student motioned to the pay phone, off the hook. Willie Joe ran to the phone.

"Uncle Ben! Good to hear from you. How's—"

He stopped in mid-sentence, as Uncle Ben cut him off abruptly.

"When? How? Did she suffer?"

Aunt Agnes had passed peacefully, during the night.

"Have you made any arrangements yet? I'll take the next bus—"

"You don't need to do that son. I've taken care of everything. You just stay where you are. She's in a better place. Now she and your mother can look after each other. I got to go now."

Just like that. The finality hit him hard. Willie Joe worried about Uncle Ben, all alone. Hey, if he survived the war, he can handle this. He should go home. He felt guilty not attending the funeral. His uncle was the only one left in the world that cared about him. That hit home.

CHAPTER 24

TRUST BETRAYED

Freshman year seemed to move at light speed for Willie Joe. He had a stellar academic record, dispelling any myths about tokenism or Affirmative Action. He had earned his way on campus—as he always had. Word got around Easton fast that the kid from Newark worked as hard in the classroom and the library as he did on the basketball court. Chamber Higgins had warned him that they would watch his every move, and they did—with awe. Nobody on the Easton athletic faculty or coaching staff had ever seen jump shots like Willie Joe's, flawlessly executed. He had that rare combination of strength and grace that makes for a perfect basketball player. The bleachers in the gym began to swell with crowds watching the elegant teamwork Coaches Miller and Higgins had put together. Even students that never cared about sports began to show up, just to watch.

The name Willie Joe Cunningham began to show up first in campus newspaper headlines, then in the community papers. That never happened to freshmen players at Easton before. Girls would stop him on campus and invite him to parties. Most of the time, he politely declined. He still felt uncomfortable as a Black man in what he perceived as a White world. Finally, he became friends with just a few other Black students, members of the only nationally chartered Black fraternity with an Easton chapter. Known as Groove Phi Groove, they spent evenings in the parking lot practicing coordinated dance steps—with moves as elaborate as any executed by the Easton varsity basketball team. One night, Lee Brown, the chapter President, invited Willie Joe to his dorm room.

The whole Groove Phi Groove membership passed beers, joints and shared stories. Willie Joe learned that they arrived at Easton from the most diverse backgrounds. A few came from middle class suburban backgrounds; other came from cities like Philadelphia, Cleveland and Detroit—places very much like his hometown of Newark. They had all heard about Willie Joe's reputation on the court, even though only a few of them had ever seen him handle the ball. Most of them had followed professional basketball. They recognized talent when they saw it. And they saw it in Willie Joe.

Invariably, the conversation found its way around to women. Willie Joe listened as the brothers described their exploits. The stories contrasted sharply with those of his White roommates—and rang much truer.

"Smacked that White bitch's ass good. Made her get on her knees and give me head. Took her from behind and rammed her till she screamed like the pig that she was."

"Shit. That ain't nothin', bro'. I had this White girl was comin' on to me at a party, right here in this room. She kept grabbin' my balls. I took her inside there. She unzipped her jeans; then she unzipped mine. I didn't have to do nothin'. She had a pearl necklace in no time—and she liked it. She come back here the next night and we was diddlin' half the night."

"You guys ain't seen nothin' till you see a White woman pull you into the shower, bend over and beg you to boff her. Hey, Willie Joe, you ever had any White pussy?"

"He looks like a vanilla virgin, but I'll bet he's fixin' to. Here's the deal, see; when we see a sister with a White man, that's just disrespectin' her. But it's different when a brother takes a White girl. It's a payback, man, for slavery, for Jim Crowe, for lynchings and all that shit. We deserve to have the prize."

Willie Joe got up, excused himself and walked back to his dorm room. Alex and Craig were out. He tried to remain as quiet as he could, so as not to disturb Evan, but Evan sat up in bed when he came in. Evan exuded a strange combination of innocence and wisdom. Willie Joe wondered how someone could just intuitively know so much when he had experienced so little. He sensed Evan wanted to talk, so he listened.

"I struck out with Sandy, big time. I guess she just doesn't care for me."

"Or maybe she just has her eye on someone else. Women do that. It may have nothing to do with you at all. They get fixated on some guy, and they don't notice the person right under their nose. I guess we do it, too," Willie Joe tried to soothe the hurt.

"Yeah, I'm guilty of that. There was this girl in high school. I didn't even realize that she was interested in me until we graduated, because I was so hung up on this other chick that lived right down the street from me. I was almost obsessed with her. I used to walk past her house, call her up on a pretense—you know, like asking for help on a homework assignment—but she would never go out with me. I probably should have paid attention to Stacy instead," Evan admitted.

Suddenly, the conversation took a radical shift.

"Hey, did you know there's a rumor on campus that Coach Higgins is recruiting that guy they call The Altoona Assassin—I think his name is Breezy Smith. I heard from one of my classmates that they want him as a guard on your team," Evan's words woke Willie Joe right up.

"No, I hadn't heard that. I know of the guy, but I've never met him. Could be a good thing. I'll check around. You see, a guard and a jumper are two critical parts to a team. Without both of those positions well covered, your team has both a weak offense and a weak defense," Willie Joe explained.

The next day, Willie Joe did check around. He went right to the source. He walked in to Chamber Higgins' office, unannounced. At first, Coach Higgins seemed startled to see Willie Joe standing over his desk. Then, he seemed almost put off.

"What can I do for you, Willie Joe? Is everything all right?"

"Sure. Fine. Just wanted to confirm a rumor. A friend of mine says you might be bringing some new blood onto the team—Breezy Smith, The Altoona Assassin, to be exact. Care to fill me in?" Willie Joe surprised himself, since he seldom ever got confrontational. He didn't intend to be, but he figured it might be taken that way, any way.

"Rumors can be true sometimes. Just the same, they are just that— rumors. You did right, to come and ask me. You know I would have told you when the time was right. As soon as we seal the deal, I'll tell you—*if* we seal the deal," Coach Higgins rose from his desk.

"Always good to see you, Willie Joe. Always. See you on Thursday, at practice." Chamber Higgins turned and walked away, leaving Willie Joe standing there, still wondering.

Chamber Higgins did in fact bring Breezy Smith to Easton. The Altoona Assassin lived up to his name. He and Willie Joe worked well together. The team began to rack up some impressive wins. Still, the rumors continued. Willie Joe sensed some unrest in Chamber Higgins. It seems he had to pull some strings to get Breezy Smith's financial aid approved. He didn't have the grades or the standardized test scores that Willie Joe had. Willie Joe decided to check around and try to confirm the continuing rumors. He dropped in to visit Lee Brown.

"Yo, Willie Joe, my man, what's happening? Your timing's good—the pussies just left. So what brings you here, bro'?

"Lee, you know we lead different lives. I don't do the fraternity thing, the weed or the beer. But you are on my team. I respect your ability—and your insight. I need some intel here. What do you know about these rumors—that Chamber Higgins is getting restless? I hear he might leave and take Breezy with him. Do you have anything solid on this?"

"Willie Joe, my man, I thought you'd never ask. See, I was gonna tell you as soon as I confirmed it myself. But I did you one better. I heard it for myself. Here's the deal. I went to shoot some hoops by myself the other night after my last class. Higgins was havin' a argument—a real blowout. I could hear it from out in the locker room when I come out of the shower. He and Head Coach Baker was really getting' into it. I swear, I thought someone was gonna get decked right then and there."

"So what happened? Come on, give it up."

"Well, Coach Baker says that after the cuts, he was gonna have to divide the money between you and Breezy, which I thought was fair. Then, I heard it. I couldn't believe it at first, but I did hear it. Higgins says 'We need to fight for Breezy more than we do for Willie Joe.' Well, that ended it right there."

"What happened, Lee?"

"Higgins stormed out of Baker's office. I swear it. That's how the shit went down, Willie Joe."

"Then, this is no rumor any more. He's bailing on us. And he's gonna take Breezy with him. That's gonna mess up *my* game, big time.

He's a combo guard. Without Breezy, I don't get my hands on the rock. Thanks, bro'. I needed to know that."

Willie Joe slipped out and returned to his dorm, across the quad from Lee's.

In spite of the rampant tension, the last game of the season had a surreal quality to it—you know, when everything seems to fall into place exactly right, and everything feels like it's happening in slow motion. Everything was riding on it. It was the last home game for the conference championship, Humanitarian League versus Marywood. Willie Joe made every jump shot, every free throw; the team trounced their opponent; the crowed cheered, rising up from the bleachers. He had never quite seen anything like it. Everything Coach ever taught him came into play. He anticipated every move, and it went down exactly as he had pre-visualized it before the game. Finally, as the fourth quarter ended and the last foul shot swished through the basket, the crowed went wild. Two seconds later, the buzzer sounded and the fans stormed the court. They surrounded the team as they made their way out the gymnasium doors. Willie Joe felt an adrenaline rush like he had never felt before. He felt powerful. Then, he saw the faces of his family members flash in front of him. Unable to share the moment with them, his emotional high crashed to the ground.

As the crowd began to disperse, Willie Joe spotted Grace. She blew him a kiss. At first, it felt good. Then, he became cautious and put up his guard. He did not want to set himself up for a letdown. He headed for the locker room, quickly undressed showered and changed back into his street clothes. He avoided the other team members, knowing they would probably want him to join them for a celebration. They invited him; he declined and left.

Arriving back at the dorm, Willie Joe entered the darkened suite. Evan, Alex and Craig had strung up a homemade banner reading, "Home of WJ, the Jump Shot King". Willie Joe looked around at his smiling roommates. Someone snapped on the lights. Suddenly, cheers came from every corner. There were students everywhere. Willie Joe felt overcome. Someone turned up the music. Beer bottles appeared. Smoke filled the room. Willie Joe ducked into the hallway. Grace's door opened part of the way. A hand reached out and grabbed his, pulling him into the room. A single candle flickered in the dark. He saw the outline of Grace's face draw near. He leaned over to kiss her. She had a towel wrapped around her. It dropped to the floor. She had nothing on under the towel.

Grace began quickly undressing Willie Joe. He felt himself becoming aroused. In no time, he had her on the bed. He had never felt anything quite like her. He had never seen a White woman naked, except in pictures. Her skin glistened like alabaster; she looked like the statue of a goddess, perfect all over. Her skin was so smooth to the touch. Willie Joe was afraid he would climax too soon. He wanted it to last. Before he could mount her, she climbed on top of him and went down on him. With every stroke of her tongue and every motion of her lips, he felt ready to explode. He made every effort to hold back. He rolled her over. He could feel her heat up like a furnace. She instinctively rolled him back over and thrust his head down to her crotch. He had never tasted anything so sweet in all his life. He could not believe this was happening to him.

Finally, he rolled her over and began to lick and kiss every inch of her body, from her shoulders on down. His penis throbbed. He probed with his fingers. She was soaking wet. He turned her on her side and entered her slowly. With every thrust, he felt her muscles contract and grab at him. He knew he couldn't hold out much longer. Grace moaned. Willie Joe pulled out and came like a river. They embraced. She probed his mouth with her tongue. Grace blew out the candle.

Sometimes the lines and the spaces between reality and fantasy just seem to blur. For Willie Joe, the boy from the projects in Newark, he had just entered that dream space. He savored the moments and the hours. But he knew it would not last. Sandy knocked, and then entered the room. Willie Joe slipped into his clothes under the cover of darkness, leaned over and kissed Grace, and made his way across the hall. The party seemed to wind down just as he entered the suite. People drifted out in small groups. Willie Joe dropped into bed. Evan followed. Both of them knew they would fall asleep at any moment. Evan propped himself up on his elbow, facing Willie Joe.

"Well, did you make her?"

Willie Joe smiled at him.

"Gentlemen don't ask, and gentlemen don't tell."

What about you?

"I melted the iceberg; that's all," Evan confided in him.

Final exams rolled around. Willie Joe had spent more time in the library than any place else on campus for the last month of the semester. The pace of nearly everything had picked up. He and Grace spent more time together—in and out of bed. But he felt uncomfortable with her in public. She never seemed to feel it, but he insisted that Easton just didn't accept mixed race couples.

Between exams one day, Willie Joe decided to take a walk over to the gym and just practice shooting. He suited up. Before he left the locker room, as he stood in the doorway, he froze. He overheard Coach Higgins having a somewhat heated conversation. He knew he wasn't supposed to hear it, but he couldn't help but listen.

"Dean, you know how hard I've worked to bring the best talent to this campus. You know how hard they've worked to bring pride to Easton. We're building a reputation here. Now, you tell me you can't get us any more money because of these Federal program cuts. You've got to be able to raise it from somewhere. What do you want me to tell Breezy Smith? You'll have to quit school because the funding dried up? Or transfer someplace else where they have the money to pay your tuition? I'm sorry, but I'm going to have to move on. That's just the way it is," Coach Higgins dropped the receiver.

Willie Joe got dressed and left. He felt betrayed. He had trusted Coach Higgins. What would happen now? He headed back to the dormitory. Alex and Craig played an electronic basketball game on the TV screen. They waved to him.

"Where's Evan?" Willie Joe asked.

Alex motioned across the hall. Willie Joe figured he was still trying to persuade Sandy to pay attention to him. He knocked on the door. Grace poked her head out. Seeing Willie Joe, she stepped into the hallway.

"We've got company. I'll see you later, okay?"

Willie Joe had a sinking feeling. He didn't want to know who "company" was. He just knew that if Grace didn't invite him in, it had to be her company, not Sandy's. He had had enough for one day. He headed for the library. Perhaps Mr. Shakespeare, Mr. Baldwin or Mr. More had some answers for him.

CHAPTER 25

WHAT PRICE, PARADISE?

Final exams were finally over. Students trickled off campus to disperse around the country. Most came from middle-class homes in small towns. They spent summers with their families, taking vacations, visiting relatives and seeing the rest of the world. Not Willie Joe. He decided to keep his campus cafeteria job through the summer, for as many hours as he could get. He needed to earn the extra money to make up for the financial aid cuts the Reagan Administration had swept the country's campuses with. Evan, Craig and Alex had each decided to spend the summer with their families. Still, they had made a pact to return to Easton before the summer was over—and to remain together as roommates for the coming Sophomore year. Willie Joe joined their pact. It just felt right.

He had second thoughts about not going back to Newark for the summer. Maybe Uncle Ben needed him. He wrestled with the thought. Every time he turned it over in his mind, he came up with the same answer. Stay in Easton; wait and see what would happen. Besides, what would he do in Newark? Go back to the supermarket? He felt bad about leaving Uncle Ben alone after Aunt Agnes's death, but he kept coming back to the same conclusion—or justification. If the man could survive a foxhole war, he could certainly go on living, even without his wife of many years.

Willie Joe began to actually enjoy the time alone in the dorm suite, after his roommates left for home. He felt freer and more powerful—more his own man, coming and going as he pleased and not answering to anyone. Although he felt a kinship with his roommates, he still felt somehow different and apart from them. He felt he was a man surrounded by boys. It was all about experience. He enjoyed their company, but he didn't feel he could learn that much from them. He wanted the challenges that came with the company of men with more worldly experience than he himself had. That's probably why he sought out Lee Brown. Lee had that unusual combination of rough-edged street smarts and intellectual curiosity—not that he was an academic. He had the ability, but not the discipline to apply himself the way Willie Joe did. Lee had decided to spend most of the summer on campus, as well—largely for the same reasons as Willie Joe. There was nothing to go home to.

Willie Joe awoke on Saturday morning and decided to see what Grace's summer plans were. He hadn't seen her much those last few weeks—just coming and going. He knocked on the door of her suite. Nobody answered. He decided to slip a note under the door. The note simply read, "Call me. Willie Joe." She never called.

Willie Joe sauntered over to Lee Brown's building and bounded up the stairs. When he arrived, Lee stood in the doorway, drinking coffee. He welcomed him in.

"You look like a lost dog, Willie Joe. What's eatin' you? Coffee?"

Willie Joe graciously accepted the offer of coffee. Lee closed the suite door behind them and the two men slipped into the living room chairs.

"It's Grace. I haven't seen her and nobody answered the door when I went looking for her."

"Well, Willie Joe, you came to the right place. Uncle Lee has got the answers. Not always the answers you want, but I've got 'em, just the same. Here's the scoop. I heard it on good authority that your Grace has left the building—for good. I got this from someone reliable. Just don't ask me who spilled the beans, bro'. The rumor is that she found out she was pregnant, dropped out of school and went home. That's all I know. Do you think it's yours?" Lee stared him down as he asked.

"No, I don't think so. I think she was seeing somebody else these last few weeks. I'm a little more careful than that. I think you know," Willie Joe returned the stare, coldly.

"Don't shoot the messenger, man. I'm just doing my job as your trusted friend and advisor," Lee could feel the hurt in Willie Joe's voice.

"She's a woman. They play the game by their own rules, man. You know that. Don't expect a woman to act like a man. They don't tell you what they're gonna do, or why they doin' it. They just do it. Look, you didn't make no deal with her, right? I mean, about seein' anybody else or nothin', right? Then, she's free as a bird. And so are you. Move on, man; just move on," Lee clamped his hand on Willie Joe's shoulder.

"Thanks for the coffee. I got to get to work. Let me know if you want to shoot some hoops later, when I get off," Willie Joe knew Lee was right. Still, the idea of Grace just taking up with someone else, never breaking it off with him, not saying goodbye and leaving for good, was more than he was prepared for at that moment.

Grace never called, and Willie Joe never saw her again. Sandy and the others in their suite had left for the summer, so there was no one else to ask. That was it. Lee was probably right. She just up and left. He would probably never know about the pregnancy rumor. He just had to get on with it—and get over it.

Summer evaporated into a series of practice shooting session with Lee Brown, half-days of work at the Easton campus cafeteria, an occasional hour in the library—and a once weekly phone call to Newark, to check on Uncle Ben. He always insisted everything was "Just fine, just fine," and that Willie Joe should stay right where he was. Still, he always had that pit in his stomach after he hung up, like he had neglected one of the only people in his life that ever really cared about him. Guilt can destroy a man. It really can.

The August heat reached new highs that the sleepy little town of Easton had never quite seen before. Even so, it didn't compare to the summers Willie Joe remembered back in Newark—especially during his youth in the projects. There, the heat reflected back from the pavement and the tall buildings and filled the air with the stench of factory smoke held down by the temperature inversion. He remembered the sensation of the sometimes-unbreathable air that hung over Newark. This was nothing like that. Easton still had grass and trees and open spaces with fields and farms. At least the nights were cool, for the most part.

Willie Joe waited with anticipation for the school year to begin. He had already gotten his class schedule in his campus mailbox. He had signed up for the most difficult courses he could take—German, Biology Lab, Statistics, Shakespeare and Human Physiology. Something told him these courses would even help his game. Maybe they would. He had gotten over Grace by the end of the summer. He looked forward to seeing the return of the co-eds to campus. The scenery lacked something without the magic of those hundreds of beautiful women roaming around. He looked forward to the return of his roommates, as well. By late August, Willie Joe had confirmed that indeed Coach Higgins had left Easton—and did in fact take Breezy Smith with him to his new school. He went to see Head Coach Baker —out of his genuine concern for the team.

Coach Baker had just returned to campus after a two-week vacation with his family, touring the national parks and camping. He arose from his desk and smiled when Willie Joe entered.

"Good to see you, Cunningham. I hope you enjoyed your summer— and I hope you're ready to get down to some serious work, because we're going to need you to give us your all again and perform. The team needs you, and Easton needs you," Coach Baker confided in him.

"Yes, sir. I am ready to work. I really just stopped by because I'm concerned about how we're going to keep winning—I mean after Coach Higgins and Breezy left. So, what's the game plan?" Willie Joe asked, sincerely.

"Well, since you're here, I will tell you before I share our news with the rest of the team. I will ask you to keep it confidential for now. I need to keep this out of the papers until the season starts. Then we can make the official announcement. So, here's the deal: I've hired Coach Pete Miller from over in Reading, not far from here. I don't know if you've heard of him, but he has an excellent reputation for team building. I've watched his teams play. I think you'll like his coaching style. It reminds me a lot of our mutual friend Coach, back in Newark. He's an intuitive, if you know what I mean. Coach Miller should be on campus next week, so you'll meet him then. Until then, mum's the word, okay?"

Willie Joe assured Coach Baker the news would remain under wraps. He felt privileged that Coach Baker respected him enough to confide in him. More than anything, he looked forward to getting back on the court with someone who would mentor him. He secretly hoped that Coach Miller would not disappoint him like Coach Higgins did. He would just have to wait—and to trust, until he gave him a reason not to.

The last week of August rolled around. Willie Joe walked across campus after finishing his shift at the cafeteria. A sudden storm broke out. Thunder crashed and lightning pierced the blackened sky. Then, the downpour followed—like someone had just turned on a shower, full force.

In a few short minutes, Willie Joe's cafeteria uniform became soaked. Plastered against his dark skin, the white cloth became transparent. His underwear showed right through. He sprinted the last hundred yards, reaching the quad of dormitory buildings. Drenched, he climbed the stairs. His sneakers squished on the carpet. Just as he reached the door of the suite, it swung open. Evan, Alex and Craig greeted him. There would be stories to tell; he was sure of that.

In minutes, while Willie Joe toweled himself off and stepped into dry clothes, Evan, Alex and Craig unwrapped a three-foot sub sandwich and began to crack open the proverbial beers. The rain continued to pour down outside for a brief five minute spell. Then, the sun beamed down and steam rose from the puddles on the sidewalk outside the dorm. Willie Joe studied each of his roommates as they gathered around the table, ready to devour the mammoth sandwich.

"You first," Willie Joe pointed to Evan. "I can tell you've got news to share."

"You're too busy looking at the mustache I grew over the summer. Here. Check my belt. See anything new? Yes! The notch. My first conquest. I still have some catching up to do, but I'm in the game now," Evan beamed. He wore the loss of his virginity like a Boy Scout merit badge.

Alex and Craig began to spin fantastic stories about their summer exploits. Willie Joe knew better than to take them literally. Nonetheless, they entertained him. As the practical joker, Alex's stories might have actually had a grain of truth in them. Still, Willie Joe always felt like he was listening to kids around a campfire, trying to outdo one another, when he heard these yarns. According to Alex, he had laid nearly every prostitute in Paris. Not to be outdone, Craig had to detail his supposed exploits on the nude beach at Sandy Hook, New Jersey. They made short work of the sandwich—and the beer. Willie Joe confessed that he had nothing much to tell. It was an uneventful summer. Nobody believed him. They would rather hear made-up exciting stories than the boring truth. With their sophomore year just ahead, they would each undoubtedly write their own stories. Sundown came; the boys unpacked and settled back in to their dorm rooms—and they quietly watched the rest of the students find their way back to the cocoon they all called Easton.

CHAPTER 26

THE GREAT AWAKENING

Every college and university campus in America had its own character—just as every town and city had a unique flavor. Easton lay at the crossroads of small town America, while still in the shadows of both New York and Philadelphia. This created a strange mix; a blend of the hard-edged cosmopolitan world we call urban America, and the naïve, pristine world we call suburbia. The hybridization of the two reflected off of everything about Easton. The student body consisted mainly of rural and suburban students, fresh out of high school, and mostly the first generation in their families to attend college. The urbanites like Willie Joe and Lee Brown stood out—not so much for their color as for their character. Shaped by the forces of broken families, broken spirits and their downtrodden ancestors, they bore the mark of their worldliness at a young age. Somehow, though, it didn't always show in their decisions. Lost and without guidance, these students often fell between the cracks. Not so for Willie Joe Cunningham. He always instinctively sought out mentorship. Maybe because it was missing during his youth, he craved it and was determined to keep it in his life.

Sophomore year proved much more demanding for Willie Joe academically. He had to shift his schedule around, spending more hours in the library, fewer hours at his cafeteria job and far less time in the dormitory, in order to maintain his practice time and his game time on the court. He was both excited and apprehensive about meeting Peter Miller, the new Assistant Coach. He had checked him out the best he could, researching library microfilms for newspaper clippings, and networking informally with anyone that might have connections to Miller's former campus in Reading. He had learned that Pete Miller had more friends than enemies, had the praise and respect of both colleagues and competitors alike within the college basketball community, had coached winning teams and several players that went on to become pro's. Still, he wanted that one last bit of reassurance before he placed his future career in Coach Miller's hands. He had to ask the one person he knew he could trust for an unbiased opinion. He called Coach.

"So, to what do I owe the honor of a call from the great Willie Joe Cunningham?"

"Come on, Coach. I really need your insight here."

"Insight, eh? My insight says you ain't never gonna come back to Newark, an' you gonna be tryin' out for the big time in a couple years. What else you need from an old man like me?"

"Coach, I'll get back to Newark when the time is right. Right now, I need to know whatever you know about a coach named Pete Miller—"

"The Red Herring from Reading. Now you're talkin', boy. 'Bout time they got themselves some real talent. Son, you got the right guy, now. Stick with 'em; you'll do okay. An' I still say we ain't gonna see your ass in Newark fo' at least a year. Got to go; I got some kids who need me. Oh, and say hello to your uncle—if you happen to see him befo' I do."

Willie Joe hung up the receiver with that mixed set of feelings in the pit of his stomach. He should go home, if only to see Uncle Ben—and Coach. At the same time, he had the comfort level he needed to trust Coach Miller.

Finally, the first practice date rolled around. The team suited up and waited, seated on the bleachers. Coach Miller marched past them like a drill sergeant, whistle around his neck and clipboard under his arm. He surveyed them. He knew he had the goods. Willie Joe at first wondered how a man as short as Pete Miller could know so much about a tall man's game like basketball. That thought evaporated minutes after they hit the floor. Coach Miller set them up, let them play and stood back to observe. His eyes operated like an instant replay video camera. He never missed a detail.

The real surprise came when Coach Miller showed his stuff. He stole the ball in one deft move, dribbled around the guard and sunk a basket—without even jumping. He had the whole team's attention. Willie Joe knew he could learn from him, quickly. Learning his style of cut, move, shoot would pay big dividends on the court—especially when a player with Willie Joe's skill executed it. His philosophy of life equals basketball and basketball equals life appealed to Willie Joe. It reminded him of his old friend Coach from the Boys' Club in Newark.

Success came with a price tag—a big one. One called total devotion. Coach Miller was extremely demanding. He insisted you had to "Pay the price to be the best." And he only wanted the best on his team—the best players, the best students—and the best human beings. Not that he had any great holiday plans, but it all really hit home when Coach Miller called for a two and a half hour practice on Christmas Day. No one said a word. They just showed up and gave him everything they had—as if it was a Final Four game and winning the Conference title depended on it. Maybe it was his working class background that made him more relatable to players like Willie Joe and Lee Brown. He was White, but not "white".

Coach Miller tuned in to Willie Joe's intuitive playing style of anticipating his opponent's moves and pre-visualizing his own moves. On a time-out, he took him aside.

"Willie Joe, listen to me. You need to get this. You're probably the smartest player on this team. But the smartest guys aren't always the strongest. The reason why they're the smartest is because they understand how the strongest became strong. For you, it's not how many points you score, but how you score the points—and how you keep your opponents from scoring."

Coach Miller had a more cerebral outlook on basketball, and it permeated his coaching style. It was completely compatible with Willie Joe's playing style. Together, a cerebral coach and a cerebral player make a deadly combination.

That winter brought killer snowstorms that threatened to keep the Easton team home. One ice storm forced their bus to turn back after nearly careening off the road and into a ravine. They had to reschedule three of their away games. Finally, they hit the road again for the last one. It had warmed up just enough to turn to rain—driving rain. It didn't dampen the team's spirits. They played well against Colgate, known for its high scoring team. The teams ran neck in neck during the first half. In the third quarter, the tide turned. The reporters would have a field day with this one. Willie Joe scored 35 points on 15 shots. He stole the ball four times, provided eight assists and picked up ten rebounds. The tension mounted as the fourth quarter came to a close. Willie Joe got his opening and took the last shot. It sailed through the net just before the buzzer. The two-point lead won the game for Easton.

The season came to an end abruptly after that game. Willie Joe returned to his dorm, tired from traveling—not from playing. As he entered the suite, he sensed a heaviness. He knew something had gone terribly wrong. Evan, Alex and Craig all stood up when he dropped his gym bag on the floor. He scanned each one of them. The silence nearly deafened him. Finally, Evan stepped forward and looked up into Willie Joe's eyes.

"We got a phone call a couple of hours ago, while you were on the way back. The hospital called. It's your uncle. He passed away last night. We're sorry. We're here for you."

Willie Joe just stared past them all, at the window. Feelings of guilt overwhelmed him completely. He felt he had neglected his uncle. The one person left in the world that had really cared about him was gone. Now, he would probably never go home. There was nothing there for him. Nothing at all. Finally, after an awkwardly long silence, he looked at Evan, Alex and Craig.

"Thank you."

He walked out the door. He wasn't sure where he was going. Some unknown force tugged at him. He headed for the athletic building. He entered the quiet building, hearing the same sounds he had heard the very first time he came to campus—the sloshing of the swimmers in the pool. He made his way to the coaching staff's offices. He found himself face to face with Coach Miller. He confronted him, like an animal cornering its prey. Willie Joe could hardly believe the words that fell from his own lips.

"You knew, didn't you? You knew my uncle passed away, but you didn't tell me."

"Come on, Willie Joe. We all depend on each other here. We're a team. More than that, we're a family. If you had gone back home, we would have lost the game and the tournament—"

"I lost the only family member I had left that really cared about me. You want to talk about losing; you want to talk about family? What do you know about it?"

"I'll tell you what I know. I know that Newark is your past; Easton is your future. Do you think the rest of us had it easy? Let me enlighten you, Willie Joe. My mother gave me up for adoption when she became pregnant at the age of sixteen. I never even knew who my father was. I still don't. My adoptive family was killed in a plane crash. That's right, I was orphaned when I was thirteen; lived in foster homes until I was eighteen and joined the army. I went to college on the G.I. bill. It's what you make of it. I'm sorry for your loss. I'm sorry I didn't tell you, but that's the cruel way life works sometimes. We all had a job to do at that moment, and we needed you to do your part. I heard your uncle was a great man, a decorated war hero."

That was as close as Willie Joe would ever get to an apology. He just had to move on.

A month later, as Willie Joe checked his mail in the campus mailbox, he opened a letter from the law office of Mr. Oppenheim, who had processed his guardianship years before. Uncle Ben's estate had just settled, and he was the sole beneficiary. At least he had the security of knowing he could pay for the rest of his education, regardless of how the government played with the financial aid numbers.

CHAPTER 27

NEW WORLDS TO CONQUER

The summer after sophomore year was even less eventful than the previous summer. In a strange sort of way, Willie Joe almost missed the sweltering heat of a Newark summer—the smell of a summer rain as it hit the pavement; the steam vaporizing when the cool rain percolated into the waiting heat of the concrete. He still felt like a stranger in Easton—especially on those rate occasions when he left campus to go into town. So few Black faces greeted him. Everything seemed unfamiliar and uncomfortable. A Black man in a White world. Willie Joe wondered if he would ever adjust. In Newark, at least he felt he belonged. Still, he desperately wanted to become part of his new world.

Once again, the campus became a sleepy little enclave, nestled in the womb of small towns and farmland. Not only did so many of the students leave campus for the summer, but so many of their families left town for vacations. Willie Joe had never been on a real vacation. He could only go by what he had seen in movies and television. He imagined his fellow students' families packing up their cars to tour national parks; he envisioned them boarding cruise ships and jet planes to far away destinations. Then, the knock at the door of his dormitory suite pulled him from his daydream.

Willie opened the door. To his surprise, he came face to face with Grace. He instinctively looked down. A stroller with a beautiful baby. He could hardly believe his eyes. He took a double take. The baby was not White. Overcome, he invited her in. Grace spoke first.

"I felt really bad about just leaving and never saying goodbye. I felt I at least owed you that."

"You never owed me anything," Willie Joe smiled as he looked down and motioned toward the baby.

Before Grace could speak, there was another knock at the door. Willie Joe jumped up to answer it. The second shock was even greater than the first. Lee Brown came in and took Grace in his arms. All the missing pieces of the puzzle suddenly fit together. That's why Lee knew so much. He had been Grace's new lover—and the father of her child.

"Well, I'll be a son-of-a-gun. Look at the happy family," Willie Joe flashed a smile at Grace, Lee and the baby.

"We named him William, after you," Grace offered the baby to Willie Joe, as if he was a peace offering.

"I am honored; honored to have both of you in my life as friends; honored by your integrity and respect for me; and honored to have this handsome little fellow named for me."

Willie Joe had never even held a baby before. Something warmed him inside as little William fell asleep on his shoulder. Questions began pouring into his head. He felt compelled to ask at least a few of them.

"How did your families accept—"

"The race issue? They didn't. We're on our own here," Grace confided.

"Listen, man, we really got to be goin'. We got us a little apartment off campus, so you'll still see me around. We gonna make it all work; you'll see," Lee gave Willie Joe that penetrating look that only he could give.

"See you on the court, man. And thanks, Grace, for caring," Willie Joe saw them to the door and let them out.

Willie Joe lay on his bed for at least two hours after Lee and Grace left with the baby, with memories and visions spinning around in his head. The bright sunset threw off a piercing glare. He got up, dropped the blinds, fell back onto the bed and lapsed into a deep sleep. He began to dream. He saw himself first as a child back in the projects in Newark. He saw his brother, his mother, his father, his aunt and his uncle all around him. He noticed how vulnerable and powerless he was. Then, he saw himself suddenly fully grown. He saw himself with Lillian, with Grace and with countless nameless, faceless women. Somehow, the sex in dreams was even better than in waking life. Willie Joe felt powerful. In an instant, he was back in church, a little boy, with the Reverend Pearl admonishing him. The stained glass window he remembered so well from the Beulah Baptist Church shattered. The fragments came crashing down on him. He stood up, now fully grown again. Next, he was back on campus. He saw himself naked, shooting baskets. Then, he was in bed with a White girl. No one he could recognize; it could have been anyone. When he looked up, he saw his mother's face angrily staring him down. Then, with a start, he woke up.

The end of summer rolled around, and as usual, Willie Joe returned from his cafeteria job to find the dorm suite piled high with Evan, Alex and Craig's belongings. He anticipated the stories of their exploits that were sure to follow—and they did. Evan had a couple more notches in his belt, Alex spun a wild tale of how he almost ended up in a Jamaican prison and Craig detailed the adventure of a supposed road trip with his band—and all the requisite groupie girls that came with that package. After devouring the predictable pizzas and beer, the boys began to unpack and settle back into dormitory life. When he had completely finished unpacking, Evan reached into his steamer trunk and pulled out a wrapped package.

"This is for you, Willie Joe. I hope you like it."

Willie Joe didn't know what to say.

"Just open it, man; just open it."

Willie Joe fumbled with the ribbon, then tore the wrappings off of the flat package. His eyes widened. Evan had prepared a scrapbook chronicling every basketball game Willie Joe had played since he came to Easton—scorecards, newspaper clippings and sportscasters' color commentary. Willie Joe was overcome. Nobody had ever paid that much attention to him. He just never felt that important to anyone before. It just cemented the friendship even more. He didn't know what to say.

"You are a true friend. I will guard and treasure this always. Thank you."

The revelry wound down as the stars came out. The Easton sky blanketed them in a protective covering.

Willie Joe had really loaded up on his course work for junior year. Everyone traditionally regarded it as the most difficult and the most critical academic year. It would be difficult to keep up his stellar grade-point-average, maintain Coach Miller's demanding basketball practice and game schedule and still work part-time at the campus cafeteria. But Willie Joe had developed excellent time management skills. If anyone could do it, he could. He and Evan, Alex and Craig walked to the Student

Center Building. They each checked their mailboxes. Evan withdrew a care package from his parents, who were traveling overseas. All four of them removed their class schedules and went back to the dorm to review them. Sure enough, Willie Joe and Evan had one class together, Anthropology.

As the weekend drew to a close, the campus population began to swell again. Most of the students had returned a full week before the start of classes, to give them time to get into the swing of campus life. For Evan, Alex and Craig, that meant a full week of girl watching. Now that they had become upper classmen, the landscape had changed. They felt a powerful sense of mastery over the Easton female student population— as if they could pick and choose whomever they wanted to fraternize with...and sleep with. The fantasy would fade when they realized how many other upper classmen they competed with.

Willie Joe didn't share that same feeling. He had come to a place of letting life happen to him—especially when it came to women. Not when it came to his education or his future career; that he took complete control over. But he sensed that he just didn't have the same control over his personal life. He would have to wait and see.

The first week of classes had the campus bustling with activity. Guest lecturers, military recruiters, students' family members all rounded out the usual campus community. After a long wait in the bookstore lines, Willie Joe and Evan attended the first session of the Anthropology class they had together. With only 20 students in the section, in a regular classroom, they would have a more intimate experience than the lecture hall type classes they had become accustomed to during freshman and sophomore years. Students of all descriptions filed in. Most everyone seemed to know at least someone in the room. Professor Mercer, clad in an army flack jacket, khaki pants and a sweater, took to the blackboard. Willie Joe couldn't help notice that every move the man made was so purposeful and deliberate. He had everyone's rapt attention. Willie Joe hardly noticed as the last student entered the room and took her seat— right next to him.

A few minutes later, Dr. Mercer called for a five-minute break. Then, Willie Joe could not help but notice the young woman seated next to him. If goddesses walked the earth, she qualified. He tried not to be too obvious as he took in her beauty. She was one of the only female students that dressed like a woman, not like a girl. Everything about her was perfect. Her hair was perfectly coiffed, her make-up applied just right, her satin blouse pressed neatly, her skirt revealing a perfect pair of legs sporting patterned stockings.

A minute later, Evan leaned across Willie Joe.

"Robin, I would like you to meet my roommate and one of my best friends, Willie Joe Cunningham."

He turned to Willie Joe.

"Willie Joe, I would like you to meet one of the smartest girls on campus, Robin Whiteside. Robin and I had a class together last semester. We worked on a project together. Oh, and yes, she aced the class."

Willie Joe could hardly believe what had just happened. He finds a perfect woman and of all people, his roommate Evan knows her and introduces her to him. No worries about the usual awkward stumbling around to introduce himself.

Dr. Mercer resumed the class at the conclusion of the five-minute break— which ended precisely at the close of a five-minute interval. The man must run on military time—or have a stopwatch in his head, Willie Joe mused. He could have sworn Robin had been eying him up during the rest of the class, but he dismissed the thought. He never believed that women found him that attractive—even after his experiences with Lillian and with Grace.

Dr. Mercer threw out a series of questions, challenging the class to discover for themselves whether individual psychology or the larger culture had the greater affect on a person's development.

"Take a side, develop your argument—and support it with whatever evidence you can find...anywhere. Use your textbook, use films, newspaper clippings, whatever you can find. I want to know how you think, not what you know."

Most of the class filed out of the room slowly. Willie Joe and a few others formed a knot around Professor Mercer. They felt an instant bond. That was how it went with many of the Easton faculty members. The lines sometimes even blurred between student and teacher. Friendships forged easily, yet still with the requisite respect. Willie Joe just wanted to thank the professor and acknowledge his impact. Evan and Robin joined the knot. Professor Mercer invited them to walk and talk with him, as he crossed the campus to his next class.

Willie Joe and Robin began to exchange protracted glances on the walk. Evan hung back, sensing the almost chemical reaction between the two. It was going to be very difficult to stay focused on class, no matter how riveting Dr. Mercer's teaching style, with Robin in the same room as Willie Joe. His inner voice told him to stop anticipating, and to just go with the flow, wherever it takes him. Easier said than done. Finally, everyone had asked their questions and Dr. Mercer ascended the stairway into Wilfred Hall for his next class. The group began to disperse, each going their separate ways. Willie Joe felt compelled to say some parting words to Robin.

"Robin, it was a pleasure meeting you. Evan is a great friend, and I thank him for introducing us. I do look forward to seeing you again, and I know we're going to enjoy this class."

Robin looked him right in the eye, as someone who clearly knew what she wanted.

"The pleasure was mine, William. Oh, and by the way, I knew who you were, even though we hadn't met. Evan spoke very highly of you, and I had seen your picture in the papers. I guess you didn't recognize me out of uniform. I'm one of your team's cheerleaders."

With that, she turned and walked, swinging her hips. Willie Joe was stymied. She had been there all the time, at each of his games, and he never even noticed her. Evidently, she noticed him. He laughed to himself. So that's how life works. He couldn't wait until he saw her again.

CHAPTER 28

YOUR FUTURE CALLS

Willie Joe was right; it became increasingly difficult to concentrate on his studies with Robin in the picture—and in the same classroom. He felt so powerfully drawn to her. Modest as he was, he never assumed anything about her feelings—he just sensed the mutual attraction. He wondered about the race issue. Would it build a wall between them? Would she truly fully accept him, or would there always be a barrier between them? He would know, soon enough.

Wednesday came around, and with great anticipation, Willie Joe knew he would see Robin again in Dr. Mercer's class. Evan watched as Willie Joe seemed to spend just a little extra time on his appearance. He approached him, at first gingerly. Then, he got up his nerve.

"Wear the white shirt with the black pants; it will contrast more with your skin tones and make you look really sharp. Trust me; Robin will like it. I know her."

Willie Joe grinned, nodded his head and took Evan's advice. Amazingly, they had become that close—friends, like brothers, that can read one another's thoughts. They both finished dressing, sat down to a quick breakfast and left the dorm, headed for Professor Mercer's Anthropology class. Evan and Willie Joe arrived first; the other students trickled in, in small clumps. Everyone seemed to gravitate to their usual seats as Dr Mercer began writing his usual battery of thought provoking questions on the board, his back to the class. As before, Robin arrived last, slipping into the empty seat next to Willie Joe. His heart raced. She sensed it. He felt her glances; he returned them, cautiously. Finally, their eyes met. She smiled first. Time seemed suspended. Even Dr. Mercer's engaging style of Socratic questioning seemed distant, quiet and removed for both Willie Joe and Robin. Finally, as he perambulated throughout the room, Dr. Mercer stopped right in front of them, snapping them both out of their reverie.

"And the answer to my parting question of last week, Ms. Whiteside?"

Robin opened her loose-leaf notebook, withdrawing several neatly typewritten pages.

"You can leave that on my desk on your way out. I want to hear your thinking. Which dominates the formation of the individual—nature or nurture? One's own mind or the surrounding culture?" Dr. Mercer queried as he held his position, his pose and his glance.

Robin rose from her seat.

"Abraham Maslow says society rules; Margaret Meade agrees, that the larger culture shapes us. Most psychologists and psychiatrists disagree. Freud says it's your parents; Adler says it's your family unit—but Jung departs from his fellow psychiatrists and theorizes that we each carry the entire history of our race, and are all inextricably connected. I cannot accept the idea that we are each predetermined in our genetic material. When identical twins were separated at birth and grew up in different environments, they each developed completely differently. I believe that the forces surrounding you—family and society, will override your individual personality."

"Well done. Who wants to refute that position?" Dr. Mercer had returned to the front of the classroom.

Evan stood up.

"In spite of proper upbringing and a lawful society, most serial killers simply defy the forces around them. They operate outside of the accepted norms; they fail to embrace the larger culture's standards. Are these people 'defective'? I don't think so. They simply have a strong, overriding ego that propels them to place themselves above all others."

And so it continued, until each student had articulated his or her position, with Professor Mercer adding no comment; just facilitating the discussion like an orchestra conductor or a film director unfolding his story. Finally, Dr. Mercer handed out a single mimeographed sheet of paper with the same questions he had posed on the board. Now, he challenged the class to define whether the differences or the similarities among the world's races were greater.

As they left class, Evan hung back with Professor Mercer. After the rest of the students had left, Willie Joe approached Robin, ever so cautiously.

"I enjoyed your answer to the professor's question. You obviously did your research—and gave it a lot of thought. I was wondering, would you maybe like to—"

"Yes."

"I didn't ask the question yet. Be careful what you agree to."

"I think I can trust you. What did you have in mind?"

"A date, obviously. Would you care to stop up to my dorm room and—"

"No, that's not my idea of a date—certainly not a first date."

"I was going to say, we could study together. We could go to the library if you prefer."

"Still not my idea of a date. Dinner and a movie would be fine."

"Okay. Dinner and a movie then."

"*Out* to dinner and to a movie."

Flashes of his first encounter with Lillian came back to Willie Joe. He wondered with anticipation just how that first date with Robin would go.

"You can pick me up in the lobby of my dorm at six P.M. Friday."

"Very well, then. Six P.M. Friday, at your dorm."

Robin intrigued Willie Joe. She knew just what she wanted; she took control of the situation; and she imparted a lesson in the process. With Robin, it was all about propriety. She grew up in polite society, and she seemed determined to educate Willie Joe in the ways of her upbringing—an advantage he never had. He was content to just go along for the ride.

Thursday flew by in a flash for Willie Joe—classes, basketball practice, his cafeteria job and a few hours in the library. Friday became a blur, with more of the same. As Friday drew to a close, Evan noticed Willie Joe nervously preparing for his date with Robin.

"Just be yourself and just be gentle and patient with her. Everything will work out. You'll see."

Willie Joe took one last look in the mirror, buttoned his shirt, grabbed his wallet and keys and bounded out the door. When he arrived at Robin's dorm, he found her seated in the lobby, looking devastatingly beautiful. She stood up to greet him. He nervously approached her, not sure quite what to do. She took his arm and placed it on her waist. Willie Joe was sure he sensed the other girls staring at him. He felt lost and embarrassed in the sea of white faces. It didn't seem to bother Robin.

They walked out and she took his hand, leading him to a row of parked cars. They stopped in front of a silver BMW.

"Get in. Yes, it's mine."

Willie Joe just smiled at Robin.

"You are full of surprises, aren't you?"

"Silly. How did you think we were going to get into town—hitchhike?"

Robin fiddled with the radio until she found a station she liked. Motown music. Good choice, Willie Joe thought. In minutes, they pulled up in front of an Italian restaurant.

"Like Italian? I love it."

"Sure."

As they waited to be seated, Willie Joe looked around the restaurant. Again, he felt the stares. He saw a Black couple in the corner, but no mixed race couples. He was going to have to get used to this. After they ordered, Robin clasped his hand. He just stared into her eyes, not knowing what to say. When the meal arrived, Willie Joe uncomfortably looked down at the place setting in front of him.

"The small fork is for the salad; the larger one for your entrée."

He didn't mind Robin's guidance at all. After all, he lacked the social graces and she was so willing to help him acquire them—without belittling him in the least. He could not take his eyes off of her as he asked her about her home and her family.

"Boston is just the greatest city; you must come and see it soon, William."

She was the only one that called him that. She never asked; she just did it. No matter; he would get used to it quickly. She went on to describe her father's seafood importing business, her mother's charitable work in the community and her older sister, Christine, whom she idealized.

"And what about your family? I would love to hear about them."

Willie Joe's heart sank. He didn't want to bring down the mood, but he didn't want to be evasive either.

"Unfortunately, they're all gone now. My brother died rather young; both of my parents are gone; my aunt and uncle, whom I lived with during high school, have also passed on."

The pain of acknowledging his aloneness in the world passed quickly.

"Then I feel compelled to admire you all the more for going through all of these difficult experiences on your own," Robin offered.

By the end of the dinner, Willie Joe felt at least some of the barriers—real or imagined, had come down. They got back into Robin's car and drove around the block to the theater. As they stood in line outside, it began to rain lightly, then more heavily. Robin held her purse over her head. Willie Joe shielded her from the rain. During the movie, Willie Joe slipped his arm around Robin and instinctively began to fondle her breast. She immediately moved his hand away and shot him a look of disapproval. Nothing was said.

When they arrived back on campus, Robin pulled the car into her assigned parking space. Willie Joe waited for a cue. He did not want to blow the evening by making a second presumptuous mistake. Robin needed to remain in charge in order for things to progress. She leaned across the console to him, put her arm around his neck and pulled him close. She kissed him, cupped his face in both of her hands and looked him in the eye.

"William, I like you very much—and I find you very attractive, but I'm not that kind of a girl. I'm not sleeping with you on our first date. If you have feelings for me, you'll have patience. Let's see what develops," Robin kissed him again.

They got out of the car. Willie Joe walked her to the door of her dormitory, leaned over and kissed her again.

"Thank you for the best night of my life," he expressed, with all the sincerity he could muster, and walked back to his dormitory.

CHAPTER 29

REACHING FOR THE STARS

There were many dates. Willie Joe and Robin began to spend nearly every free hour together. The relationship progressed at its own pace, and took its own shape. They had become a familiar fixture on campus—the star athlete and the cheerleader. Everyone accepted them as a couple at Easton. Of course, college campuses only masqueraded as microcosms of society. The real world still had its cold reservations about mixed race couples. Still, Willie Joe became more comfortable with Robin out in public, despite the small town stares. They became a familiar sight in town, as well. Easton the community would just have to accept them.

Junior year drew near to a close. Willie Joe and Robin studied together, dined together, took long walks across campus together. Except when each of them attended classes, basketball or cheerleading practice, they spent most of their waking hours together. Sleeping was another matter. Although it seemed the natural next step for Willie Joe, he did not want to risk losing Robin by coercing her into a sexual relationship before she felt ready. It frustrated him every now and then, but he knew they would eventually end up there. He sensed that she not only exercised that proper upbringing and conditioning of hers, but she needed complete and full assurance that he truly cared for her in every way, and intended to remain with her—and her alone, for the long haul.

Robin had gone home for Easter weekend. His roommates had taken off for the holiday, as well.

Willie Joe found himself suddenly alone for the first time in months. After a brief practice session on the court with Lee Brown, he returned to his dormitory room. He began to doze as the Easton sun set. He had just begun to dream about Robin. In the dream, he met her family for the first time. Strangely, they had no faces—expressionless. Suddenly, the phone rang and Willie Joe awoke with a start.

"Long time, no speak, Mr. Cunningham. It took some doing to track you down."

He recognized Lillian's voice.

"Rutgers and I get along well. They have a very demanding pre-law course. By the way, I heard about your uncle's passing from the Reverend Pearl. I'm sorry for your loss; everyone spoke very highly of him. I never did get to know your family. So, what about you? How is Easton treating you?"

Willie Joe thought carefully and composed every word deliberately before speaking. He felt a twinge of guilt, but more nervousness.

"Easton's been good, Lillian. It's a far cry from Newark, but I've managed to make the adjustment. I'm doing well and enjoying it."

He sensed the awkwardness on the other end, as though Lillian was waiting for him to invite her to see him. And she was.

"So, I guess you won't be goin' home too soon. It must get lonely there."

Willie Joe calculated and anticipated the outcome of his reply before making it.

"Sometimes. But I've managed to make some really good friends here. I've got good company."

Lillian read between the lines. She knew he would not invite her to Easton.

"Well, you take care now, Willie Joe. And don't be a stranger. If you do get to Newark, just let my folks know you're coming, and I'll see if I can make it home. New Brunswick isn't all that far from Newark."

"Thanks for the call, Lillian. It was nice hearing from you."

He dropped the receiver in the cradle of the phone, nearly breaking a sweat. She was his first love—the first woman he slept with, and he couldn't put enough distance between them. He was just glad she called when Robin was away. Try and explain that one. He still had a lot to learn about women, but he knew they could become very possessive and very jealous.

The team ended another great season, with Willie Joe among the high scorers. Coach Miller praised them, but warned them not to get over-confident, soft or sloppy before the start of the next season. Now, he had the ammunition he needed to go before the administration and the alumni to ask for additional funding. He would lose at least one graduating team member and needed to replace him. Scholarship and grant money made all the difference when it came to finding talented players. Very few of them came from the privileged class.

Final exams drew near and even Alex and Craig had to hunker down to study. They studied together, tag team style. Each would quiz the other in preparation for their exams. Evan preferred to hole himself up in one of the tiny carrels on the third floor of the campus library where you could hear a pin drop, and study alone. That left Willie Joe and Robin alone in the dormitory suite each weekend in May. That's when it happened.

One warm May Saturday, Willie Joe and Robin had spent nearly the entire day studying together. They took a few short breaks, but diligently ploughed through their books and their notes, quietly preparing for each exam. They ordered in Chinese take-out and had it delivered. Willie Joe studied Robin as she delicately twirled her lo mein around the fork. Every move a picture. She was perfection in the flesh. Never a hair out of place. She looked up to notice him staring.

"What? Did I do something wrong?"

"Not a thing; not a thing. I'm just admiring you."

She smiled, pushed her dinner plate aside and stood up. He wasn't quite sure what to do, so he just waited. Robin got up, closed the open door to the suite and locked it. She sat on his lap and began to unbutton his shirt. Willie Joe felt a rush of pleasure as she buried her tongue inside of his mouth and swirled it around. He began to unbutton her blouse. He watched with anxiety as her breasts heaved. He felt her heart pounding. He heard his own heart echoing in his ears. Without any warning, he picked her up and carried her into his room, carefully laying her on the bed. Robin kicked off her shoes, unhooked her bra, took his hand and placed it high on her thigh, under her skirt. Willie Joe got up, stood over her and got undressed. He closed the bedroom door, not out of modesty, but to make Robin feel safe and comfortable. He slid her skirt down; then, gently slid her panties off as she lay quietly, waiting. He gently fondled her breasts, and then massaged her genital area to relax her. She drew a deep breath and began pushing his hand deeper inside of her. By now, she was thoroughly lubricated.

Without any warning, Robin suddenly rolled on top of Willie Joe and grabbed his throbbing erect penis. To his complete surprise, she thrust it deep inside of her mouth and began to go down on him with speed and with force. He felt himself nearly ready to climax. Robin instinctively withdrew, wrapping both hands around the head of his penis, gently stroking it until Willie Joe could no longer hold back. He exploded. Gasping for breath, he got up and returned the favor, tonguing her until Robin practically screamed with pleasure.

Both of them got up, hand in hand and headed for the shower. The warm water bounced off of their bodies, making every nerve tingle. They locked in an embrace. Then, they each scrubbed the other with a bar of soap, savoring the smoothness. They gently caressed one another. Robin wrapped her legs around Willie Joe. He lifted her out of the shower. After drying off, they both lay on the bed, their bodies highly sensitized. They could feel every nerve ending. Now, Willie Joe took charge. He finally felt in control. He sensed that Robin knew what she was doing, but had not slept with many men. He slowly mounted her and began gently thrusting. In seconds, she began to moan. He raised her legs. He penetrated deeper. They both felt the earth move. They climaxed together in a passionate explosion. They lay side by side, staring into one another's eyes, breaking a sweat and breathing hard.

Nothing cements a relationship like true passionate lovemaking between two people who connect psychically, as well as physically. Especially young people, who are still largely unspoiled by the lies and deceit that come with age. Willie Joe and Robin, now inextricably linked, knew their futures were intertwined. It seemed strange at first; the debutante from the proper Boston family and the boy from the projects in Newark. Two different worlds to conquer; two paths that converged into one in a cataclysmic thunderclap of emotion. They knew they belonged together, and that was all that mattered.

CHAPTER 30

LIFE AT LIGHT SPEED

Willie Joe and Robin could hardly find enough time to spend together. Every day seemed to draw them closer. It fascinated him that Robin did not see color; race just didn't matter—his or hers. She had little tolerance for people that lived petty lives and engaged in race baiting. One evening in early June, they sat outside of the dormitory. Nearly everyone had left; the campus seemed to close its eyes. Crickets chirped as the Easton sun set quickly. Fireflies swirled around them. As they sat together on the grass, arm in arm, Willie Joe studied Robin. His intuitive sense kicked in. He could almost read her thoughts, but he asked any way.

"What are you thinking about?"

"That game you played against that college from West Virginia— the one where those people on the top row of the bleachers started taunting you with racial epithets. You stayed so cool; you never broke your concentration. You focused, you ignored them, you stayed on your game—and *you won it* for us. It looked like they didn't even bother you… but I'm sure deep down, it did."

"You're right. It bothered me. But my coach back home always taught me to stay with my game, no matter what."

"That just endeared you to me even more. You know, I've been thinking, it's time you meet the family."

Willie Joe almost physically pulled away. Robin sensed his discomfort.

"I know; it's going to be awkward. It always is. But it's really important for me. I need them to approve."

"Approve or accept?"

"Well, I would *like* their approval, but I *need* their acceptance. They will always be my family. We don't know how they will react; we just have to go with the flow."

She could see it concerned Willie Joe. If it meant that much to her, he knew he must meet them. Still, he dreaded the experience. At least he didn't have to worry about whether his family would accept her. There was no one left.

By the end of June, the entire campus shut down for one week. Every year during that week, the whole staff had a paid vacation while the facilities managers performed maintenance on all of the systems in each and every building. They chose that week for the trip to Boston. Willie Joe had tried to imagine himself fitting in with Robin's family for the week. He struggled with the thought, knowing they came from such different worlds. It wasn't the race issue alone. He simply lacked the social graces. He had never even been to a country club, let alone played polo or cricket or golf or done any of the things he imagined people from Robin's family's social circle do. He tried not to let it show, but as the week drew near, his nervousness got the better of him. He could hardly contain it. Robin sensed it.

"You want them to give you a chance, don't you? Well, then you've got to give them a chance, too. Don't prejudge them, please. Remember, we're going to be together whether they like it or not."

He heard those reassuring words—exactly the antidote for the uncertainty he felt. Finally, the day came. Willie Joe and Robin packed up her car, swung by the gas station, filled the tank, checked the air in the tires and began the trek to Boston.

Nothing thrilled Willie Joe like the feel of the open road with Robin by his side—maybe because he had spent so much of his life trapped and confined in the urban landscape. The sensation of freedom that came with no walls produced exhilaration like nothing he had ever known. Robin sensed it. Anything that made him happy made her happy. Mile after mile of highway flew by. They crossed state lines he had never seen before. Suddenly, the world seemed to have grown so much bigger for Willie Joe. He felt that childlike wonder he had missed out on for so many years while growing up. After a few hours of driving, they stopped at a rest area in Connecticut. For the first time, Willie Joe felt like no one was staring at them. He noticed couples of all sizes, shapes, ages and ethnicities. The license plates gave it away. Mostly New Yorkers, these diverse families and couples came from the great urban megalopolis—an extension of his birthplace. They were just like him—not small-town provincial people. They took a long break, enjoying the fast food restaurant's best offering. Funny how different the menu looks when you're really hungry.

Robin tied her hair back, rolled the window down and adjusted her seat. Willie Joe pushed his seat back all the way, allowing him to stretch his long legs. He began to feel drowsy. Robin encouraged him to sleep. He chose not to. The sky began to darken as they finally crossed over into Massachusetts. Robin exited the freeway and made her way onto the local highway. Garish lights from the chain stores flashed at them, like clowns grinning in the dark. Willie Joe had never driven a car. He wondered how Robin stayed so alert for so long; how she instinctively knew every turn to take. Just at that moment, traffic slowed down. They inched their way forward. The smell of the diesel exhaust from the truck in front of them overwhelmed them. Robin switched lanes to avoid it. Everyone ground to a halt. They inched along until they finally saw the flashing lights of the tow truck; then the ambulance; then the police patrol car. Emergency personnel scurried around like mice. Then they saw it—an overturned vehicle appeared to be stuck under a truck. It would take a miracle for anyone to survive.

Traffic began to move. Willie Joe and Robin both felt it—how tenuous our lifelines are. At any time, our fragile lives could just end—smashing our illusion of immortality. Robin steered her way around the wreckage of the crash, to where the traffic flow began to move again. Suddenly, Willie Joe felt the panic of anticipation once again overtake him. He tried to mask it, changing the station on the car radio. At least the music kept them awake.

Finally, they left the highway. As they entered the sleepy little town of Holyoke, it looked like something out of a 1950's television show. Everywhere he looked, Willie Joe saw white Cape Cod homes with white picket fences, trimmed green lawns and sidewalks lined with trees. They slowly turned down one street after another. To him, they all looked the same. It was just too cliché. Sure enough, when they reached the center of town, the street sign caught his eye—"Main Street." It looked like something out of a drugstore calendar—the barber shop, the Post

Office, the hardware store…oh, so Americana—so unlike his home city of Newark, New Jersey.

At last, Robin made the final turns to the long, winding road along the river. Then, at the end of the road, she took a left onto the last side street. Slowing down, she rolled into the driveway of the house numbered 38. Slightly imposing, it seemed to dwarf the others on the block, as if to say,

"Somebody important lives here." Two tall maple trees lined the walkway up to the front steps. The ample veranda wrapped around the side. Willie Joe remembered the nights he spent at Aunt Agnes and Uncle Ben's, on the much smaller veranda of 63 Mapes Avenue in Newark.

They got out of the car. Willie Joe instinctively went to open the trunk and retrieve their bags, but then stopped. He looked at Robin. She had already started to make her way to the front steps. He followed suit. Just then, the panic gripped him again. He took a deep breath, standing behind Robin as she opened the door. Her mother threw her arms around Robin, looked Willie Joe up and down and beckoned him in. He breathed a sigh of relief.

"You must be William Joseph. I'm so pleased to meet you. Robin really has not told me much about you at all. I'm afraid you'll have to tell me yourself. You two must be exhausted from the drive. Let me get you both a cold drink. Robin, your father must be around somewhere."

She went into the kitchen, leaving them alone for a moment. Willie Joe anxiously looked at Robin, waiting for her approval. She squeezed his hand under the table as they sat in the well-furnished dining room. Willie Joe looked around, eying the antiques, the paintings and the classic Colonial furniture. Just then, a figure appeared at the top of the winding staircase, clad in a tennis uniform, with a sweater tied around the waist.

"Christine bean—"

"Robin bobbin'—"

Robin's older sister Christine seemed to float down the stairs with that same genteel grace Robin always exhibited. She barely looked at Willie Joe. He felt the coolness instantly. Robin broke the awkward silence.

"Christine, this is William Joseph Cunningham; William, this is my big sister Christine I told you about. Where's dad?"

Christine motioned toward a room with double doors, tightly shut.

"In his study, I guess. I wouldn't disturb him if I were you. You know how he gets. He'll come out when he's ready."

Robin's mother returned with a tray full of drinking glasses and a pitcher of iced tea. She poured one for Willie Joe first. Robin plopped a coaster in front of him just before the glass landed on the table. Willie Joe reached for the glass; Robin placed her hand on his arm, stopping him until everyone had his or her glasses. Then she nodded. Willie Joe smiled, and then took a long draught.

"This is really good, Mrs. Whiteside; really good."

"It's my own special secret recipe, William. My mother taught it to me. I'll make sure and pass it on to Robin so you can continue to enjoy it."

Robin noticed Christine seeking her attention and rose from her seat.

"William, you don't mind if my sister and I just slip away for a few minutes and catch up on some girl talk, do you? I don't see her much. You and mom get acquainted. I'm sure dad will be out soon."

Robin and Christine slipped out the back door like a couple of little schoolgirls. Mrs. Whiteside proceeded to give Willie Joe the house tour, explaining the history of all the heirlooms. From time to time, Willie Joe noticed Christine and Robin through the window at the umbrella table in the backyard. He wished he could hear what they were saying.

Christine studied Robin, and then just dropped it on her, like a bomb.

"Robin, what *are* you doing? What do you expect to come of this? Surely, it can't be a good outcome. Don't tell me you're really serious about him."

She never gave Robin a chance to get a word in edgewise. Finally, Robin spoke, leaning across the table and looking her sister straight in the eye.

"Since you asked, I will tell you. Yes, we both care for one another very much. William is the sweetest young man I have ever met. And before you ask, the answer is yes—I have slept with him."

Christine looked away, sighing deeply.

"I guess there's nothing I can do or say to make you see how this will end."

"You don't know how this will end, and neither do I. I do know that nobody has ever really cared about me like William does. And don't tell me how I'm going to break dad's heart; mom seems to accept him just fine."

Christine stood up, shaking her head.

"Let's go inside. We'll just have to play this out, come what may."

Robin followed her.

"Yes, we will."

The girls returned to the dining room as Willie Joe and Mrs. Whiteside looked at the family Bible that had been passed down for generations. The Bible recorded the entire family history of births, marriages and deaths for over a hundred years. Mrs. Whiteside closed the Bible and looked at Willie Joe.

"William, are you a religious man?"

Willie Joe at first seemed taken aback by the question. Searching for words, he chose them carefully.

"My family members were avid churchgoers. I attended at an early age. I admit I haven't gone since I started college."

Mrs. Whiteside smiled.

"I appreciate your honesty. Religion has always meant a lot to us. Robin and Christine always attended church regularly. It does contribute to the moral fiber of society. If everyone remained faithful, I do believe we would not have so much lawlessness. Will you excuse me, please? I do want to see if my husband is all right. Thank you."

Mrs. Whiteside inclined her head toward the study doors, listening for a moment. Hearing nothing, she knocked, and then entered. It seemed like a long time passed. Willie Joe could only hear muffled voices. He could not make out the words. He thought he heard a faint classical music background. Finally, Mrs. Whiteside emerged, alone. She kept her composure. The room fell quiet. Willie Joe looked at Robin. Robin looked at Christine. Christine looked at Mrs. Whiteside. Finally, Mrs. Whiteside spoke, with hesitation in her voice, looking directly at Willie Joe.

"I'm very sorry, but he's not going to come out. You'll have to give him time. He's not going to accept this so readily."

Robin began to tear up. She straightened up and reached over to take her mother's hand.

"Mom, I think it best we leave. This is just not going to happen yet."

Willie Joe stood up, rising over Mrs. Whiteside.

"Ma'am, I fully understand. Your husband is just not ready to accept our relationship. I do hope he will come around. I thank you for your hospitality."

Robin embraced her mother, then kissed Christine on the cheek and headed for the door, with Willie Joe in tow. He felt the depth of her pain, but he didn't see it until they reached the car. Tears streamed down her cheeks. He wanted to console her, but she insisted on leaving promptly.

"Let's just get out of here. I am so sorry. I knew it wouldn't be easy, but I didn't think it would be *this* hard. I had really hoped they would accept us together. I really wanted to show you the sights in my town. Let's just head back to Easton."

"Robin, it's late and you drove a long way. Maybe we should get a room. You'll be refreshed in the morning; better able to make the drive, okay?"

Robin nodded, and they left the town of Holyoke behind.

CHAPTER 31

WITHIN MY REACH

The end of summer drew near and the usual student population trickled back to the Easton campus—along with the newbies; incoming freshmen and their families poured in, cars loaded up with all the trappings of a new life on the quiet little campus. Willie Joe and Robin had enjoyed their time alone together. Now, they would have to readjust to the somewhat chaotic life of roommates and dormitory parties criscrossing their days and nights. Much had changed over the past three years, but the bonds of friendship had only grown stronger. In spite of the loss of privacy, Willie Joe looked forward to the return of his roommates. It was Sunday morning. Robin had just come out of the shower wrapped in a towel when they heard the door to the suite swing open. Willie Joe instinctively and protectively closed the bedroom door and ran out to the living room. He greeted Alex and Craig; Evan followed right behind.

While Robin got dressed, he caught up with them. Something seemed different. Alex and Craig did not display their usual over-the-top exuberance. As they began to unpack in their bedroom, Willie Joe pulled Evan aside.

"Any idea what's up with them? They don't seem like themselves."

"From the few minutes we spent together unloading the cars and bringing everything into the lobby downstairs, I caught some bits and pieces about a trip to Mexico over the summer that went sour—something about them getting caught in the middle of a drug bust. Sounds like they were really traumatized. They seem pretty tight-lipped about it, but I'm guessing they did a little jail time and it wasn't pretty."

"Hey, we'll just give them some time to readjust and settle in. What about you, Evan? Anything eventful, or just the usual family vacation and another notch in the belt?"

Evan smiled.

"You nailed it. A little sailing; golf at the Cape; a lot of beach time, and more girls than you could shake your stick at. And how about you, Willie Joe? Did you finally get around to meeting my family?"

Willie Joe looked at Evan, puzzled.

"Meeting my cousin Robin's family."

Willie Joe's jaw dropped. He flashed a glance at the closed bedroom door.

"Robin's your cousin? You never told me."

"I didn't see what difference it would make."

Just then the bedroom door opened and Robin entered, toweling off her still damp hair. She threw her arms around Evan's neck and gave him a hug. Willie Joe stood there, shaking his head. Robin approached him, wrapping her arm around his waist and looked up at him.

"So now you know, silly. It matters?"

"No. He'll still be my best man."

Evan beamed a smile at them. They all laughed.

"Let's all go to the mailboxes and pick up our class schedules," Evan suggested.

They took the walk over to the student center, then back to the dorm and compared notes. As seniors, they all had a lighter course load. For Willie Joe, this year would determine his future. He had to beat his own record and outperform himself—both on the court and in the classroom. He was ready for it. This year, he had Robin's full support, as well. They had grown so close and so dependent on one another. They had one class together this semester—"The Psychology of Winning."

Everything seemed to move like clockwork that first semester. October 15th marked the first basketball practice on the schedule. Classes flew by; practice after practice ticked away and then the basketball season kicked in. On a Friday afternoon, Evan came running in to the dorm room waving the latest issue of the campus newspaper, "The Clarion."

"Extra, extra, read all about it. Easton scores and wins another title; Cunningham leads the team to victory." Willie Joe could hardly believe it. Evan handed him the newspaper. Larger than life, in big bold type, the headline read, "Easton's Cunningham Named Pre-Season All-American 1st Player in the Humanitarian League." Evan snatched the paper and read the rest of the article aloud.

Willie Joe stood there listening, in his usual modest fashion. Students began pouring into their suite. Someone stood on a kitchen chair and anointed Willie Joe's head with beer. Robin began to perform her cheerleading moves, landing in a split in front of Willie Joe. A few weeks later, another win, another title and the madness of celebration again descended on Willie Joe's dorm suite. This time, the local press picked up the story, with Willie Joe named Most Valuable Player of the Quaker Tip-Off Classic and the DC Holiday Festival. Even Coach Miller showed up to congratulate him, the rest of the team in tow. Alex and Craig took charge of the festivities, wheeling a keg of beer up the stairs on a hand truck.

The second semester began with a bang. The Easton team won every game —except the conference title. Here they were, little Easton, the unknown, unsung dark horse team, seeded 8th in the NCAA. The play-by-play announcer's voice rang out over the loudspeakers—and the local radio station, as Willie Joe scored 27 points, grabbed 8 rebounds and 6 assists—not to mention several steals. In the post-game wrap-up, the sportscasters said it was a miracle the team *didn't* win. When they interviewed the opposing team's coach, Villanova's Rollie Massimo, he took the high road, calling Willie Joe "One of the finest players in the country!" He wondered how his Wildcats missed him, and how he ever ended up at Easton. After the final buzzer sounded, Willie Joe looked up into the bleachers. He spotted the scouts. They were easy to pick out. He could hardly believe it—the Celtics, the Knicks and the Bulls all sent scouts. These teams had some of the most sophisticated defenses in professional basketball! When the crowd dispersed, one of them approached him.

"Mr. Cunningham, my name is Chad Phillips. I'm a scout for this team and I would like to arrange a private meeting with you to talk about your future in professional basketball. Would you call me to arrange a convenient time— that is, if you're interested?"

Willie Joe felt a sweat break out as he stared down at the business card. He could hardly believe his eyes—the Boston Celtics! If you're interested? He couldn't believe his ears either. He suddenly understood the meaning of the phrase "butterflies in your stomach." He nervously replied.

"Absolutely. Yes. I'm interested. I'll call you."

"Good. We've been watching you play and we like what we see. This year's draft pick will be critical for our success. Our coach saw you play a few weeks ago and was very impressed. He said you move like Bill Bradley. Don't underestimate yourself, son. You were named All-American, and that's no small feat. I'll expect your call later this week."

"Thank you, sir. Thank you."

Willie Joe wished his mother could see him now. He bowed his head as Chad Phillips walked away. To himself, he silently said,

"Thank you, God. Thank you, God."

When he emerged from the locker room in his street clothes, he met Robin.

"I saw you talking to that man. He's a scout, isn't he? How did it go?"

Willie Joe handed her the business card. Robin's eyes lit up.

"He wants me to call him for a private meeting. I think they want to draft me."

Robin turned to him, threw her arms around him and kissed him. She knew it meant he would be away from her for long periods, but she knew it meant everything to him. She was willing to make the sacrifice.

Over the next few days, Coach Miller received several calls from agents wanting to sign Willie Joe. He passed the messages along so Willie Joe could return their calls. Willie Joe asked Evan to serve as his agent. With his family connections, he could probably help land a deal to play in New England. At any rate, he knew he could trust Evan to watch his back and help him secure the right deal. Evan deferred to his father, a contract lawyer, who graciously accepted the job.

A week later, Willie Joe found himself across the desk in Coach Miller's office—from the Celtics scout Chad Phillips...and the Celtics coach. The meeting went well. Still, it seemed so surreal. He kept having to refocus his attention on the moment. He felt like he was dreaming. Willie Joe thanked them as they dropped him off in front of the dormitory. He felt like he had just won a Nobel Prize.

The meetings came and went, one after another, scout after scout, coach after coach. Several weeks went by, but no firm offer materialized. The end of the semester and graduation approached. Willie Joe sat with

Evan and his father to explore his options. In spite of his lack of sports-world experience, Evan's father displayed the skills and the knowledge to steer Willie Joe in the right direction.

"I've researched this thoroughly. Even though you remain undrafted, you can still go to the Celtics Training Camp up in Waltham, at Brandeis University. We'll get you in as a free agent. If we're successful, we might even get you a signing bonus. Are you game for it?"

"Absolutely, man; absolutely," Willie Joe placed his full faith in Evan's dad's judgment and went with his recommendation.

"I'll take care of all the arrangements and the formalities. You just do what you do best—play ball, keep learning and growing—and do some winning along the way."

Although he still felt like it was all a dream, it did happen. Officials from the Celtics came down to Easton to administer a competency test. The test seemed ludicrous at first. Some of the questions just didn't make sense. They wanted to test Willie Joe for aptitude. Like every test he ever took, he passed. And Evan's father made it happen—a sweet two-year deal with a $20,000. signing bonus! Willie Joe wanted to know what he owed, but they insisted he was family and refused to take a dime from him.

"We just want to say 'We knew you when.'"

He didn't know how to thank them. No one had ever treated him so well.

CHAPTER 32

REAL WORLD; REAL CHALLENGES

If Willie Joe thought that learning the politics of college athletics presented a challenge, and acquiring the social graces of the upper classes would take some doing, he discovered that the world of professional sports rolled over everything else in life like a steamroller. He needed Evan's dad to navigate the business end of things, but learning the etiquette and the protocol of working the team and the coaches offered a learning curve all its own.

In any case, the basics always ruled. Willie Joe reverted back to everything he had learned from Coach at the Newark Boys' Club. He knew he needed preparation—the right preparation, to make it through training camp and to go pro. He left nothing to chance. To get ready, he decided to play in the famed Sonny Hill league. The best way to improve your game always involved playing against the best. This experience would pit him against players from St Joseph's, Temple University, Villanova, Penn State, Princeton and La Salle. It proved to be the best possible training he could ever get.

Basketball had to become more important than anything in his life, in order to make it. That meant even Robin had to take a back seat. It became more like combat than sport for him. He had to make every day count. And he did, scoring nearly 18 points per game. In time, he just settled in like a well-oiled gear in a playing machine. Even though he was a rookie, he had begun to find his groove, beating all the players in the famed Celtic Run. He dashed up and down the court 35 times in three minutes—an unheard of feat. The coaches watched in awe, shaking their heads as he beat the other players—Ainge, Johnson and the other rookies. Rumor had it that even Larry Bird praised his performance. It was the second to last day of training camp, and things really ramped up fast.

Then, as the action got even more intense, Willie Joe stole the ball from Cedric Maxwell. He felt a twinge in his knee. Going in for a thunderous jam, just as he landed, he heard a pop. The coach blew the whistle. Everything stopped. No amount of ice would take the pain or the swelling down. He had blown out his knee. As he hobbled off the court, all Willie Joe could think about was, "What now? Was his career over before it had begun?"

The doctors showed him his X-rays and his MRI's. The soft tissue damage would take months to heal, followed by more months of physical therapy. Would he ever play basketball again? They wouldn't even speculate. Willie Joe was crestfallen. He felt like a wounded bird. Robin comforted him at his hospital bedside. She knew the less she said, the better. She also knew he needed her there. The cast made his injuries look worse than they really were. Evan showed up, chipper as always, still with a positive outlook. He knew it would take time before Willie Joe could sort this out and figure out his next steps.

Robin had landed a good job just after graduation, not far from the training camp. She had found an apartment in the area as well. It looked like a long road ahead for them, but they would have to make the adjustments and begin to build their lives together. Willie Joe hobbled out of the hospital on crutches, leaning on Robin on one side and Evan on the other. Loss of his physical prowess was the one thing he had never had to worry about. He had never felt more powerless.

When a man's body breaks down, it's extremely hard for the mind not to follow suit. Even with all his discipline and training, bouts of depression overcame Willie Joe periodically. He had difficulty sitting still in the apartment—especially knowing Robin had become the breadwinner. None of it seemed right to him. He wanted to make it right. He began to read again, voraciously—mostly self-help books. As he read, he kept putting the good stuff into his head. As his in-home physical therapy helped him to become stronger and he became more self-sufficient, his attitude began to turn around. Things seemed brighter. He stopped worrying. He still played basketball—in his mind. But the stronger he got, the more frustrated he became.

Months went by. The cast had long since come off, his mobility improved, he hardly used the crutches. He was careful not to undo any of the healing. Still, he ached to get out and go. He continued to wonder if he would every play ball again. Finally, Willie Joe went to the doctor for his follow-up exam and more tests. Robin stood by, anxiously as Dr. Weingarten spoke.

"I've read your physical therapist's reports and they are encouraging. I've compared your new scans with your original ones and they do show some nice improvement. However, I'm still cautiously optimistic about the outcome. You've exhibited a good range of motion, but I would not recommend any strenuous activity yet—and still don't recommend you put your full weight on that knee. There is nothing we can do surgically; it's just going to take time. I know that's not what you wanted to hear."

Willie Joe continued his regimen of mild exercise, resumed cane walking and began to take an interest in natural healing modalities. He studied herbalists and began to change his diet. There had to be something that would help him heal better and faster. If traditional medicine didn't offer anything, maybe he could find some alternative. After several weeks, it seemed as though his efforts had paid off. He put the cane aside, began to walk normally, letting his full weight fall on the injured knee and lo and behold, the pain had subsided.

One Friday evening, Robin came home from work looking piqued. Willie Joe surprised her with a home-cooked candle light dinner. Afterward, to her surprise, he slowly dropped to his knee. Her mouth dropped open with joy as she saw he was able to perform this simple movement. A moment later, her mouth dropped open again.

"Robin Whiteside, will you marry me?"

Willie Joe reached in his pocket and withdrew a ring, presenting it to her. He had been sending a small payment in each week to the jeweler, since his injury.

Robin took his outstretched hand, stood up from the table and beckoned him to stand up.

"Oh, yes. This is the happiest day of my life."

She threw her arms around his neck. For the first time in months, he once again felt powerful.

They didn't know quite how they would put it all together, but like most young people, their belief in the power of love would somehow carry them through everything and light the way. They debated about whether to tell Robin's family about the engagement yet. They decided to wait. There was no need to even set a wedding date yet. Somehow they knew everything would work out. It always did. Then, a phone call came. It was Coach Miller. He had heard about Willie Joe's injury and wanted to know how his recovery was progressing.

"I don't know if I will ever play again, especially pro. But I've come a long way and the doctor says things look good. Thanks for asking."

"Listen, Willie Joe. That's only part of why I called you. I've got an offer for you. Do you think you can tear yourself away from New England and get back to Easton? Here's the offer; if you enroll in grad school here, I can get you in as an Assistant Coach to me—as my graduate assistant. I'm sure you'll want to think it over, but I do need an answer by next week. We could really use you here. I mean that."

"Thank you. Really, that's good news. I promise I'll get back to you in a couple of days."

Willie Joe looked at Robin, searching her eyes for a sign.

"What? What is it?"

"Would you be willing to quit your job and move back to Easton? Pete Miller just called me and offered me a graduate assistantship. It probably won't pay that much, but I would come in as his assistant coach—"

"If it's what you want, then start packing. I would never stand in your way. I'll give notice and look for a job around Easton."

"There is one more call I need to make before I can decide."

"I understand."

Willie Joe began dialing. He hadn't called the number for so long, he had to look for it in his wallet.

"Coach? That you? Willie Joe Cunningham—"

"Well, well, I'll be. If it ain't my boy Willie Joe himself. Been a long time. Always good to hear from you. So tell me how things been goin' fo' you?"

Willie Joe described his college basketball career at Easton; the titles the team won; then, he told Coach about his training camp experience and about the injury. Finally, he asked his advice on whether he should take Coach Miller's offer and return to Easton.

"How fast can you say 'Yes', boy? That's how fast I would take that offer if I was you. What you been through is only an upset—a setup for a comeback, son."

Willie Joe detected a tiredness in Coach's voice, in spite of the cheerfulness. He hung up the phone and looked at Robin, who had just finished drying and putting away the dinner dishes.

"We're going to Easton!"

She threw her arms around him.

"We're going to Easton", she repeated.

That night, for the first time in months, Willie Joe slept peacefully, without the restlessness—or the disturbing dreams he had become accustomed to.

CHAPTER 33

A BEND IN THE ROAD

Willie Joe and Robin both understood that Coach Miller's offer arrived like divine intervention itself. What else could he possibly do that would fulfill him? What else had life prepared him for? If he couldn't play the game he loved on the court, at least he could train other deserving young men to play their best game. Robin gave notice at her job, began sending resumes to recruiters around the Easton area and they packed up the apartment. While Willie Joe loaded the rented truck, Robin went on ahead to find an apartment in Easton. They would have to live modestly for a while. Graduate assistants didn't earn much.

When they arrived back in Easton, Coach Miller had a surprise for them. Willie Joe reported in to learn about the lay of the land. Coach Miller reached in his desk drawer and handed Willie Joe a small envelope. He opened it. Two keys with a tag attached, bearing an address.

"Don't sign that lease. We got you an apartment on campus, subsidized by the college. Welcome back. I'll see you here on Monday morning. I know I can count on you."

"Yes, sir; you can. I don't know how to thank you."

"Just do a great job; help us win and make us proud."

Willie Joe returned to Robin, held up the keys and told her to stop unpacking. Just then, there was a knock at the door. Two Easton students, still in their basketball uniforms, showed up with a van.

"We're here to help you move, Mr. Cunningham."

In no time at all, they resettled into the staff quarters on campus. Robin spent the next week calling around and interviewing for jobs. Finally, her efforts paid off. A factory in Allentown had opened a branch office in Easton and needed someone with take-charge organizational skills to support its sales staff. The pay didn't compare to what she earned in Boston, but it would do fine for now. Willie Joe perused the graduate school catalog, trying to decide what courses he should start with. Something told him he needed to learn more about business and management, so he decided to sign up for those courses. He needed to keep his schedule flexible, with the team's practice and game schedule. As a recent graduate of Easton, he knew the demands placed on the team members. Those same demands—and more— would go to the coaching staff.

Now that they had some order in their lives, each with a job to perform, Robin and Willie Joe needed to begin planning their personal future. They had to think about their wedding. Willie Joe knew they could no longer avoid the inevitable. They had to confront the hard reality that her family ultimately might not accept their union. He knew this would place a great strain on Robin. He also knew that she was committed to going ahead with their marriage, whether her family approved or not. He remembered her words on that difficult trip they took to Boston, when her father would not even come out and meet him. She had said she "Hoped they would accept it, even if they didn't approve of it."

Robin knew what she had to do. She nervously dialed her parents' home.

Her mother answered.

"Mom, I hope everything is fine with you and dad. Is he home? I need to speak to him."

Her mother handed the phone to her father without even speaking— an uncharacteristic move for her. Somehow, her intuition told her she needed to do just that.

"Hello, sweetheart. Everything okay? Good to hear from you. Do you need anything?"

Robin held her breath before speaking; then launched right into it.

"Yes, as a matter of fact I do. I need your blessing. William and I are getting married."

After a brief pause, she heard a deep sigh. Then he spoke.

"We only want your happiness. I think you know that. We're going to have to trust your judgment; that you know what's right for you. So

I guess we need to meet your young man then. Have you set a date yet? Would you like us to come down to you?"

Robin quietly hung up the phone, turned to Willie Joe with tears streaming down her face.

"He wants to meet you, William. They're going to come down to see us. I can't believe this is really happening. It's so wonderful."

Willie Joe enveloped her in his arms, cradling her face against his chest.

He knew how much it meant to her for her parents to accept their marriage.

Two weeks later, the Whitesides arrived for their visit. They went to dinner at that favorite Italian restaurant in Easton where Willie Joe had taken Robin on their first date. The nervousness evaporated as Mr. Cunningham and Mr. Whiteside began to learn that, although they came from different worlds and although they looked very different, on the inside—where it counts—they resembled one another very closely. Their value systems aligned; their priorities jived. As the evening progressed, they toasted one another, sharing a glass of wine and breaking bread together. Mr. Whiteside had a keen interest in sports and had met a few professional athletes in his time. He had great respect for Willie Joe's accomplishments. He felt compelled to tell him about his own humble beginnings.

"My father fished for a living. He had a small boat and a crew of one. We had lean years and we had fat years—kind of like Pharaoh's dream in the Bible. We learned to save, not spend. My mother had to make do with whatever the catch of the season yielded...and she did. When I finished high school, my father expected me to join him on the boat. So, now we had a crew of two. I learned more about business on that fishing boat than any college could teach me. After a few years, I decided to go to school at night. What I learned there helped me to parlay my father's humble beginnings into a substantial fleet of fishing boats. Now, we export most of our catch. Your turn, son. Tell me your story."

Mr. Whiteside sat back and listened. Willie Joe faltered, not sure what to say. He wanted to be kind to his parents' memories, yet still truthful.

"My father worked in a factory; my mother worked as a domestic. Both of them—and my older brother—died young. We grew up in a project; we attended church every Sunday. When they passed on, my aunt and uncle took me in and adopted me. I could not have been happier. My uncle took me to the local Boys' Club and introduced me to my basketball coach—my first mentor. I learned what I needed to know from this very giving man. I thought I would play pro ball, but God had other plans for me. He was kind enough to offer me this wonderful opportunity. Now, it's my turn to give back."

Willie Joe now sat back and waited.

"Son, I would be lying if I told you I thought your lives would be easy going forward. It will be the most difficult for your children. We want the best for you and Robin, but we live in a cruel and often unforgiving world. I'm sure you've already experienced that. Just be strong and look out for Robin. Now, we've got a wedding to plan, so I'm going to be quiet and let Mrs. Whiteside do what she does best."

Willie Joe and Mr. Whiteside got up and walked outside, leaving Robin and Mrs. Whiteside to begin formulating the wedding plans.

Willie Joe looked Mr. Whiteside straight in the eye and spoke.

"Sir, you have no idea what it means to Robin and I, you coming here to spend time with us—and giving us your blessing for our marriage."

"Son, I said it before. I don't need to say it again. If Robin loves you, that is what matters most. I was never in favor of the mixing of races. That doesn't make me a racist. I just believe it makes life more difficult because the world is still not ready to accept it. I'm being brutally honest with you. I have absolutely nothing against you as a person—or as a future son-in-law. I just know it's going to be difficult—especially for a child of a mixed race marriage. But I have every confidence that you will do right by my daughter."

Mr. Whiteside withdrew a pipe from his jacket pocket, and began to fill it with a fragrant cherry tobacco. He lit it and began to puff on it. He looked like the images of sea captains Willie Joe had seen in movies. He had never met a real seafaring man before this.

"Robin means the world to me. I think you know that, sir. I would never do anything but the right thing by her. I have learned so much from her. I intend to earn your respect, sir."

"You already have. Just look after her for us, please. That's all that matters. Let's go inside and see what these ladies are up to."

When they returned to the table, Robin and Mrs. Whiteside had gone to the ladies' room, so they waited for them to return.

"Are you staying for the rest of the weekend?" Robin asked.

"No, I think we'll head back to Boston in the morning. We need to get back to our hotel and get some rest. We had a long drive down and we've got a long drive back," Mrs. Whiteside acknowledged.

"It was a pleasure and an honor, sir," Willie Joe stood up and extended his hand.

Just then, the waiter presented the check. Mr. Whiteside and Willie Joe both reached for it and pulled, tearing the check in two.

"I guess this means we're going to split it," Willie Joe offered.

"Not this time, son. Not this time. It's on me," Mr. Whiteside insisted.

CHAPTER 34

SEARCHING FOR THE HORIZON

Life seems to accelerate and kick into a higher gear as we age. Willie Joe observed this. He could hardly believe how much the pace of his life had picked up since he and Robin arrived back in Easton. And it just kept spinning, faster and faster. Robin worked by day, kept in touch with her mother as the wedding plans progressed, while Willie Joe learned the ins and outs of coaching by day, and attended his graduate school classes by night. It seemed dizzying at times; there just didn't seem to be any letting up. Still, they always managed to find quiet time for one another.

Willie Joe learned day by day that the mechanics of playing basketball on the court were only the tip of the iceberg when it came to recruiting a team, financing a team, coaching a team and putting it all together to create a winning season. As the Assistant Coach, he focused mainly on working with the players at practice. Still, any time Coach Miller had to handle a personal emergency or go on a brief hiatus, the rest of the coaching duties landed solidly in Willie Joe's lap. He didn't mind. It all contributed to the learning experience he knew he needed to gain.

The team grew steadily better; they piled up the wins as that first season progressed. Still, the world was, as Robin's father said, a cruel place. Willie Joe experienced it again, firsthand, when he went to the homes of two wealthy White students. The parents met him with cold stares, shunning him. Had nothing changed in the hundred years since slavery was abolished in this country? Would the color of a man's skin always determine his place in our society, or the heights he could rise to? Willie Joe hoped not. These things he would not even share with Robin. He just kept them buried deep down inside. And they ate away at him.

The beginning of that first season took a toll on Robin and Willie Joe. Those first few away games became painful—a pain that would later become a dull ache—one they would just have to learn to live with. It had nothing to do with trust; they had simply grown so close that spending time apart caused them both pain. But they knew it would pay off. Finally, their wedding date drew near. It gave them both a feeling of lightness. Willie Joe nonetheless felt discomfort. Although Robin's family had accepted him, would the family's friends feel the same way? It would have to remain a mystery until that day. Willie Joe found this nerve-wracking.

At last, the weekend had arrived. Willie Joe and Robin packed up the car and made the trek to Boston. Somehow the trip seemed much faster than that first time they drove up together. Willie Joe had just gotten his driver's license, so at least he could share the driving and relieve Robin at the wheel this time. When they arrived in Holyoke and pulled into the driveway of the Whiteside residence, Christine greeted them at the door. It seemed like night and day, compared to Willie Joe's recollection of their first meeting. Finally, his future sister-in-law had accepted him. A big and important step. This time they did not hesitate to unload their bags from the car. After Mrs. Whiteside parked their bags in the guest room, Mr. Whiteside ushered Willie Joe into his study. Quite a contrast from his first visit, when the man would not even emerge to meet him. Robin, her mother and her sister went upstairs to review the wedding plans.

Willie Joe stared around Jack Whiteside's study. He had never seen anything like it, except on television or in movies. Dark wood paneling graced the walls; brass sconces mounted at either end of two tall built-in bookcases, and model ships everywhere. Everything seafaring hung on the walls—paintings, nautical instruments, porthole mirrors and a model bathysphere. Jack Whiteside stood up from behind his massive carved mahogany desk, leaned over, clasped Willie Joe's hand and motioned for him to take the chair opposite his. Willie Joe sank into the tufted green leather chair and extended his long legs under the desk.

"So, how was the ride up, son?" he asked, genuinely interested.

"Not bad at all—in fact, rather pleasant. You know, growing up in a city like Newark as I did, we never had a car and I only just learned to drive. At least this time I could share the driving with Robin," Willie Joe offered.

"Well, I know you've waited anxiously for this day, son; we all have. Welcome to our family."

Willie Joe felt overcome to hear those words.

"You know there is nothing I have wanted in my entire life more than to have Robin by my side as my wife, sir."

"I believe that. I thoroughly and completely believe that, William. I do have a question for you, however."

"Please, Mr. Whiteside, ask it—anything," Willie Joe implored.

Jack Whiteside sat back in his chair, re-lit his pipe, took a long puff and looked up at Willie Joe. Will you think any less of me if I tell you that I did not invite my business associates to the wedding—only because I believe *they* could not accept an interracial marriage? Will you believe me when I tell you that decision has nothing to do with *my* acceptance of the marriage?"

"Mr. Whiteside, sir; you said it when you first met me—it's a cruel world. Enough said."

Jack Whiteside smiled at Willie Joe, stood up, poured a glass of Scotch and offered one to Willie Joe.

"I know you're the athletic one and you probably don't drink, but I'll ask you to make an exception on this occasion. It's almost a kind of a ritual. We need to seal our bond as father and son."

Willie Joe rose from his chair to accept the glass and spoke.

"I am honored beyond my wildest dreams to have you as a father-in-law, Mr. Whiteside."

"After tomorrow, it's just 'Jack'. Are we okay with that?"

"Yes, sir. Perfectly okay with that," Willie Joe beamed a smile at him as they clinked their glasses and downed the shots. It was true. Willie Joe had never drunk liquor before. The sensation of the hot whiskey going down gripped his throat. He felt his face flush. It felt wrong, yet it was so right. He was proud to seal the deal. Jack Whiteside reached into his blazer pocket and slid an envelope across the desk to Willie Joe, his hand still on top of it.

"This is for you and Robin. Please don't open it until you get home from the wedding; that's all I ask."

Willie Joe had never encountered situations like this before. He didn't know quite what to tell Robin. He decided to keep the details of the meeting between her father and himself quiet. When he emerged from the study, he found Robin, Christine and Mrs. Whiteside at the dining room table, poring over seating diagrams, photos of the reception hall and floral arrangements.

Everybody seemed to find an adrenaline rush that kept him or her going. Eventually, they gave in to hunger, not to fatigue. After feasting on the best home cooked dinner he had ever eaten, Willie Joe retired to an easy chair in the living room. The ladies continued their discussion of the arrangements for the big day tomorrow. Mr. Whiteside retreated once again to his study.

Finally, the hour grew late, the grandfather clock in the living room chimed, keeping Willie Joe awake and Robin came to fetch him. They fell into a deep sleep, locked in an embrace.

The Church overwhelmed Willie Joe. He had never seen an edifice like it. It looked like a miniature version of the famed St. Patrick's Cathedral in New York City. As he scanned the gigantic stained glass windows and the high pulpit, Willie Joe's memories flashed back to his days as a child attending services at Newark's Beulah Baptist Church. Suddenly, he remembered the time when he had felt the presence of what he unmistakably believed to be an angel. The long buried spiritual part of him seemed to awaken. For just a moment, he closed his eyes and imagined his parents and his brother standing before him. If only they could see him now, but wishing wouldn't make it so.

People slowly filed in to the church, taking their seats. The anxious murmuring grew to a crescendo. Robin had gone over to meet the priest and approached him, escorting him over to meet Willie Joe. Willie Joe felt the awkwardness as he found himself surrounded by a sea of White faces. He felt judged; he felt somehow unworthy. That would change. Father O'Reilly looked up at him and the serenity in his eyes just melted Willie Joe's fears and discomfort away. Everybody took his or her places. Willie Joe felt more at ease when Evan, his best man, approached.

The ceremony went smoothly, like a picture book wedding—right down to the throwing of the rice as they exited the church. Suddenly, Willie Joe had yet another flashback. As they stood on the steps of the church, he remembered that day during the Newark riots when the police arrived in full riot gear at the Beulah Baptist Church. He never forgot the tension of that moment. Robin tugged at his arm and broke his reverie as the photographer shot one photo after another. Willie

Joe wondered if this was what celebrities felt like when faced with the paparazzi.

The limousine whisked Willie Joe and Robin back to the Whiteside residence. They had decided to drive back to Easton the next morning before taking a brief honeymoon. They planned to fly out of Newark Airport for a few days in the Bahamas. Newark Airport had undergone major expansion several years ago, and was now an international airport with multiple terminals. When they arrived back in Easton, Willie Joe and Robin unpacked their wedding baggage and re-packed for their island trip. They sat at their kitchen table, looking over the cards and gifts. Then, Willie Joe remembered the envelope Jack Whiteside had given him—along with the instructions not to open it until they arrived home. He ran into the bedroom, rifled through their suitcase and presented the envelope to Robin. She looked at him with excitement.

"Go ahead, you open it."

"No, it's from your folks. You should open it."

"William, they're your family too, now. Go ahead and open it."

Willie Joe nervously fumbled with the envelope and tore it open. He read the note aloud.

"To our dear children, we wish you all the best that life has for you. Since the wedding was a small one, the gift will be a large one. Perhaps it will help you buy a home. Love, Mom and Dad.".

The check cascaded out of the note as Willie Joe opened it. He stared at it wide-eyed, stunned, in disbelief , then handed it to Robin. Thirty thousand dollars! Willie Joe had never seen a check for that much money in his entire life. He and Robin hugged each other and then ran to the phone to thank her parents. That night, they slept as if they did not have a care in the world.

Before the morning sun penetrated the curtains in their bedroom, the clock radio alarm woke Willie Joe and Robin. Allentown's own rock and roll radio station nearly blew them out of bed with the hard driving rhythm of Country Joe and the Fish. A little blending of cultures had broadened Willie Joe's musical listening habits. Something about a college community just rubs off on everyone. The coffee pot hissed and gurgled; the shower poured down and the two lovebirds prepared to hit the road for a weekend of island fun in paradise.

CHAPTER 35

IN HIGH GEAR

There's something about putting money in a man's pocket that just changes his outlook—and his self-esteem. Willie Joe Cunningham was no different. It didn't change him. He still remained the same modest, unassuming man. It just raised his feeling of self-worth, quietly, inside.

It started out like any other day, with William kissing Robin goodbye as they each left for work. William need only to walk across the campus; Robin, take a short drive across town. It continued like any other day in Easton. Robin performed the duties of her job diligently; called her mother at lunchtime; William coached the team and worked with the players one-on-one to improve their skills. As always, William came home for dinner; Robin cooked, and William once again trekked across the Easton campus for his evening classes.

But something felt different in the air. Both William and Robin sensed it. Sure enough, when Robin arrived home, she could hardly contain her ebullience. She had just enough lead-time to take a shower, change her clothes, prepare dinner and greet William. When he entered the apartment, he caught the fragrance of the candles before he even reached the kitchen table. He scanned the room; everything had been very carefully prepared. He looked at Robin, dressed just perfectly.

"What's the occasion?"

She just smiled back, pulled out his chair and beckoned him to sit.

"I got a raise and a promotion today. You are now looking at the Assistant Office Manager."

"That's wonderful, baby, just wonderful."

"There's more good news. Open this."

Robin handed him a piece of mail.

"It's our first college reunion. We should go, don't you think?"

"No question. We *have* to go. What? There's more?"

"Remember the wedding gift from my folks? Well, I think we're going to want to use it very soon."

William looked at Robin quizzically.

"It's time we started to look for a home—a real home, where we can raise our family."

"I suppose, but what's the hurry? Wait a minute? Are you trying to tell me something?"

"Yes. I went to the doctor; I'm pregnant, William."

Willie Joe could hardly contain himself. He jumped up from the table and embraced Robin.

"Do your folks know yet?"

"No. I wanted to tell you first. We can call them after dinner."

Willie Joe just kept staring at Robin, shaking his head. He felt overcome. He finally felt like he really had a *life*. After breaking the good news to their family, Robin and William decided to contact a real estate agent the next day and start searching for a home. He could hardly concentrate in class that evening; the excitement of becoming a father trumped everything in his mind. When he arrived home, he found Robin doing what pregnant wives do. She had begun looking at magazine ads and catalogs for baby clothes, voraciously poring over lists of names. Willie Joe sat next to her on the living room couch and encouraged her to slow down.

"We've got time to do everything; there's no hurry. Just relax and let it all happen. Everything will work out just fine."

And everything did work out just fine. Reunion night came and William and Robin anxiously entered the gym, decorated with streamers to welcome them all back. They could hardly wait to see their old friends. The band played all their old favorites from Kool and the Gang, from the Isely Brothers; it felt like a scene from a movie. William greeted Alex and Craig, amazed at how they had matured in such a short time. Evan arrived with his fiancée. William scanned the crowd, spotting Lee Brown and Grace. He escorted Robin over and introduced them.

"I want you to meet two of my favorite people, Lee and Grace. They both played a special part in my life. And this is my wife Robin—"

"So you all went and married the cheerleader, Willie Joe—"

"I go by 'William Joseph' now—"

Before he could say another word, Charisse and Karyna, the two Black girls who wouldn't give him the time of day a few short years ago, grabbed his hand and began dancing with William. It began to get a little intense. As the pace and the beat of the music changed to a driving disco number from Chic, Charisse and Karyna began to surround William. They each performed a bump and grind against him. He went with it, one in front of him and one in back of him. The music stopped. William looked up to find Robin standing alone. She looked unhappy. He approached her.

"Don't say anything, please. Just don't say anything. Can we go now?"

William had learned this much about women. It's best to just let it go. Explanations don't work. They just muddy the waters and cloud the issue. In truth, he hardly even knew the sisters. They had nothing going on; it was just a dance. But he knew better than to try and dismiss it. He had to see it from Robin's viewpoint. They had gotten just a little too close and a lot too physical for her to just dismiss it. She felt threatened. Maybe he had been with one of them before they met. She didn't know. She didn't want to know. She would just have to get over the incident. He married her; he loved her; they were about to start a family together. She had to trust him. It really came down to a cultural thing. In Robin's white, Anglo-Saxon world, married people just didn't get physical with other members of the opposite sex. In William's cultural context, Black people did. It had nothing to do with remaining faithful to one's partner. William wished he could explain that, but he felt Robin just wouldn't understand. He let it go, and hoped she would do the same.

Robin continued to work for the first few months of the pregnancy. On weekends, Robin and William went house hunting. Finally, they found the perfect home, just minutes from the Easton campus. An older couple had lived there, raised their children there and retired. Now, they needed a smaller home without all of the responsibilities and maintenance. They had found a retirement community. Robin and William liked the brick colonial the first time they saw it. They felt drawn to it. It reminded Robin of the home and the neighborhood she grew up in. For William, it was everything he never had growing up— exactly what he wanted for his children. They returned the next evening to take another look—and to make an offer.

The excitement of moving to their new home seemed to consume Robin and William. They did not have a lot to pack up. Scheduling the move would present the biggest challenge to them. William now had a team to coach, practices to attend and games to manage—including a slate of away games, as well as the home games. The basketball season at Easton had just kicked in. Somehow, they knew they would manage.

This season would truly test William like no other. The new Assistant Coach, he had to assure the team could and would win. He taught the players everything he had learned—the intuitive, psychological game he had learned from Coach back at the Newark Boys' Club, and the physical fine points he had learned from the Celtics' training camp coach. It all started to come together.

The team functioned as a unit; Coach Miller knew he could trust William to work the plays while he worked the Administration for money and equipment. The road schedule began to become grueling. William and Robin began to feel the tension from the time spent apart. Robin's pregnancy had progressed nicely. She passed all of her doctor's exams with flying colors. Secretly, she wished William had been able to go with her. She never said it, but he sensed it any way. Robin began to become resentful and irritable. William wondered if her mood came with the normal hormonal changes of a pregnancy, or if he truly had an issue to deal with. He chose not to confront it, for fear of upsetting her. Robin, on the other hand, began to wonder if she could fully trust a husband that spent so much time away from her. The stories of coaches on the road hooking up with women permeated the sports world. Anyone connected with collegiate or professional sports had heard them—especially Black men trolling for White women. In spite of it all, Robin dismissed her suspicions. But the rift between them began to grow. Finally, Robin took the initiative to address their concerns. They lay awake one night, both of them unable to sleep. She began the conversation.

"William, we have always both tried to see the other's point of view in every situation. We need to work through what's going on right now in our lives. I'm feeling a little neglected; you're feeling a little overwhelmed. I'm a little scared about having our first child; you're worried about supporting a family. What are you *feeling* right now?"

The way Robin emphasized the word "feeling" jarred William. He had cut himself off from his feelings. He thought carefully before replying, composing his words carefully.

"I guess I'm feeling a little bit of fear myself. I hadn't really faced it. I've just been forging ahead; you know, thinking more than feeling."

"And what were you thinking?"

"Just that this situation is temporary—that it won't always be like this. I guess I'm a little worried about what will happen when you stop working and start caring for the baby. We put all of our money into this house, and I'm still not earning that much. I guess I should also concern myself with seeing my child grow up."

"Well, as usual, I guess you read my mind. Those are exactly my concerns, but we haven't really addressed them yet. I spoke to an old friend of the family yesterday. He's actually a friend of Father O'Reilly's—a Jewish Rabbi. They're very wise and learned, you know. He said 'The Bible says Hashem will provide.' That's an old Hebrew word for 'the Lord.' I would like to believe he's right, but my practical side says we have to think this all through and prepare."

"We will. I promise you, we will. Now you just get some rest. You're not only eating for two, you're sleeping for two."

Willliam placed his hand on Robin's belly, feeling the little life inside of her. With that, they both fell asleep.

CHAPTER 36

THE SILVER LINING

William sat in his hotel room miles from home, composing in his head what he would say to his pregnant wife. He genuinely wanted to be by her side, to share every kick the baby made, but he knew he simply could not. Robin knew it, too. This is what she signed on for—like it or not. The loneliness and the longing haunted both of them. William remembered the words his uncle Ben imparted to him:

"Son, this ain't no dress rehearsal. This is the performance—and the curtain ain't waitin' for nobody. It's goin' up, if you know your lines or if you don't."

Peasant wisdom. Simple but wise words from someone that lived life with his eyes open—as if he still had to look out of the foxhole and watch for the enemy every day of his life. Professor Mercer used to tell his class that "Awareness only starts the process of living; self-awareness completes it."

William lifted the receiver and began dialing. He held his breath as he waited for Robin to pick up. Any time the seconds ticked away, he feared something had gone wrong—something he felt powerless to stop, so many miles away. The warm Florida sun created a glare that penetrated the curtains. Finally, Robin picked up, sounding groggy.

"I hope I didn't wake you baby. I just wanted to check in with you before I get back from dinner and it starts getting late. Everything okay?"

"Yes. I just wish you were here, William. I'm okay; I'm just tired. The doctor says that's normal."

"I miss you, too. Just get some rest. I'll call you again in the morning, before our final practice."

He felt a pang deep in his stomach as he heard Robin replace the receiver on the cradle. He pictured her lying on their bed alone. It only made him feel worse, knowing she needed him—and their unborn child needed him. The road to success is paved with responsibility; don't let anyone tell you differently, he thought. William left the room and took the elevator to the restaurant in the lobby, where his team waited for him. His mind instantly flashed back to the elevator in the projects. What a difference. He remained torn between his obligation to the job, and to his family. Such a short trip seemed so long. He knew there would be many more like it.

No sooner did William arrive home bearing the newspapers with headlines of the Easton team's wins than he had to turn around and leave for yet another away game. He felt like he rode a merry-go-round. At times, he awoke with a start, disoriented and not sure even where he was. Months passed and Robin's due date drew near. William departed nervously for the next game of the season. A lot rode on the success of the team. They could win the Eastern Conference if they won this game. Fortunately, he only had to go to Ohio this time—still within striking distance of Pennsylvania.

Sure enough, all the stars seemed to align for this game. William stood on the sidelines, anxiously watching his team members—and the clock. The tension mounted when the fourth quarter arrived. His best shooter had to make the foul shot. The entire game rode on that one shot. The crowd rose up in the bleachers as the ball rolled around and kissed the rim, dropping through the net two seconds before the final buzzer sounded. Everyone from Easton cheered. The local play-by-play announcer shouted over the din. William quietly left the gym, his heart pounding. He felt like he owed God a thank you for letting him win. His mother would be proud.

In minutes, William had driven from the Ohio campus to his hotel room. He checked for messages when he arrived in his room. The red light blinked on the phone. He listened to the playback. Robin's sister Christine sounded breathless. They were on their way to the hospital. He had to leave immediately. He quickly packed, checked out and drove to the interstate. He nervously surveyed the horizon, hoping no State Troopers were around. Then, he cranked up the radio, opened the window and floored the accelerator. William wondered if the police were lenient with expectant fathers. After all, they had pregnant wives, too. He hit the scan button on the car radio. Springsteen came on. It reminded him of New Jersey. For the first time in a long time, he began to really think about Newark. He even wondered what Lillian was doing. He quickly dismissed the thought, like changing the channel on the TV. He crossed the state line into Pennsylvania and began to head South toward Easton. The reality of becoming a father suddenly gripped him. He had waited for this moment and nothing could take it away from him. He noticed the flashing lights of a State Trooper ahead of him. Better ahead than behind. Only a half hour left to go. He checked the gas gauge. Almost running on empty. He fully intended to make it, no matter what. He pictured Robin in the delivery room. He had never even been in a maternity ward before. He found himself overcome with excitement. He punched the radio dial again. More Springsteen; more thoughts of New Jersey.

With just enough gas in the tank to spare, William pulled into the now dark parking lot of the hospital in Easton. He dashed into the main entrance, feeling a twinge in his bad knee. No matter. No stopping us now. Out of breath, he strode up to the volunteers at the information desk. A pretty young Black woman with the nametag "Ivy" smiled at him.

"The maternity ward is on the fourth floor; go right when you exit the elevator."

William smiled and took off, wondering if he wore an invisible tag that read "expectant father." He nearly collided with a nurse when he slid out of the elevator. She pointed him in the right direction. At the nurse's station, they directed him to Robin's room. He had missed the delivery. Christine sat by her bedside. Robin held the baby in her arms. William leaned over to kiss her and stared into the eyes of his daughter. Her cocoa complexion glowed. She stretched her tiny hands out as William cradled her in his arms. Robin chose the name Brandi, like the girl in the popular song. Robin motioned for William to sit on the bed.

"Did you win?"

William looked at her, still in awe at the miracle in his arms and answered,

"We won. We have a baby girl."

"The doctor says she appears to have an ear problem. Everything else seems fine. We'll have to deal with it," Robin cautioned.

William and Robin got into a rhythm, taking turns feeding the baby. Unfortunately, the ear problem persisted. A chronic infection, it caused a throbbing pain, keeping Brandi awake—and of course, William and Robin. At times, it seemed like more than either one of them could handle—baby care, a home, a job, graduate school. They cherished the few hours of quiet they managed to get on weekends. Robin's mother offered to come and stay for a few weeks. They graciously accepted. A little stability in the household would go a long way. Angela Whiteside came from that generation of super moms that could cook, sew, diaper and decorate the house, all at the same time. At least it gave Robin a breather and William a chance to get caught up with his class work. He still wondered how he handled graduate school on top of everything else.

Something new seemed to gnaw at William as he got his bearings. He began to feel disconnected. As much as Robin's family had accepted him, he felt disenfranchised, as though his family tree had somehow withered. Indeed it had. No one remained, other than himself. He understood that he had just begun to create his own family, yet it still didn't seem to fit right. For the first time, he began to worry about Brandi. Who would accept her, Black people, White people…or neither? He called his old friend Lee Brown, who had a mixed race marriage. He knew Lee would set him straight.

"Bro', you got it all goin' on. You got your wife's family on your side. Neither of our families accepted it at first. The kids? Kids got to be taught prejudice. If nobody teach it to 'em, they don't see no color. We take 'em to the playground and the other kids play with 'em—just like that. Don't be creatin' problems before they happen, man."

Lee was right. William had to stop trying to protect an infant from a cruel world. When the time came, he and Robin would deal with it. If only the rest of the world could act like the children. William stood over Brandi's crib— his little miracle, he called her. He remembered Jack Whiteside's words. Life would be difficult for Brandi. He thought about how fortunate he was, to have risen above his humble beginnings. He couldn't have done it without Coach and Uncle Ben. He took in the scene, marveling at his wonderful new life. He lived in the world of his beloved sport of basketball, he had a beautiful wife, a great home— everything he touched had turned to gold—or at least silver. William got undressed and fell into a deep sleep. For the first time in months, he began to dream vivid dreams. Not haunting dreams, but vivid dreams, nonetheless. He saw himself steering a ship through a storm. When he came out on the other side, rainbows glowed on the horizon. Robin and Brandi were at his side. Every time the dark clouds rolled in, the sunshine blasted them away. Schools of fish of every color would leap out of the water, sparkling in the sunlight. When the waves crashed on the shore, they played musical notes. What a world!

CHAPTER 37

CAREER IN GEAR

Under William's leadership, the Easton basketball team flourished. Coach Miller had pretty much left him alone to handle the day-to-day, week-to-week, game-to-game duties of a coach, while he himself handled the Administration, the politics and the fund raising. Life continued to move too fast for words. William worried about missing his daughter's most formative years. He longed to see her take her first steps, but the demands of coaching a traveling collegiate basketball team meant going on the road again and again and again. Robin began to show signs of wear, as all of the responsibilities of a home and a child fell upon her while William traveled. As much as she tried to hold it all inside, sometimes the dam just broke.

"Baby, what's bothering you?"

"You're here and you're gone, just when I need you the most."

"I'll be home soon."

"And you'll be gone again, just as soon. Are you sure you're not fooling around on me?"

"Like I would ever do that, when I have you."

"I just need reassurance. Hey, we just got the invitation for the next Alumni Day. We're going, aren't we?"

"Sure, sure. We're going. You can let 'em know. I love you baby; I'll be home soon. Kiss Brandi for me, okay?"

William gently let the receiver down. It felt like it had heavy weights on it. He couldn't get the picture out of his head, of Robin and Brandi fending for themselves. He wondered how long they could live this way before something would crack. He looked in the hotel bathroom mirror.

He never noticed the worry lines that had started to form on his forehead. No matter; they would work it out. They always did.

That year drove Easton to the top. Coach Miller received a special citation from the President of the college. Nothing for William. That's how it works in this world. Somebody on top always takes credit for the work you do and for the accomplishments you make. Part of the price you pay, William thought; one of the lessons he had to learn. The more games William helped Easton to win, the easier it was for Coach Miller to go out and raise money from wealthy donors and corporate underwriters. At least that allowed William to go out and offer a few more scholarships to deserving underprivileged students—future team members for William to coach. So the wheel keeps turning.

Finally, he was going home again. This time, the basketball season was winding down, so the final games were home games. William pulled into the driveway, noticing the property needed work. The shutters needed repair, the gutters needed cleaning and the leaves he never had time to rake were still plastered to the lawn, long after the last winter snow had melted. As he walked through the doorway, Robin greeted him. She looked tired. Brandi reached her arms out; he picked her up and lifted her to face him. Her eyes glowed with excitement as she wrapped her tiny hands around his neck. Nothing melts a father like his little girl's kisses.

William sank into the living room couch with Robin by his side, casually sifting through the mail. One envelope caught his eye. He opened that one first. The invitation bore the college seal. He read it aloud.

"You are invited to the groundbreaking for the expansion of Easton's new addition to the gymnasium, to be named 'Miller Hall', in honor of Coach Peter Miller, for his contribution to the growth of Easton College's athletic programs."

"Well, well, I'll be a—"

Robin touched her finger to William's lips.

"We know who deserves the honor. That's just how it works in business, in life and in politics. I learned that from my father—and from my uncle. You know—Evan's father. Hey, I'm going to ask my folks to come down the weekend of Alumni Day. They can baby sit for Brandi, so we can attend all the festivities. It will be great to catch up with our friends and see what everybody is doing, don't you think?"

"Sure baby, sure. It'll be fun. And we miss your folks. I'm sure they miss Brandi. She seems to have really bonded with them the last time they came.

And your dad's getting ready to retire, so he's got more time now."

The phone rang, piercing the quiet suburban Sunday afternoon. Robin answered it, handing it to William with a suspicious look.

"It's a woman. She didn't give her name. She sounded upset. Go take it in the other room."

William glided into the kitchen, rifling the refrigerator as he answered the call. Suddenly, he froze.

"When did it happen? How? What can we do? I'm sorry; I'm so sorry."

William nearly dropped the phone, returned to the living room and stood speechless as Robin looked up at him.

"Who was that? What happened? You look terrible."

"You remember Grace. It's Lee Brown. He hit a telephone pole with his car and bled to death at the scene. They have two young children. He might have been drinking. I don't know what to do."

William crumpled into the chair opposite Robin. He looked devastated. He looked over at Brandi, then at Robin, wondering what would ever become of them if anything happened to him. He dismissed the thought in his usual fashion—like changing the channel on a TV set or the station on a radio dial. Since he had been with Grace before Lee, he felt somehow responsible for her. It gnawed at him. He couldn't get the thought out of his head. What if that first child was really his? What if Lee had claimed paternity when he married Grace? He would never know.

Alumni Day came. William and Robin dressed up—he sporting an Easton blazer, she in a long black dress. They arrived on campus to find the burgeoning crowd had taken nearly every available parking space. Ever the gentleman, William let Robin out in front of the building and went to search for a place to park. When he returned, he found Robin talking to Coach and Mrs. Miller. They scanned the crowd briefly. Then, Coach Miller motioned to a small group of students to join them. These three were just about the only other Black faces in the room. They were the new incoming freshmen students that William had recruited on scholarships. One came from Trenton, New Jersey; one from southwest Philadelphia and the other from Paterson, New Jersey. William knew they wanted him to recruit more students, but it was still a struggle to find the funding. Somehow they always managed to squeeze money out of the budget for buildings, but it seemed like there was never enough for people.

Robin smiled as a beautiful young lady waltzed over and hugged her. Liz Sommers had just been voted Homecoming Queen. Robin had held the same title herself when Liz first arrived at Easton. The Sommers family had generously endowed the college. They had a long history with Easton. The rumor Robin heard involved Liz's grandfather, a wealthy banker whose real name was Sommerstein. She heard they had changed it after World War II to avoid anti-Semitism. Robin whispered the story to William. Prejudice lives on. White people even hate other White people. William shook his head in disbelief. He felt a tap on the shoulder. He swung around to find Alex, Evan and Craig all raising champagne glasses and toasting him. What a moment. A quick flash blinded him momentarily, as William saw the roving photographer capture the shot for posterity.

William slipped away to the men's room. He glanced under the stall. Something didn't look right. He thought he recognized the rubber-soled shoes. He approached, and heard a strained groan. He opened the stall door to find Coach Miller hunched over, his face contorted and his hand on his chest. His pupils appeared dilated. William ran out frantically, looking for a campus security guard.

"Call an ambulance. It's Coach Miller. He's in the men's room. I think he had a heart attack."

The commotion interrupted the ebullient crowd. People began to move toward William. He ran back into the men's room, feeling Pete Miller's clammy hand. He moved his hand to the neck, feeling for a pulse.

"We're gonna get you help. It's on its way. Just hang in there, Mr. Miller. Just hang in there."

William remained by his side until the ambulance crew arrived. By this time, everyone had moved to one side of the room. Robin comforted Mrs. Miller. The crowd buzzed. The room seemed suspended, frozen in time.

William and Robin returned home, a pall hanging over them. They didn't know what to expect next. An hour later, the phone rang. Robin handed it to William.

"Yes, President Connolly. Yes, I understand. I will not disappoint you. You know you can count on me."

Robin waited as William hung up the phone.

"They want me to take over as interim Head Coach. It's a lot of responsibility, but I think I'm ready for it."

Robin secretly hoped it would not take William away from her and from Brandi more often. She knew it meant a great deal to him, so she said nothing. He sensed her apprehension.

"Baby, it could be good for us, really. Let's just see how it plays out, okay?"

She knew deep down she could not take his dreams away. This is what he always wanted. She acquiesced, quietly.

CHAPTER 38

REV IT UP!

A hard rain pounded down from the Easton sky, sloshing through the streets.

Rivulets ran down gutter pipes and poured into nearby storm sewers. A rare, quiet Sunday afternoon for William, Robin and Brandi, they stared out their living room picture window, taking in the majesty of the scene. Brandi sat wide-eyed, peering at the droplets forming on the window. She followed each one as it dripped down the glass like a liquid icicle. The three sat transfixed and quiet.

The ringing telephone broke the peacefulness. William excused himself and went to the kitchen to answer it. He did not recognize the voice. At first, he panicked inside; it sounded like Lillian. A few seconds later, he realized it was not. A similar intonation, but an unknown Black woman.

"I am so sorry to call you at home on a Sunday Mr. Cunningham, but I really do need your help. I work all week so I couldn't call you until now. The Athletic Department at the College gave me your name and number. My name is Liz Gilson. I'm calling about my son Tyrone. You see, the only thing that matters in his life right now is his dream of playing basketball. He would give up *everything* for it; he really would. He's a senior in high school now and he's been accepted to Easton, but the only way we can afford it is if he gets a scholarship. I'm a single mom, you see, and I'm working two jobs, but we just can't swing it on what I earn. His grades are good, but he doesn't test well and I'm afraid he might not make the cut. The Financial Aid office told me they have so few athletic scholarships. I'm hoping maybe you can help us. Do you think you could just spend an hour with Tyrone and myself, and see if there's anything you can do? We would so appreciate it."

She hadn't given William a chance to say a word yet. The story struck such a familiar chord with him. He had met so many Tyrones and so many Liz's. But he couldn't say no.

"I'll meet you at your home next Friday evening. What time do you get home from work?"

"That would be wonderful; it really would. Come at six o'clock; I'll cook dinner. I'm a really good cook. Thank you so much."

She rattled off the address. William knew exactly where they lived—just across the bridge in Phillipsburg, New Jersey, the only low-income community near the College.

William returned to Robin and Brandi with a tray full of snacks.

"So who is she?" Robin inquired, as William placed the tray on the coffee table.

"How do you know it was a 'she'?" William asked, studying her.

"A woman always knows. A woman always knows," Robin smiled, kneeling behind him and massaging his neck as Brandi reached for a cracker topped with cheese.

"Just a student's mother looking for some reassurance for her son. You know I can't turn these folks away. This kid is probably just like I was years ago."

"I know, I know," Robin nodded, adjusting Brandi's ponytails.

That week whizzed by in a flash, with William's practices, department meetings and night classes. He made sure to remember the invitation to meet with the Gilsons. Crossing the bridge into New Jersey, he turned down the narrow streets of gray little Phillipsburg. He could imagine the miners who settled that community, trekking home after a day in the darkness of their cavernous existence. Row upon row of attached houses greeted him. He pulled the car up in front of the address Liz Gilson had given him. In a moment, he stood at the door of the nondescript downstairs apartment. He knocked first, and then rang the bell. A deep-throated dog barked twice. The whole scene reminded him of his encounters with Lillian at her parents' Newark home during their high school years.

The door swung open, breaking his reverie. A young Black boy with a spindly build gingerly greeted him. Before William could cross the threshold, a big-boned German Shepherd lunged for him. The boy grabbed the dog's collar in mid-air.

"Down, King, down."

The dog obeyed, acquiescing and slumping into the corner by the staircase.

"You must be Tyrone," William extended his hand.

"Yes, sir, Mr. Cunningham, I am."

He heard the familiar voice call out from the kitchen,

"Tyrone, bring our guest into the kitchen. Dinner is almost ready."

The smell of down home cooking wafted its way to William. He hadn't had soul food since he had been with Robin. Secretly, he kind of missed it, but he never said anything. It reminded him of his mother's and Aunt Agnes's cooking. William followed Tyrone. When he reached the kitchen, he nearly did a double take. Before she turned, Liz reminded him of Lillian. When she turned to greet him, he froze. She reminded him a lot of Lillian— just older and a little more flamboyant in her dress.

Liz Gilson would stand out in a crowd—not just because of the hot pink, low-cut, tight sweater and the tight jeans—but the perfect complexion and the big deer-like eyes. William could not help but notice her womanly figure and her provocative walk. She invited him to sit down next to Tyrone. For the first time since he left home, he said grace over a meal. Liz had done a good job of bringing up Tyrone, all on her own. William didn't want to know her story. He could probably have written it himself. He just wanted to know if he could help Tyrone.

After a sumptuous meal of pork chops, collared greens and sweet potato pie, they moved into the tiny living room. It had only one easy chair. Liz insisted William take it. Tyrone pulled up one of the kitchen chairs while Liz perched herself on the arm of William's chair. Her cologne drifted over to him, penetrating his nostrils.

"You see, Mrs. Gilson—"

"Please call me Liz."

"I've been struggling with this problem ever since I came to Easton. They want me to recruit the best talent, but the financial aid is so limited and they insist on such high academic standards that it makes it really hard for me to get students like Tyrone on the team. Make no mistake; this is exactly what I want—more kids like your son here. I'm just going to have to take up the good fight and see what we can do. May I take this transcript of Tyrone's grades with me? I promise I will do my best for you, Liz."

"I believe you, Mr. Cunningham. I believe you will—and we thank you for it."

She leaned over as she stood up from the armchair. William could not help but notice her full breasts, mostly exposed. He felt a twinge of excitement, and then caught himself. Tyrone extended his hand and thanked William. Liz led him to the front door. She stood blocking the door, taking his hand in both of her hands and squeezing it hard. She stood on tiptoe and gave him a quick peck on the cheek, pressing herself against him.

"If there is anything at all I can do to repay you, please let me know. I will do anything for my son."

William believed her—which scared him. He imagined someone less scrupulous than himself taking advantage of the Liz Gilsons of the world. But then, he suspected that was just what she wanted. After all, it did not appear that she had a man in her life. He wondered if she had come on to him even stronger, whether he could have resisted her advances that easily. Deep down, he admitted to himself that he did find her attractive. He slammed the car door and headed home.

It had started raining during the ride home. William stepped inside. Robin greeted him with a cold stare.

"Your shoes are wet. Take them off. Don't track mud in here. I've been cleaning this house all week."

Her words felt like a cold wet slap in the face. What had he done to deserve this? He waited for the other shoe to drop, so to speak. Robin stood steadfast, her hands on her hips.

"Well, did you solve her problem?"

William stared back at her, incredulous.

"I can smell her cheap cologne—and that sure looks like lipstick on your collar. Please don't make any excuses; don't insult me. I don't want to know."

"Baby, there's nothing to know. I met with an incoming freshman and his mother. Look, here's his high school transcript. They live right over the bridge in Phillipsburg."

"I'm sorry, William. It's difficult for me, knowing that you're with other women all the time, when I'm here taking care of your home and your daughter. I guess I got jealous. I'm allowed."

"It just means you love me; I know that. I'm trying to help these kids. Someone has to care about them. I never would have amounted to anything if someone didn't care about my welfare. And as for you, young lady, it's bedtime," he gave Brandi a pat on the behind and pointed toward the stairs.

William scooped Brandi up and carried her up to her room, tucking her in.

William and Robin settled in for the night, sitting on their bed, her head against his shoulder.

"Do you ever regret not going back to the team—to the Celtics, trying to make another go of it?"

"Not for a minute. I have everything I could want right here. I've got my beautiful wife, my lovely daughter, a great home—and I still spend all of my days with a career in basketball…just not on the court. I mean, think about it, baby—how long of a career do you think I could have had playing pro ball, even if I never had a major injury? After a few years, I would have been looking for something else to do anyhow. So, I just started doing it sooner. I really feel the love from the kids; they *want* me coaching them. They relate to me. Like this kid Benny Johnson from Trenton, New Jersey. He hangs on my every word and my every move. And I guess it doesn't hurt that I'm going to get a Master's Degree soon. That will qualify me for a higher salary, which will make things easier for us. I've moved on with my life—no baby, no regrets here."

He wrapped his arm around Robin and gave her a hug.

"Let's go look in on Brandi. I love to watch her sleep," William motioned to Robin.

They both slid off the bed and deftly made their way across the hall, peering into Brandi's room. They watched in awe as her tiny hands cupped her teddy bear. With each breath, they observed her little nose wrinkling like a rabbit's, her chest rising and falling. Everything about her seemed so perfect. Only the chronic ear infection problem ever disturbed her peaceful sleep. They crept back to the bedroom.

William stood behind Robin, cupping her breasts in his hands and gently stroking her nipples. She arched her neck back so he could kiss her shoulders. She felt him become aroused, then turned and pushed him back onto the bed. They both quickly undressed and got under the blanket. Robin grabbed William and thrust him inside of her. They both released their pent-up desire in seconds. Robin had never achieved an orgasm that quickly. In a moment, they both fell asleep, locked in an embrace.

CHAPTER 39

COUNTING YOUR BLESSINGS

A man in his thirties ought to feel like a man, look like a man, walk like a man—and make his own decisions like a man. William's uncle Ben always said that to him when he was in high school. The years had kind of just crept up on William. He felt so much a part of Robin and Brandi's life, he seldom thought about himself as an individual. With his whole family gone, and Robin's family so far away, he felt somehow isolated and disconnected at times. Now he had his own family, but spending so much time away from Brandi and Robin seemed to weaken that bond. He found himself in a peculiar place—always having to explain himself to Robin made him uncomfortable. He just wished she would trust him more. All the stories of Black coaches hooking up with White women— they called it the "WPC—the 'White Pussy Club'" only helped to drive a wedge between them. He never joined in those romps. He had what he wanted. He just wished the subject would stop coming up. What had made Robin so insecure? He had never given her any real cause for concern. It just got under his skin.

William finished his coffee, kissed Robin and Brandi goodbye and headed off to the campus. The "check engine" light flashed at him from the dashboard. Not having grown up around cars, he had never been real attentive to them. With their busy schedule, and his frequent out-of-town travel schedule, he never seemed to have the time to get the car serviced. He would probably have to get a newer car soon, when he completed his Master's Degree and qualified for a raise. For the first time in his life, he had begun to think he deserved better things. The newer cars needed less maintenance anyway, he thought, justifying his desire. For the first time ever, he had actually gone to a dealership and "kicked the tires" of a late model BMW. He had driven Robin's older BMW and liked the way it handled. After all, the 1990's cars performed much better than the ones from the 1980's.

The news bulletin on the car radio interrupted William's train of thought. We were preparing to send troops to the Persian Gulf to stop a Middle Eastern warlord named Sadaam Hussein. President Bush made the announcement himself at a special White House press conference broadcast live from the Rose Garden. Iraq seemed so far away, yet suddenly became so important. William flashed back to about ten years earlier, when Jimmy Carter had to deploy special operatives to free American hostages in Iran. At that moment, basketball became so insignificant. William began to question whether he and his life really mattered. It wasn't really depression; he just questioned his own importance when people were dying in uniform to preserve our way of life. How important could sports really be? As he parked the car and entered Miller Hall, he looked around at the students—like little insects wrapped in a safe cocoon, insulated from the harsh realities of the outside world. Then he thought about all the boys he had saved from lives ruined by drugs and crime. He thought about his brother Carlton—how he wished somebody could have saved him. He felt a shift; suddenly, it all made sense. What he did mattered. It counted for just as much as anyone else's work. Save one kid from a life of poverty and you save a whole family. Devote your life to saving kids and it adds up to a lot of lives saved.

William sat down at his desk and glanced at the weekend mail, just delivered. He saw the pink envelope, hand addressed to him personally, and opened it first. Liz Gilson had written to thank him for his efforts on Tyrone's behalf. William had to turn up the heat under a few people, but finally, the papers got shuffled and the financial aid had been approved. Another one saved. The official looking envelope with the gold seal caught his eye next. It came from Easton College President Connolly's office. William's eyes widened as he read the words.

"We are pleased to announce the return of Coach Peter Miller, following the recovery from his period of illness. We invite you to join us at a reception to celebrate this momentous occasion on Saturday September 17th. RSVP to Jane Stillman, Assistant to the President."

He didn't know at that moment whether to consider it good news or bad news. It could go either way. He would just have to wait and see.

Another more nondescript envelope marked "Personal and Confidential" caught William's eye. He slit it open. A small college in West Virginia expressed interest in meeting with him for a possible position. He smiled and tucked the envelope in his briefcase. It's nice to be wanted, he thought—even if he had no interest in the position. The rest of the mail consisted of more students looking to come to Easton. All of them had heard about the acclaimed athletic program; all of them needed financial aid. It continued to frustrate William. He really didn't want to leave Easton, but he had to go and plead the case for every disadvantaged student he wanted to recruit. They all had the desire and the commitment; many of them had reasonable academic skills, but it always came down to the same thing. They just couldn't quite reach the required grade-point-average and standardized test scores that Easton demanded—and none of them could afford the tuition. Yet, they had the star quality to become the players that would make the team win game after game, title after title. Without the winning, the other side of the equation would fall apart. Easton wouldn't get the grants and the donations that funded those scholarships. What a vicious circle.

William and Robin attended the reception for Coach Miller's return, as did nearly the entire Easton campus community. Robin couldn't help remark to William that Peter Miller appeared to have aged noticeably since his heart attack. The scene struck an eerie chord; it reminded them too much of the day he had the heart attack. William remembered discovering Pete Miller hunched over in the men's room toilet stall. He seemed in good spirits, but William noticed he didn't have the quickness of step and the energy level he had become accustomed to.

That year flew by, with William focusing on developing the new talent on Easton's basketball team. The practices seemed endless; the games came and went, but it all paid off. Finally, everyone at Easton recognized that William's attention to the players resulted in wins. President Connolly had pulled a few strings and gotten William a pay raise, even before he completed his graduate studies. In fact, he became the highest paid Assistant Coach in the Humanitarian league. More offers poured in; in discreet mailings. He tucked them away, but remained loyal to Easton. He had found a home for both his career and his family. He finally achieved some contentment, and that was worth the price of admission.

So what was next? In the world of college athletics, most of the coaches and Athletic Directors were either former players or those who had aspired to become professional players. With that comes a certain high level of competitiveness. Most of them leapfrogged across the country for better jobs—and most of them didn't care whom they stepped on to get those jobs. William was still learning how those decisions were made. He often felt like a pawn in the game, adrift and not at all in control. He never knew how secure his position would remain—despite all of the wins he was directly responsible for through effective recruitment and training.

The season ended abruptly, without much pomp and circumstance. William looked forward to his graduation. Robin had already planned a party, inviting just a few of their closest friends and her parents. Sure enough, the day before the graduation, Brandi's ear infection went out of control.

"I've got to take her back to Dr. Moore, the ear-nose-threat specialist, and see if he can at least get her some relief. She literally cries herself to sleep. William, I really need you to come with me," Robin implored.

"We've got it covered, baby; don't you worry. I'll be there. You can count on me."

William hung up the phone, and then looked up from his desk with a start. Pete Miller stood over him. He looked tired. William invited him to pull up a chair.

"What's on your mind? You look a little piqued."

"I'm packing it in for good this time, William. I really can't keep up the routine any more, and I can't just dump it all on you. As you know, this can be a very demanding job at times. The heart medication just knocks me for a loop. I'm done well before the day ends. Doctor says it will be the best thing for me. Listen, I don't know what's gonna happen from here. I promise you I'll put the word in for you, but these decisions are made at the top. You know that."

"When are you leaving?"

"Two weeks; just two week more weeks and I'm done. Listen, you've done a great job. I'll make sure they know."

William watched as Pete Miller disappeared out the door, wondering what would happen now. Once again, he felt powerless. The whole campus community wondered what would happen now. Most everyone assumed

William would take over as Head Coach of the Easton basketball team. After all, he had led them to victory, time after time. Even the local sports reporters speculated in their columns, after the news got out. The Alumni Association President even visited William, just to let him know they would endorse him as Pete Miller's successor. But how much clout did they have with the Administration? Probably not enough. William told Robin nearly everything, but he just couldn't tell her about this. Her parents were coming; she had worked so hard to plan his graduation party—he just didn't want to put a damper on things. Still, it gnawed at William from the inside. He could feel the uncertainty in the pit of his stomach. He had no idea what would happen next. He could only wonder and speculate.

Then, it felt like somebody dropped a bomb. William opened the final issue of the "Easton Clarion", the campus newspaper, and there, in big bold letters, emblazoned across the page, the headline hit him between the eyes.

"Chamber Higgins Returns to Easton; Future Staff and Direction Unknown."

He went on to read the rest of the story. Evidently somebody had leaked the news, but not filled in the blanks. Nobody knew what other decisions, if any, had been made at the top. They only knew that Chamber Higgins would return as Head Coach. William had no fondness for him, but would certainly work for him—if Chamber wanted him. William wondered whether the wealthy alumni would accept a Black coach. He wondered whether the talented players would still want to come to Easton, knowing Higgins' reputation. William had learned to play the game. He had his spies, too. He discreetly placed a call to the Vice-President of the Alumni Association, who served on the Selection Committee. He told him point blank what was said behind closed doors.

"My Alumni President promised Chamber that 'they could always talk you into being his assistant.'"

At least he knew he had some support. William needed to probe deeper. He continued to call around to his closest allies on campus. Evidently they had coughed up a hefty salary to attract Chamber Higgins back to Easton. That rubbed William the wrong way, knowing how he had waited so long to receive a small raise, even though his performance topped all previous records of any Assistant Coach. As things often happen, William accidentally passed by Chamber's office as he was meeting with the Director of Development. He overheard their conversation.

"What do you think? Will he stay? Can he sustain the winning streak?"

"Foster, I have every confidence in Cunningham. I see what he's done. I'm willing to give him a shot."

And so it went. William continued to lead the team to victory; Chamber continued to squeeze more money into the budget. The 1992 season broke all records. Under William's coaching, the Easton basketball team won five league titles and averaged eighteen wins per season. Easton had never achieved that level of prominence before, and everyone knew who produced those successes—the Administration, the Alumni, the public and the news media. William had built a reputation for recruiting and training the best players—and they never let him down. Team loyalty trumped everything, and he truly felt the love.

CHAPTER 40

WHAT GOES AROUND

Nothing ever proved truer than the old adage, "What goes up must come down"—or her sister, "What goes around comes around." But it became a hard reality for William to swallow. To know a thing intellectually is not the same as to *experience a thing emotionally*. William always loved Sunday mornings. They had evolved into his only real family time and catch up time. But that too seemed to have come to an end. His whole world just seemed to have developed cracks. He sat on the living room couch, coffee cup in hand. Robin and Brandi still slept as he stared at the coffee cup. For the first time, he noticed the fine cracks in the ceramic—as if the kiln only pretended to fire it full of vitality and strength. William stared at his image in the spoon, distorted by the curvature. For the first time, he noticed a few gray hairs creeping in. He felt like they didn't belong there—intruders that showed up before their time. Suddenly it struck him. He had heard this story before. His mind flashed back to his youth. Sitting in the Beulah Baptist Church in Newark, he recalled the Reverend Pearl's sonorous voice booming from the pulpit.

"And Joseph did interpret Pharaoh's dream. There were seven lean cows and there were seven fat cows. And they stood for seven years of plenty, and for seven years of poverty—"

Robin and Brandi appeared and broke his reverie. William looked up. For the first time he noticed that Robin, too, had gray hairs. He waited. She just motioned silently for him to come to the breakfast table. He could feel the tension. Had the love gone out of their lives, like some liquid poured out of a glass? No, but they had become more distant. Not cold, but a cooling, like molten lava, before it becomes rock. He thought about it. It began to make sense. He needed to take responsibility for the widening chasm in their relationship. All was not as it should be. His team's winning streak had ended. He began to brood, often. Robin sensed his mood and mirrored it. He would have to figure out how to rekindle the flame. He looked at Brandi. Other than the chronic ear infection, he felt blessed for her good health.

"Are you going to tell me about it?"

"Tell you about what?"

"William, I know you too long. I practically know your every thought. What's bothering you?"

"Nothing, Robin. Nothing I can't fix."

But he knew it was a lie. And so did she. Brandi studied him quizzically. He looked up from his plate, saw her pleading look and forced a smile. Her eyes lit up. Robin silently got up and began to clear the table. William remained lost in thought, as he built a silent wall around himself. And so it remained.

That week, William coached the team hard for the upcoming game with Clarion State. He wondered if it would make a difference. He had lost confidence in himself and the team. Clarion would be tough to beat, no matter what.

Everything came in a rush—a whirlwind. The Clarion players dominated the court for the first half. The Easton team kept looking to William for guidance. It was as if he was hollow—like he wasn't really there. He was so accustomed to winning; he had become paralyzed with fear when the tide turned. Finally, his team began to score. The clock ruled this game, and it had decided to treat the Easton players harshly. Everyone felt it. As the second half drew to a close, Easton was down by one point. The final seconds took the breath out of everyone. The crowd hissed. You could hear the ball bounce. Then, Clarion State froze the ball. William stalked the baseline as if he had stolen someone's wallet. He wondered if anyone had noticed. Suddenly, a quick hand steals the ball and heads for the winning basket. Easton's Gordon Riley deftly went for it.

At that very moment, William saw himself in his high school jersey, sprinting down the court and rising above the outstretched arms of his opponents, as he laid the ball in the basket.

Gordon reached for the rim. Seemingly out of nowhere a black arm knocked the ball into the bleachers. A Black forward from Clarion State stared at William for the longest time. William's shoulders slumped from the weight of yet another loss. All he can do is to turn away. Gordon makes a valiant effort to inject his lanky six foot-three frame between his coach and the forward, shoving his chest out in defiance. At that moment, the Clarion State teammates swept away the forward in celebration. William mopped the sweat from his brow and from his mouth. It tasted as bitter as the defeat itself.

The downward spiral just continued—on the court and off. William brooded; Robin withdrew—even Brandi seemed to hang back. Little things began to set him off. The car not starting; the neighbors' dog barking. Irritability had become the order of the day. He instinctively knew what would follow as he entered Chamber Higgins' office that night, after the loss to Clarion State.

William felt spent—like an elephant had sat on him and refused to leave. Chamber hovered over him like a fighter moving in for the kill, hammering him. He went right for the jugular.

"Do you like losing? Is that it?"

William stewed, nearly ready to blow up.

"Look, Cunningham. We need to make the dance. A third year without that revenue could sink us—you, me, the team—all of us. I know what you're thinking; you don't have the players. The humanitarian league is tough but Breezy Smith seems to win every—"

William rose to his feet.

"I don't want to hear about Breezy. He has players."

Just at that moment Gordon poked his head in, realizing it was a mistake.

William settled down and invited Gordon in. He addressed William directly.

"Excuse me, coach. I just want to let you know I'm gonna be late for practice. I have an exam."

William replied without pausing a beat,

"That's fine, Gordon."

Gordon turned, ready to leave, when William caught his glance.

"Gordon, you played a heck of a game tonight."

"Thanks. We would have won if I had hit that three down the stretch."

William continued to encourage him.

"Listen to me. You played great. Keep it up."

Gordon flushed slightly, then quickly retorted,

"We will. We're gonna make the dance this year; I can feel it."

Gordon shot a quick glance at Chamber, and then winked at William as he took off.

"If I just had three more of him we'd be fine."

Chamber held his icy stare at William.

"You do. I've been trying to tell you. Just show them how it's done. That's your job."

"Chamber, I can't *make* the lay-ups for them," William stammered.

Chamber responded with a nod of understanding and a tired smile.

"That's your problem. They can't do things that you could do. Or what lots of Black players can do. But it doesn't mean they can't play and win. Show me what kind of a coach you are. This isn't Cheyney State, this is Easton."

William pondered Chamber's words for what seemed a long moment before answering.

"That's nice, Chamber. But they can only do what they can do."

Chamber scowled back at William.

"You're not hearing me. You're here now. You chose to play this hand. Now play it."

The weight of the losses didn't seem to lighten up. If perception is reality, then everything in William's world seemed like a loss at that moment. The week dragged on after the loss to Clarion State and the subsequent browbeating in Chamber's office. William wanted to believe that Higgins just had it in for him, but he couldn't deny the reality of his team's downward spiral. Still, he felt that he just didn't have players who could deliver—no matter how well he coached them. The basketball court operated just like a courtroom drama. Whoever maneuvered the best won the game—no matter what their education and training. Finally, the weekend came. Robin had planned a cocktail party.

They sat outside on the patio as their guests arrived. Brandi played with their dog Buck, a husky mix with a great temperament. Robin emerged from the house with a tray of hors d'oeuvres. She carried herself stiffly, almost formally, almost as if she was trying too hard to impress people. William stood out among the sea of White faces. Robin lay the tray down and sidled up to William, who sat by himself, idly stirring the melting ice cubes in his drink. She attempted to break through to him and pierce his brooding.

"I'm just tired of Chamber riding my ass about not winning."

"That's your cross to bear, Coach."

"What?"

Robin shot William an icy glance.

"I'm just saying that coaches are *expected* to win."

William looked up at her, meeting her glance with an equally cool one.

"And stockbrokers have to hit their numbers."

Robin held her stare, not about to yield the point.

"And their numbers are big. You can do anything you want to do."

Robin smiled warmly as Steven Grant grabbed a stuffed mushroom. He smiled back.

"No whispering spouses allowed."

Robin lightened up and responded warmly to Steve.

"William sometimes thinks basketball is all there is to life."

Steven let out a suppressed laugh.

"Hell, I envy a man that loves what he does. I stare at spreadsheets all day long."

William shot Robin a look. She ignored it and continued the conversation with Steve.

"Does Judy miss her job?

Steve slid into the lawn chair opposite William and Robin.

"Yeah, right. She's busier now raising her kids than she was running a bank."

Robin snapped a look back at William. William stepped up to the challenge as if he had gone for a lay-up.

"That's 'cause she likes raising her kids."

Steven finally began to read between the lines. Sensing the tension between William and Robin, he drifted into the house and sank into a chair in the living room. Robin forced a smile, patting William on the shoulder.

"Truce. We are having a party."

William nodded, returning the gesture and the smile.

"Truce."

Robin leaned forward. Before rising from the chair, she quietly addressed William.

"By the way, I moved up your therapist session to seven so you can meet Brandi's teachers at eight. And don't forget, you have Orientation tomorrow night."

William slumped into his chair, holding his watered down drink in one hand and a pig-in-the-blanket in the other. The late afternoon sun burned his eyes. His guests cast long, eerie shadows across the lawn. He wished they would leave.

CHAPTER 41

YOUTH IS WASTED ON THE YOUNG

Not much had really changed around the Easton campus since William was an undergraduate there himself. Sports, studies, fraternities and "cherchez la femme"—girls, girls, girls. When they weren't on the court playing or practicing, or in the library studying, Gordon and the other members of the Easton basketball team hung out in their dorm rooms. They liked to watch Frisbee football when they caught a game. Ritchie Tucker epitomized the typical student Easton attracted these days. His blue blood kept him warm in his shorts on a cool day. He was all smiles, and why shouldn't he be? All the good things life had to offer in the privileged class came easy.

"Dad just sold a million shares of Google. Did I tell you we're buying next to Spielberg in the Hamptons?"

Colin Sanders just nodded. Everyone called him the poster boy for Ralph Lauren. He looked like a catalog model. These kids looked like someone stamped them out of a mold.

"Just make sure he has a heliport. It's a brutal ride out there," Colin replied.

Gordon stood up, spinning his ball on his finger.

"Maybe if you guys worried about basketball instead of the Hamptons we'd make the dance."

Ritchie couldn't resist the temptation to shoot back a jibe.

"Gordon has delusions of grandeur that he'll be playing in the NBA next year."

Colin chimed in, joining the repartee.

"Please, Gordon, have delusions of Europe; it's more civilized."

Disgusted, Gordon stood in the door way and shot back at them,

"Why am I wasting my breath?"

Colin got up and grabbed the ball from Gordon.

"You and me and Ritchie all know we're gonna work at Goldman with daddy, so top pretending."

Ritchie swiped the ball and dribbled it, then snapped it back at Gordon. Really, Gordon, basketball is fun and all, but—" Gordon got right in his face.

"But what? What about missing the dance for three years in a row? What do you think that does for Coach Cunningham's resume?"

Colin naively responded,

"They wouldn't fire him, would they? Affirmative Action and all of that?"

Ritchie playfully pushed Colin over the politically incorrect joke. Then Gordon pushed Ritchie hard. They stood chest to chest. Gordon spoke up first.

"I heard Higgins chewing him out. He's gone if we don't win this year."

"Bullshit. He's the best coach I ever had," Ritchie countered.

Colin weighed in.

"I don't believe it either, Gordon."

Gordon, exasperated, began to raise his voice in frustration.

"Just do me a favor and think about your game for the next few weeks. The Hamptons will still be there."

He felt a twinge of guilt and extended his hand to Ritchie.

"Sorry about the push. It's just that I know it means a lot to the coach."

Ritchie accepts the handshake and clamps his arm around Gordon's shoulder.

"We are who we are. We're not gonna grow to six-foot-nine and Black overnight."

Gordon shook his head, still miffed.

"Every year it seems Princeton beats a major team. We scrimmaged with them and we held our own."

Colin changed his demeanor and copped an attitude of feigned sincerity.

"I'm gonna ask the coach for you to address us before games."

Ritchie barked back at him,

"Shut up, Colin."

Ritchie and Gordon exchanged glances. The threesome called a truce.

William checked his watch. It had stopped. He had become preoccupied with the dialog he kept replaying in his head with Chamber, and didn't even notice. He barreled down the gym hallway, passing the shining squash courts. The tennis coach, Kip, just rounded the corner and walked by with a set of rackets and a ball cart. Kip eyed William, then spoke.

"Having a Weequahic High reunion?"

William froze at the mention of his Newark alma mater.

Kip stopped to address William.

"The guy in your office said he's a friend of yours."

William looked at him confused.

"What guy?"

"The Black guy with "Weequahic" across his chest."

William eyed Kip suspiciously.

"What's his name?"

Kip shrugged his shoulders and continued walking. William entered through the open door of his office. A weathered looking skinny Black man in a basketball sweatshirt sat on his sofa. William had no idea who he was, even as he rose to greet him with a huge smile.

"It's Tricks, Willie Joe; Tricks Johnson. Remember?"

Tricks points to his sweatshirt. William relaxed, surveyed his old friend and gave him a hug.

"I'm called William now."

Tricks nodded, then backed off. William circles him once, and then stops, holding his gaze.

"Now hold on, Tricks. What happened to the rest of you?" Tricks lets out a laugh, poking William's mid-section. "You stole it."

William stares him down.

"Man, that's muscle, not fat."

Tricks responds playfully,

"I heard somewhere that skinny folks lives longer."

William snorted. Unable to help himself, he shot back, "I thought only women get anorexia."

Tricks and William slapped hands, and William's mood lightened up.

Tricks bounced up from the sofa.

"Don't be using words I can't understand. Us JUCO guys don't talk that way."

Tricks surveyed the pictures of William's ball players in action around the office; all of them were White. He swung around to face William.

"Can they play?"

William squinted back at him.

"They're good kids."

Tricks continued, revving up his diatribe.

"Yeah, I bet they can light it up if you give them time to shoot."

William stared down at the calendar on his desk blotter and coolly responded,

"They have time in this league."

William rises, sitting on the edge of his desk to face Tricks. He is running out of things to say. His mood changes and he cuts to the chase.

"Why the fuck you here?"

Tricks keeps his balance and holds William's stare.

"Thought I'd see you at one of Savior's games."

William dropped his voice half an octave, answering Tricks impassively. "Newark is dead to me."

Tricks grinned the old grin William remembered so well.

"He's broke all your records—every last one of them."

He barely got the words out when William shot back,

"Not all."

Tricks' voice turned almost singsong.

"Could help you."

William grunted at him.

"He could if he stays alive to graduate high school."

Tricks' voice went deadpan. He let one word slip out, quietly.

"Coach."

William's ears perked up.

"Coach?"

Tricks remained deadpan.

"He's dying. Wants to see you before he goes."

William drops into the sofa. Tricks confronts him.

"Come home, Willie Joe. Come home."

William snaps out of his momentary trance, his nostrils flaring.

"Home? Newark isn't my home; hasn't been for a long time, my man."

Tricks continues to play him.

"You were born there. It's in your blood."

William grits his teeth, then answers.

"I'll tell you what's in my blood—getting stabbed after a basketball game,

my brother dying of a drug overdose in the playground at the park. Look at you. You're almost dead yourself."

William realizes he went too far. He shakes his head contritely. Tricks nods and smiles ruefully before addressing William one last time.

"Think about it."

William faces him.

"I already thought about it."

Tricks sauntered out of William's office quietly and disappeared down the gymnasium hallway, whistling.

CHAPTER 42

FIXING THE CRACKS

William turned the key, threw his car into reverse and gunned it down the driveway, nearly missing the neighbor's kid on the bicycle waving to him. Distraction: the order of the day. Dusk began to envelop the Easton sky. Faint lights from the airliners heading for Allentown airport blinked above. Splat! A sudden downpour pounded the windshield. William turned the wipers. He had forgotten to replace the blades, which dragged across the window. Just one more thing to add to his pent-up anger. He hated these therapy sessions. He only attended them for fear of losing Robin. He didn't see any progress, but he kept going to placate her. He sometimes wondered if it would help more if they went to therapy together. He often felt as if she just wanted to "fix" him. But that was all in his own head.

William sank into the chair opposite Sarah. She held her fifty years well, in an intriguing package that any man would pay attention to. William seemed intent on studying her sleek legs, rather than giving her his full attention. The pin spotlight from her high intensity miniature desk lamp outlined her sinewy calves. William imagined running his hand up her smooth thighs, right under her skirt. He couldn't help but notice how her satin blouse hugged her full breasts. He wondered if she unbuttoned more buttons for the patients she liked better. Suddenly, Sarah's pouty lips parted and she raised her voice just enough to jar William from his fantasy.

"Your anger is getting in the way of your progress."

William stewed in characteristic fashion. It had become his trademark.

Sarah continued,

"You know—"

"What am I doing here?"

William scowled at her. In his mind, she transformed from the fox to the jackal.

Sarah stared him down from behind her desk.

"You and I, we are trying to modify your thinking as far as—"

William's dark side emerged.

"I mean, what am I doing in this world? I don't belong here."

Sarah dropped the pitch of her voice, flattening it to almost a monotone.

"These feelings of inadequacy are not helpful." William instantly retorted,

"It's a fact."

Sarah dropped the cool exterior and let a faint smile cross her face.

"I don't think Robin feels that way."

"Robin understands my world about as much as Martha Stewart."

"And this is not the South during Reconstruction." William continued to stew.

"You don't know what it's like being just about the only Black man on campus. You have eyes running over your body?"

Sarah studied him quizzically.

"Excuse me?"

William felt his veins begin to pop as the blood rushed to his head.

"They ask me to support gays, women's rights, alumni functions. Show them the Black face; we must be cool."

Sarah went back into her icy mode.

"I don't appreciate your tone."

William leaned forward in his chair and glared back at her. "And I'm growing tired of your patronizing comments."

Sarah challenged him, like a cougar circling her prey.

"So leave."

William held his ground.

"I like it here."

Sarah slowly rolled her chair under the desk, placing her face in her hands and leaning her elbows on the desk blotter. She let each word fall, deliberately.

"Then stay. No one is forcing you to leave, are they?"

William copped a flippant attitude and leaned back in his chair, gripping the arms.

"No, yes, look I'll handle it. I'm a big boy."

Sarah deftly slid her glasses down the end of her nose and pointed them at William.

"Correction. A big, Black *man*."

William felt the volcano in him erupting. He wanted to grab her throat; at the same time, he wanted to lay her across the desk and take her from behind. He rose up.

"Damn fucking right I am. I'm a man first and Black second. And this bullshit behavioral therapy is trying to emasculate me and I'm sick of it."

Sarah leaned back in her chair and crossed her legs, replacing her eyeglasses.

"Please, calm yourself."

William couldn't contain himself any longer. He bolted past Sarah, headed for the door and slammed it behind him.

"I'll do better than that."

Sarah rebuttoned the top two buttons of her blouse, poured herself a cup of coffee and made a journal entry as the rain continued to pounce on her office window. She caught a glimpse of William dashing toward his car; then, she watched him peel out of the parking lot.

William felt like a bundle of nerves. He just didn't know what to do with himself. He spun around and around on a mental merry-go-round, rehashing every confrontation with Chamber Higgins, every disagreement with Robin —and every useless therapy session. He felt like going to a bar and drowning himself in booze, but he thought better of it, took a deep breath and headed for home.

Brandi, in her usual spritely manner, runs from room to room, ebullient. Robin catches her and spins her around to face her as she charges into the kitchen.

"Brandi, we're going to have dinner soon."

Brandi jumps up on one of the high stools in the breakfast nook.

"Not until daddy comes home."

As fast as she entered the kitchen, she took off. Bounding up the steps, she enters the bedroom, opens the closet and begins to rifle through boxes. She opens a plastic trash bag and pulls out a cheerleader's uniform. It bears the letters, "GO BENGALS." She tucked it under her arm and dashed down the steps, heading back into the kitchen and holds up the uniform.

"Look what I found!"

Robin beams with excitement, admiring the uniform and becomes wistful.

"Oh my...I was a cheerleader for Daddy's basketball team when we were students here in Easton."

Brandi implores her,

"Put it on, put it on, please..."

Robin laughs.

"I was going to throw it out; honestly, I was."

Brandi clasped her hands and begs,

"Please..."

Brandi plopped herself down on the sofa, full of anticipation as Robin ducks into the bathroom to change. Robin emerged, wearing the uniform. It still fits and she looks great. She does a cartwheel in to the living room. As she gets up, she leaps and recites the once-familiar cheer.

"Hey, hey, go away, the Bengals are hungry and they can play..."

Robin deftly performs another cartwheel, just as William opens the door.

Robin slips to the floor, lying on her back, laughing. Brandi leaps up, excited.

"Look, daddy, mom's a cheerleader!"

"Yes, she is."

Still laughing, Robin gets up to greet William.

"Dinner's almost ready."

William, for the first time in a long time, feels the connection he and Robin had from the beginning. He looks her up and down.

"Are you kidding? Anyone that looks that good in a cheerleading uniform needs to be taken out to dinner."

Brandi jumps up and down, unable to control her ebullience.

"I get to pick the place; it was my idea!"

So they piled into William's car, with Robin continuing to shout cheers. Brandi begins rolling down the car windows and repeating the cheers. William just shakes his head, laughing. In a few short minutes, they enter Brandi's favorite restaurant, Johnny Rocket's. Families pack the house as everyone watches the games on the TV screens. Frank, the manager, recognizes William and quickly escorts them to a table in the back. The sound of roller skates catches their attention, as Bunny approaches, menus in hand. She slides a chocolate shake in front of Brandi and skates away as quickly as she appeared. William and Robin sidle up to one another in the booth while Brandi studies the menu. William slips his arm around Robin's waist and draws a deep sigh. Robin lays her head against his shoulder, smiling, takes his hand and speaks.

"That brought back a sweet memory."

William picks up on her train of thought.

"It was after we played Colgate, late in the season. It took me that long to find the courage to ask you out. Back in the day…"

Robin ran her fingers across William's hand.

"You scored thirty-five points that night."

William dropped his voice to a near whisper.

"It felt like I scored a hundred."

She turned to him to receive a romantic, slow kiss.

Before they opened their eyes, Brandi piped up,

"Is that when you made me?"

Robin and William look at each other, shocked, and then laugh. William straightens up and leans across the table to Brandi.

"Hey…"

Just then, Brandi spots her friend Kathy at the pinball machine and runs over to greet her. Robin snatches a baseball cap from a hook on the wall behind her and dons it playfully.

"I hope your shotgun is ready."

Without pausing a beat, William pulls the cap down over her eyes.

"Locked and loaded."

They both laugh. William's tone suddenly changes. He becomes slightly detached, avoiding direct eye contact with Robin as he speaks.

"Had a strange visit today from an old friend."

Robin senses the change in his demeanor and adjusts her own, slipping into a coolness he has come to know all too well.

"Really?" she inquires, cocking her head slightly to the side.

William continues, still slightly detached and aloof.

"His name is Tricks, from Newark."

Robin suddenly sits up, as if the mere pronouncement of the word "Newark" causes her to freeze.

William responds to her, soothingly.

"Easy, Robin. He came to tell me about a kid from our high school. He's the real deal. Could help—"

Robin snapped back, glaring at him.

"What's her name?"

William responded calmly.

"Savior is a boy…"

Robin continued to press him.

"But there was also a girl, wasn't there?"

William becomes annoyed, but contains himself, trying not to take the bait. "What? When are you gonna forget that one time—" Robin becomes visibly agitated, backing away to face him.

"Never. I forgave you, but I'll never forget it."

Robin begins to tear up, but fights to keep control as Brandi rushes over to the booth.

"Can Kathy come home and play?"

In unison, both Robin and William flatly declare, "No."

Just then Bunny skates over, ready to take their order.

CHAPTER 43

WHERE IS HOME, ANY WAY?

You can never really live in two worlds, no matter how you try to. You just have to find the one that welcomes you, the one that feels right and stay there. Sometimes you have to choose. Sometimes the choices are uncomfortable, but you still have to make them. When you do, you have to turn your back on someone. That always hurts. William's uneasiness grew by the day. Somehow, basketball, recruiting and training talent and playing suburban university politics just didn't fit together for him. Still, he had grown accustomed to the life, complete with all of its social niceties.

Saturday brought yet another of the endless string of gatherings. This time, the Cunningham household hosted another garden party. William found himself surrounded by a small knot of men. He clenched a bottle of Old English beer, which began to sweat. Bruce lobbed a verbal jibe at him, motioning toward the beer.

"How can you drink that rot gut?"

William smiled, turning the bottle in his hand as he replied,

"It's like mother's milk to me."

William glanced over Bruce's shoulder as Robin pinged him with an icy stare. He could feel her seething anger. He turned away to see Brandi playing with the neighbors' kids. He lost his train of thought every time he saw Robin shooting heat-seeking missiles at him. William turned away to face his companions again. Bruce noticed his uneasiness, stood his ground and steadied William with his words.

"Man up, you can handle it."

Jeff, standing next to Bruce, weighed in, with his own special brand of light sarcasm,

"To err is husband."

Not to be outdone, Rob sneered as he made his own pronouncement, "What doesn't kill you will make you stronger."

Bruce, Jeff and Rob slapped one another in jest as they sent William to his reckoning. William joined Robin. They huddled by the roses, fingering the petals and speaking in tense, hushed tones. William took her hand.

"We're supposed to be having fun."

Robin looked up at him, torn between hurt and anger.

"Do you still have friends in Newark?"

William stroked her hair with his other hand.

"He's not...he's this guy I used to...my old coach is dying."

Robin choked on her words.

"Our marriage is dying."

William felt the barb and shot back,

"Robin!"

Tears welled up and Robin's face reflected fear.

"You promised me you'd never go back. You promised!"

William dropped his voice level and soothed her.

"Okay, that's it. I'm not going back."

Robin softened and rested her head against William's chest as he embraced her.

Robin wiped the tears from her eyes and thanked him.

"I'll just call the hospital."

Robin broke from William's embrace and ran inside the house, leaving their guests wondering. Bruce, Jeff and Rob laughed quietly as William chased after Robin. She took refuge in the pantry, facing the closet, stewing as William squeezed into the narrow space. He spun her around to face him.

"What is wrong with you? I can't call?"

Robin, still seething, confronted him.

"Don't you get it?"

William placed a hand on each of her shoulders and confronted her, eye to eye.

"I guess not."

Just then, Brandi found them and shimmied in between them. William held her gaze.

"It's just a call."

Robin continued to pout, her eyes red from crying.

"Like hell it is."

Brandi repeated the phrase exactly as she heard it. William admonished her.

"Brandi!"

Robin slowly extricated herself from William's outstretched arms and from his piercing gaze, sauntering over to the kitchen sink. She stared out at the crowd in their backyard. Her words fall out, hoarsely.

"I have a bad feeling. I'm afraid if you go you won't come back."

Brandi tugged at William's hand.

"Don't go, daddy."

William bent down, kissed Brandi and told her to leave them, promising they will be right out. Brandi hugged William's leg, then left. William leveled his gaze at Robin.

"In front of Brandi?"

Robin turned to face him.

"Newark has never left your heart."

William's nostrils flared; he gritted his teeth, containing his anger as he answers.

"You don't know what you're talking about."

Robin seized his hand and glared at him.

"Hand to your heart, on Brandi; swear it."

William clenched her hand and once again, placed his hand on her shoulder.

"Stop it."

Robin refused to back down.

"Swear on Brandi Newark is not still in your heart."

William snorted, dropping his arm and backed away.

"You should be the one in therapy."

Robin backed up against the kitchen sink and held his stare.

"You can't do it."

William felt cornered, but doesn't back off. He searched himself and mustered all the sincerity he can before responding to her.

"Hand on my heart, without Coach and the Boy's Club, I'm a dead man."

Robin refused to give an inch, but William's words sealed the conversation. She pushed him out of the way as she went back outside. William shuffled over to the refrigerator, retrieved another bottle of beer, opened it and took a belt of it.

CHAPTER 44

MAKIN' A NEW PLAN

Every time William backed out of the driveway and headed for the Easton University campus, his muscles tightened up, his throat went dry and his head ached. Today was no different. Still, he had a plan this time. A well-conceived plan. The team had practice this afternoon, and he readied himself. A little of the old confidence began to poke through as he reviewed his plan in his head. Life would always have ups and downs, winning streaks and losing streaks. If you can't win every game, then you can't lose every one either, he mused. He just needed to climb out of the downward spiral. It felt like a mudslide, on the court and at home. His thoughts turned to Sarah, the therapist. He fantasized about her again. She embodied the very definition of a love-hate relationship. A motorcycle roared past him, driven by a laughing young man with long hair flying in the breeze as his girlfriend held on to him, laughing with him. They came a little too close. William tapped into their pleasure, envying their youth and their freedom. The encounter jarred him from his reverie. He imagined the couple having sex on the pulsating motorcycle. William had never ridden on one. He wondered if the vibration would cause arousal. No matter. In seconds, he pulled into the campus, by the gym.

William perused the mail on his desk, surveyed the team as they exited the locker room and eyeballed Chamber Higgins, watching from the bleachers. Right from the get go, William began to run the team hard. Ritchie, wearing a blue mesh pullover signifying the opponents' team, stood wide open at the top of the key and nailed the jumper. William blew the whistle and all of the players stopped, holding their positions. William, heated, approached them.

"Ritchie is their leading scorer, remember? He nailed that shot with his eyes closed."

Ritchie flippantly pipes up,

"Like me."

William got right in his face.

"Really? He does it with the game on the line in front of a packed gym."

Ritchie goes to push the envelope, continuing with his cavalier attitude,

"So—"

William steamed back at him,

"You think you could do that?"

Ritchie, red-faced, responded weakly,

"If—"

William swooped down verbally, as if he stole the ball from his opponent.

"If what; if I put you in the game when it's on the line, you'll deliver?"

Ritchie responded, still tentative.

"Maybe—"

William goes in for the kill.

"*Maybe* ain't good enough."

Ritchie dropped the ball, responding sorely,

"I don't need this shit—"

William glared back at him.

"Then get the hell off my team."

Just then Chamber stood up in the bleachers. Ritchie looked over at Gordon, who slowly shook his head to signify "no."

Ritchie dropped his head and his voice.

"I'm sorry."

William calmed down, then resumed the set-up.

"Let me see it again, Ritchie."

Ritchie reluctantly retrieved the ball, dribbled it to the top of the key, took aim and made the shot, swishing it. William approached a player on the starting team wearing a white mesh pullover.

"Take it off. Go blue."

William handed Ritchie the white pullover and addressed him.

"You're starting next game."

William motioned to the team to sit on the bench. He paced back and forth before them, his hands in his pockets, deep in thought. Finally, he turned to them.

"There is a certain kind of player, team, that gives us trouble."

The team members' eyes drift up to Chamber, still in the bleachers.

William continued making his point to the team.

"So I'm considering a new offense to slow things down—one that lets us regroup."

Jason wrinkled his brow, and then speaks.

"Sounds like stalling."

William countered him.

"It's called the Princeton Offense."

Gordon picked up his train of thought, offering,

"Pete Carill. Constant motion."

William snapped back,

"That's right, Gordon. Against a certain type of team, one that is anxious, maybe not as disciplined, they might overreach—get impatient."

The light goes on for Jason, who then gets the strategy, and rejoins the dialog.

"Yeah, we keep moving the ball, get them reaching—"

Ritchie now begins to appreciate William's plan, adding,

"Or trying to deny the passing lane."

Gordon locked fists with Ritchie as they both beamed with a renewed enthusiasm. Gordon remarks,

"Took them to the dance a few times."

William now makes eye contact with every team member, then responds,

"Twenty-three times, to be precise."

The entire team rose from the bench, hooting and hollering, and slapping each other five. William directed the starters to set up the Princeton Offense and they began passing the ball around. William hovered over them, his eyes fixed on the action and keeping them focused on the new strategy.

"Let's just get comfortable. Understand, this is about patience and trust in each other to take the right shot at the right time. Make every cut to the basket precise; take what the defense gives you. Remember—slow down to move fast."

William looked up to the bleachers, but Chamber had already left the gym. The room carried a new energy; you can almost smell it as the players continued the exercise. William watched the clock for a brief moment, then blows the whistle to signal the end of the practice. For the first time in months, he felt reinvigorated. They believe in him; he believes in them.

That night, some of the tension seems to have dissipated in the Cunningham household. Still, William kept to himself, cautious of Robin and reluctant to upset Brandi with the bickering that has dominated their lives of late. After dinner, he foregoes the beer staring back at him from the refrigerator and decides to call it an early night. He tucked Brandi in, kissed Robin and fell into a deep sleep.

But that's where the real subtext of life takes place. All the unresolved issues of the day spin around you like the stirring of a soup. William succumbed to his dreams. First, he found himself on a beach, alone. Curious, since that's the one place he's never been in his whole life. Only in his dreams. William watched the waves slapping the shoreline violently. He approached gingerly. Suddenly, he sees a figure rise up out of the waves and walk toward him. Sarah, the therapist, sports a tight fitting swimsuit. Her glistening, wet body intrigues him. He studies her as she circles him like a wildcat circling its prey. She runs her fingers up and down his chest, tickling the hairs. Tired of the game, he seizes her and swings her around to face him. He can't stop. His hands caress her. She returns the gesture. He becomes aroused; then picks her up and carries her to a remote area behind the rocks. He can no longer control himself and peels her swimsuit off. She watches as he removes his swim trunks. He mounts her. Immediately, he is surrounded by uniformed police offers pointing bright lights at him. The next thing he knows he finds himself in a jail cell, still naked and pacing like an animal. A sign posted on the wall reads "Rape." He wakes up with a start, shouting, "She asked for it; she wanted it!"

Robin slept right through it all.

CHAPTER 45

HOME IS A PLACE INSIDE OF YOU

Things change; people usually don't. Once they form their life patterns, most people just stay the course; remain in their groove, wherever it takes them. Tricks was like that. When the bottle took over his life, he went adrift. It has nothing to do with your circumstances. It's a choice. You either drink and let the booze run your life, or you don't—no matter what's going on in your life. Tricks never left Newark, and Newark never left him. Like most any other day, he woke that day from his drunken stupor, fully dressed in his rumpled clothes. By sheer force of will alone, he rose from his cot, mumbling the words he had repeated so many times, with little or no effect.

"I am powerless over alcohol. My life is...not manageable."

He sat back down on the cot, rubbing his head. He noticed the bottle in the brown paper bag, reached for it and took a swig. He rose from the cot again, this time heading for the bathroom. A little cold water does wonders. In a few minutes, he found his way down to the Boys' Club. He surveyed the scene. As old and tired as he feels, the floor dulled from worn shellac and nets blackened from dirty basketballs, stare back at him. Tricks picked up a ball and positioned himself underneath the basket, laying the ball in, alternately, with each hand. He repeated the drill for a while until finally, he missed. He pounded the ball between his hands.

"Damn Mikan drill..."

Finally, he rifled through the tiny kitchen in the back of the Boys' Club until he found a jar of coffee. He brewed up a small pot and downed it, then headed out of the building. Just in time, he rounded the corner to the bus stop, as the bus pulled up. He boarded it, settling back into the seat, closing his eyes and feeling the rhythm of the bus bouncing over the bumpy, torn up Newark streets. He nearly fell as he waited by the door and the bus lurched to a stop.

Whatever a man has done, or wherever he has gone, his deeds will not go unjudged. The sum total of his worth amounts to how much he has done for others. Regardless of his station in life, his personal achievements or his amassed wealth, in the end, with all his faults, he will face judgment. And he will pass that judgment if he has cared for, given to and done for others.

The elevator door opened and Tricks shuffled down the hall just as he did every day. A few small shafts of light poked through the blinds as he stood in the doorway of the room. A young Hispanic orderly mopped the hallway floor just outside of Coach's room. Tricks pulled up the guest chair next to the bed. Coach Emmett Lockhart looked older than his seventy-two years. The disease did that to him. His once glowing dark brown skin had lost its luster. Gray stubble coated his face, like so many tiny snowflakes. He opened his weary eyes. Tricks spoke first.

"Hey, Coach. How you feeling?"

Coach cleared his throat, then answered,

"Same as yesterday, only worse."

Tricks looked around the room.

"Let's get you some food."

Coach responded, dryly,

"You need it worse than me."

Tricks let out a laugh, then continued in a jovial tone,

"That's right, Coach; your sense of humor will keep you alive."

Coach shook his head and responded,

"Not for long it won't. When is William comin?"

Tricks' smile faded quickly. He hesitated, then replied, feigning excitement,

"He's comin'; he's comin'. He's just swamped right now, coaching. If they win the next game they make the dance."

Coach mustered up whatever strength he could and leaned forward. "When?"

Tricks continued in his court jesterish manner,

"When's the game? I don't—"

Coach growled back at him, falling against the pillow,

231

"When's he *coming?*"

Tricks makes one more attempt, seeing that Coach is on to him.

"Oh, he didn't say exactly, but knowing him it'll be soon."

Coach laid his head back, closed his eyes and intoned,

"Soon I'm gonna be dead, Tricks. We need somebody to take over. Kids need a place to go; a safe place."

Tricks began to arrange the blanket and the sheet over Coach, busying himself as he responded.

"I been meaning to talk to you about that. You know, I'm sober now, been a long fight; my Pops and my Ma both—well, you know, but now I'm clean and I thought maybe…

Coach grabbed Tricks' arm and gritted his teeth.

"Get William here. Understand?"

Tricks nodded his head.

"Yeah, yeah, I do."

And he did. Tricks left the hospital. Armed with only his resolve, he boarded the express bus for Easton. He knew what he had to do. By the time he arrived on campus, night had fallen. He stood and waited outside the gym, in the parking lot. William approached his car and saw Tricks watching him from a few feet away. Tricks sauntered over and casually struck up a conversation, as though he had been expected.

"The air is so nice here. It smells like the park they took us to when we were kids. Remember?"

William softens at the memory and at the sight of his downtrodden friend. "Yeah, I do."

Tricks began wiping the condensation from William's car windows as he spoke.

"I never had the head for this kind of stuff. But you did, and here you are, living the dream."

William sighed, shaking his head as he answered.

"Look Tricks, I can't come back."

Tricks nodded his head, then answered, still massaging the situation.

"Yeah, yeah. I understand. I just wanted to apologize from the other day. It wasn't my place to barge in like that. You're a big man now."

William looked him over, trying to read him.

"Look, Tricks, you need some money?"

"Yeah, but not from you, I don't. I need help with Coach—you know, making all the arrangements."

William just stared at Tricks. Tricks used his last ace in the hole.

"Never you mind; Lillian is gonna help. She's been great."

Tricks fights to remain stoic. William can't help but take the bait.

"Lillian? She still there?"

Tricks nodded. William paused, then continued,

"Still as fine as wine?"

Tricks flashed a smile.

"She looks good as ever."

William goes deep in thought, leaning on the roof of his car. He turned to face Tricks.

"So coach, he's really sick?"

Both of them radiate smiles and slap hands. William shakes his head, wagging his finger at Tricks.

"This has trouble written all over it."

Tricks can hardly contain himself.

"Just like back in the day."

William eyed Tricks.

"You still on the wagon?"

"Oh yeah, been sober a long time, a long time."

William slapped him on the back.

"Then I won't invite you out for a beer. Come on; I'll drive you to the bus stop. I gotta get home to my wife and kid."

CHAPTER 46

GOTTA GO HOME

There are times in a person's life when nothing feels right, no matter what he or she does. But you do what your gut tells you to do. If you're right, you reap the rewards; if you're wrong, you lick your wounds. But you don't stop; you must act. Sometimes, the gnawing in the pit of your stomach tells you it must be right. The more uncomfortable it feels, the more you have to take that road. William had avoided confronting Robin for fear of losing her. Something told him that it would take more than this to really tear them apart. He had to trust that instinct. He had an obligation to others, as well. If Coach needed him, he had to go—Robin or no Robin.

William slipped the key into the lock and slid the front door open. The quiet in the house could deafen you. He sneaked up the stairs, hardly making a sound. He turned off the upstairs hallway light and opened the door to Brandi's room, just a crack. He could see her asleep, peacefully. Then he noticed the outline of Robin's figure, leaning over in the dark to kiss Brandi. Before he could enter the room, Robin swung around and strutted past him, her head in the air. She tightened the belt on her robe and continued on, down the stairs. William stood at the top of the steps, watching her as she tidied up the house before bed. He could feel the tension of the "silent treatment" as she straightened pillows and magazines. He followed her and waited until she came face to face with him.

"I'm gonna see Coach tomorrow."

Robin stopped, drew herself up and threw a towel at William.

"Bastard. Get used to the sofa."

With those words, Robin scampered up the stairs, slamming the bedroom door behind her. William eyed the sofa, too drained to even consider fighting. He slumped down to a restless sleep, tossing and turning. For the first time in his life, he felt completely overwhelmed. Sharp fragments of his life came crashing down on him—his father's drunken binges, his mother's death, his brother's drug overdose and Uncle Ben's passing swirled around him in a storm. Finally, the storm dissipated and he succumbed to a heavy sleep punctuated with dreams—disturbing dreams. William found himself enveloped by a thick white fog. As the fog lifted, he saw Black men standing in a circle. Inside the circle stood a group of young Black children, surrounding a knot of women in the center. The children moved from man to man, asking if each one was their father. At first, William just observed. Then, he joined the circle of men. He noticed Robin off in the distance, watching and taking in the scene. Then, silently, the fog came and enveloped them again. Everyone disappeared into the fog. That was the last thing William remembered before he opened his eyes.

William arose from the couch, wiping his eyes and shaking the fog out of his head. He went into the downstairs bathroom, threw cold water on his face and quietly ascended the steps. He approached Brandi's room. She still slept silently. William stood over her for a moment, and then kissed two of his fingers, placing them on Brandi's heart. He stood outside her door, debating with himself for a moment. He hesitated. He did not hear Robin stirring, and abruptly left.

William backed his Subaru wagon out of the driveway, belting down a cup of coffee. The exhaust pipe rattled. He headed for the highway and punched the button on the radio until a Bruce Springsteen song came on. He looked anything but happy. Nervously checking his rearview mirror for any sign of a police cruiser, he jammed the accelerator down. He slipped on his sunglasses as he flew down Route 78 Eastbound, right into the bright morning sun. The Springsteen song ended, segueing into another one. He felt the familiar ring of the small towns as he passed each exit. Finally, the atmosphere changed. The urban landscape drew near. William passed the airport and saw the sign for Newark. He punched the button on the radio and the soulful sound of the Isley Brothers filled the air. Still impassive and expressionless, his hand began to beat the dashboard like a drum, in time to the music. He swerved off to the right and descended the exit ramp.

Everything changed as William entered the city of Newark. He felt its pulse, its vibrancy coursing through his veins. Even the violence of the city had a luring sensation. A couple of turns and he found himself at the hospital. The bad memories came back as the doors swung open like the jaws of a whale, to swallow him. He dashed into the gift shop, picked out a bouquet of flowers and headed for the elevator. As he exited, he began squinting to read the room numbers. Finally, he stopped, squared his shoulders and entered.

Tricks arose from the bedside chair. Without a word, he threw his arms around William and hugged him. William glanced down at Coach and froze. He had never seen him like that—emaciated, withered and weathered—and clearly, dying.

Tricks whispered to William,

"He's being fed by a tube in his stomach."

William motioned for Tricks to step away from the bed, then inquired,

"What's he got?"

Tricks looked him in the eye and confronted him. Uncharacteristically stone-faced, he let the words drop like a death knell.

"Cancer of the pancreas."

William shook his head, silently, glancing over at his old friend and mentor in disbelief. Weakly, he asked,

"How long's he got?"

Tricks shrugged his shoulders. Just then, Coach opened his eyes. Seeing William, he began to cry. William leaned over and they embraced. Coach parted his parched lips and forced the words out in a hoarse rattle.

"I knew you'd come."

William felt a flush of embarrassment as he answered.

"Sorry it took so long."

William began to speak again, but Coach stopped him with his raised hand, forcing an answer.

"You came when you could."

William continued,

"Tough call you got."

Coach shook his head, then responded in his usual fashion,

"We all got tough calls coming from here. I had a good life."

William started to reply again,

"It's not—"

Coach topped him.

"It's over. It's okay."

They both fell silent. Coach continued.

"You have kids?"

William smiled, nodding as he answered,

"A little girl, Brandi."

Coach held William's gaze.

"Love your wife?"

William hesitated, and then responded.

"We're having a hard time now…she doesn't want me here…doesn't understand our world."

Coach leaned forward with an understanding look.

"You mean to say she was raised in different circumstances than you?" William fumbled with the words.

"Yes. You see, she's White and from the suburbs." Coach nods.

"She took a big chance on you, then. She must love you."

William, still off balance and trying to accept the finality of Coach's situation, stammers.

"I didn't expect this—"

Coach struggled to sit upright and confronted William.

"What d'ya want? Want to be told how great you are? How you escaped this hell we live in?"

William responded humbly,

"I couldn't have done it—"

Coach glowered back, the veins in his forehead popping.

"You're damn right you couldn't have done it without me." Tricks placed a hand on Coach's shoulder and tried to soothe him. "Easy, Coach."

Coach slumped back against the bed, his eyes darting from Tricks to William.

"Don't tell me nothing. The great thing about dying is you get to be honest. Don't have time for no bull."

William spoke next, in a conciliatory tone.

"I'm listening."

237

Coach adjusted himself and tried to find a comfortable position—a difficult task with a tube in his stomach. He pointed his finger at William as he spoke.

"I want you to come back here and take over the Boys and Girls Club."

William exhaled, then replied.

"I have a job already—a career. I can't just—"

Coach cut him off.

"This is more important."

William took it like a fighter that just got jabbed.

"Hey, I don't owe you—"

Coach mustered whatever strength he had left and went in for the kill.

"You damn well do owe me. You'd be dead if it weren't for me."

Tricks became worried.

"Coach, be careful."

Coach growled back at both William and Tricks, "Am I wrong?"

William, with bowed head, shook his head, signifying "no."

Coach continued, with all the conviction of his cause.

"The next kid you help will do a little better than you. That's what it's all about. Sacrifice. Brother Martin, Malcolm and all the rest."

William looked puzzled.

"Why me?"

Coach slowly and deliberately responded,

"You know why."

Exhausted, Coach dropped his head to the pillow and shut his eyes. Tricks motioned to William and they quietly left the room.

CHAPTER 47

HOME IS WHERE THE PASSION BEATS

"I don't know Tricks; I feel like someone just tagged me with a left hook, from out of nowhere. Let's head for the parking garage," William shook his head sullenly as they left the hospital. The doors closed behind them like jaws again.

"Don't let Coach get to you. He's been on everybody," Tricks countered.

William stopped and turned to face his friend.

"He's right."

Tricks shrugged before answering William.

"I don't know about right or wrong. I just know we need to get you to Hawks' for lunch."

William let a smile slip out, finally breaking his mood.

"That place still open?"

Tricks slapped him on the back.

"It is today."

William shot back,

"Hey, I have no time."

Tricks elbowed him, pointing ahead of them. William stopped in his tracks, as if he had just gotten clocked with an uppercut. There, leaning against a new BMW, Lillian blocked his path. He looked her up and down. Still fine as wine; still as confident and beautiful as the first day he met her. They say you never get over your first love. Lillian lowered her tinted glasses, turned and glanced at him over her shoulder.

"Ain't been back in twenty years and he's got no time for lunch?"

Still holding his gaze and glued to the spot where he stood, Lillian made the first move. She went right up to William for a hug, which he desperately needed. He kept her locked in the embrace until Lillian broke free.

"You got a wife for that, don't you?"

Tricks began to back off, raised his hand and waved to William as he took off down the street.

"I'll see you at Hawk's."

Lillian slid her glasses down her nose and pinned him with her eyes. Her stare spoke volumes, even before she opened her mouth. Just speaking his name commanded his full attention.

"Willie Joe…"

He tried to look away, but he could not. He stammered an answer, weakly.

"I'm called…"

Lillian deftly moved toward him like a Cougar ready to strike.

"Yes?"

William finally exhaled, feeling the sweat begin to break on his brow. He quickly mopped it, still in awe of her, and answered.

"Never mind. It's great to see you."

Lillian coolly responded in her characteristic manner, polishing her glasses against her blouse.

"I can tell."

William struggled to gain any semblance of composure, still watching her every move.

"It's just…look at you. Tricks mentioned you're a VP."

Lillian thrust one leg forward, laughing as she spoke.

"And you thought I would be fat, right?"

William shook his head as he attempted to answer.

"I was hoping."

They both broke into a laugh as he took her hand. Lillian tossed her head, swung her keys and pointed to the other side of the car.

"C'mon. I'll give you a ride."

The smell of the new BMW permeated the pristine car. The rich interior captivated William's attention. As they adjusted their seat belts and mirrors, he spoke.

"I thought you'd be driving a Prius, all concerned with the environment as you were in high school."

Lillian didn't hesitate a single beat before responding.

"Still am. But a girl needs to be spoiled a little, even if she needs to do it herself."

William shook his head, laughing under his breath as he turned to her.

"Now, that makes no sense to me."

Lillian slid her hand over to William's knee to get his attention.

"Maybe you forgot our promise in high school, but I didn't."

William snorted his answer, looking out the window as they whizzed through the urban landscape.

"High school? I can't remember what I did yesterday."

Lillian shot him a glance and jabbed him.

"Want me to remind you?"

William turned to her.

"I remember."

Lillian brought the car to an abrupt stop and parallel parked, easing into a space in front of Hawk's Lounge. William surveyed the scene. The tavern looked the same as it did in their day—rusty and tired. A half-baked, garish pink neon sign blinked at them, mockingly. William leaned across the roof of the BMW and gestured to Lillian.

"You sure you wouldn't rather go to the Ironbound? We might die in there."

Lillian ignored his remark and motioned for him to accompany her.

"You've been away for too long. Your Newark is almost gone."

William nodded as they entered Hawk's.

"I hope you're right."

As the door swung open, before their eyes could adjust to the dimly lit interior, William heard the sound of voices in unison, exclaiming, "SURPRISE!"

William's jaw dropped as he discerned the faces of about twenty of his old friends cheering for him. A buxom Black waitress in a tight skirt shimmied past him, laying down a tray of food on the nearby high-hat table. Her breasts jiggled as she squeezed by and returned with two more trays. William swung around to see another waitress deposit a tray of desserts. A sea of hands began passing frosted mugs of beer and wine glasses filled to the brim. Joy permeated the air. William began making the rounds, greeting old school teachers and basketball teammates. He spied Tricks, proudly sporting his old high school basketball shirt. A few of William's teammates began to tug at his polo shirt and kick at his loafers, jeering at him in fun. They could hardly contain themselves.

"Is this how they make you dress?"

"Or you want to look like a cracker?"

William took a long draught of his beer, letting his guard down as they all laughed with gusto, playfully circling him and taking turns pushing him. William straightened up, brushing himself off as he looked around and addressed them.

"It's a uniform; that's all. Look at Tricks; he hasn't taken that off in twenty-five years."

Everyone joined in the laughter as William glided over to Izza Morgan and they hugged each other warmly. He eyed his old teacher cautiously.

"Please tell me you are giving someone else hell like you gave me."

Izza placed her hand on her hip and gestured at William with the other hand.

"It's my job. Look what it did for you."

William belted down another draught of his beer and responded in a cavalier fashion,

"I'm still wondering what the Greek alphabet did for me."

Izza raised her wine glass as she extolled,

"Just so you'd enjoy the sheer beauty of the words."

William tipped his mug up to finish his beer before answering Izza.

"At least Latin helped with my SAT's."

Izza, ever the lady and the scholar, gently sipped her wine, then intoned,

"Transliteration is just as prevalent from Greek. Like 'athlete', for instance."

William waved her off, laughing.

"Oh, enough of that."

Izza changed her tone, taking on a sincere look and holding his attention.

"You look well; are you happy?"

Unconsciously, William looked to see where Lillian stood. He then realized his move. Catching himself, he answered quietly,

"I'm fine Izza, thanks."

Izza stepped into him like an umpire making a call, and waved her finger at him.

"You think Lillian can answer that with more authority?"

She begins to raise her voice and continues to gesture at him.

"Men always want to be a woman's first love—women like to be a man's last romance."

William felt a twinge, knowing Izza had just struck a nerve. He answered coolly,

"You make that up?"

Izza sipped her wine and responded dryly,

"Wish I did. Oscar Wilde said that."

William, still the scholar at heart, refuses to be outdone.

"Wasn't he…"

Izza tossed her head back.

"Yes, he was a homosexual. So what? Is it true in your case?"

William caught Lillian's eye from across the room. Unaware of the dialog, she smiled at him.

Izza gestured in Lillian's direction.

"She's always been stubborn, but it got her far."

William snapped back,

"It always kept her single."

Izza takes the bait, continuing,

"You want me to quote from another friend, Shakespeare?"

William waved her way.

"No, no, enough of that."

Izza persisted.

"One more. 'Know from whence you came. If you know from whence you came, there are absolutely no limitations to where you can go.' "

William nodded his head solemnly and replied,

"James Baldwin."

Just then, William turned and did a double take, as though he had seen a ghost. He came face to face with Leroy Watson. Knowing his life story, William assumed he had died long ago. Leroy lumbered over with a cane. The years seemed to melt away as both of them let the past slip by and embraced for a long moment. The memory of William finding Mr. Cavett bleeding in the high school staircase flashed back into his mind as if it happened yesterday. He felt embarrassed as he confronted Leroy.

"I'm sorry I had to turn you in."

"You did the right thing. I only wish somebody had stopped me. It didn't stop there, no how. I turned into a runaway train. I did the crime and the time. I guess I just finally saw the light before it was too late. Enough of that. I'm proud to call you brother, William. My hat is off to you. You did it all right."

They could not hold back the tears. Lillian began to tear up, but tried desperately to hide it. Suddenly, the jukebox began to play Luther Vandross's "Power of Love" and the room broke into dance. Leroy backed away and Lillian stepped in, dancing with William. Something about it just felt so right. For a few moments, time just stopped for William, as he absorbed the emotions swirling around him in the room. Finally, he felt like he could breathe.

Though the years, the centuries and the millennia march on, our roles hardly every change. Man hunts and gathers; woman nurtures and gives care to the sick and the elderly. All the education, the veneer of sophistication—it just doesn't change the timeless clock that ticks on. We move like figures in a tableau, playing out our respective roles. Wealthy or poor, young or old, we continue on. Robin was no different. Even with the tension in her marriage, she grew to become the rock-solid matriarch her upbringing had trained her to become. She hadn't seen William since the night before. In fact, she had no idea where he had gone or what he had done since she tossed that towel at him and banished him to the living room couch. She sipped her tea, legs crossed, in her satin robe, surveying Brandi. She noticed Brandi looked unusually sullen and quiet. At first, she attributed it to their marital tension. But, she sensed something else.

"Come on, no breakfast cereal for you? That's not like you at all."

Brandi just shook her head, staring down at the empty bowl. She twirled the spoon. Her face looked pained. Robin stood up and approached her, leaning over and placing her hands on her shoulders.

"Brandi, you don't have to suffer in silence. If something hurts you, it's okay to cry. Is this about mommy and daddy?"

Brandi shook her head, and the tears welled up.

"Do your ears hurt?"

As if the floodgates opened at the mere mention of it, the tears streamed down her face. Robin leaned over and kissed her.

"Go get dressed. We're going to the ear doctor. I'll call him right away, okay?"

"But I don't like him. He sticks things in my ears when they hurt. Can daddy come with us?"

The question cut Robin. Just when she needed William, she didn't even know where to find him. She knew she would have to take care of this herself. In minutes, she had Brandi seated in the car and began to crank the engine. The old BMW—the same one she had since college, really showed its age. It hesitated at first; then, with a crack, the starter kicked in, the flywheel turned and all four cylinders began to roar. As she backed out of the driveway, the pinhole in the muffler rumbled loudly. When she turned down Main Street, the tailpipe rattled. Finally, she pulled into the parking lot behind the professional building. They climbed the steps, Brandi, still clutching her doll and trying to feign bravery, hiding her fear. After a short wait, the nurse finally ushered them into the examining room. The doctor smiled at Brandi as he began to prod and poke and probe her ears. Robin gripped her hand tightly. Finally, the doctor straightened up.

"Could we go into my office? Brandi, would you just wait right here for a couple of minutes, while I talk to mom?"

Brandi frowned, then piped up,

"But it's about me, so I should hear it, too."

The doctor eyed Robin; she nodded and he addressed them both in the warmest of tones.

"Mrs. Cunningham, Brandi has another ear infection. She's going to need a powerful course of antibiotics. I think we need to consider the operation again. It's becoming chronic. With winter coming, the frequency and severity of these infections will only increase."

Robin stepped over to the corner of the examining room and began to dial the phone frantically, fuming. No answer. She began pacing and tapping her boot heel on the floor nervously.

More than sixty miles away, the revelers at Hawk's Lounge in Newark continued their celebration. William and Lillian slipped into the rhythm of a slow dance, arms around one another without a care in the world. Friends nodded and smiled at them as Lillian laid her head against William's shoulder. The bass notes from the jukebox vibrated the floor of the old building. William's cell phone and keys rested on a table in the corner. As the song ended, the crowd applauded and gathered around William and Lillian. He couldn't help but smile as he basked in the warmth of their admiration and support. He stepped forward and addressed the group, becoming more and more emotional.

"Thank you so much for this welcome. I can't—well, a man can't choose his family but he can choose his friends. And if he's lucky like me, they become his family. Twenty years…never again, never again."

The crowd engulfed William with hugs and kisses as Lillian stood apart from them, watching. Finally, he approached her, they find their moment and leave. They began strolling around the old neighborhood in silence. Eventually, William spoke.

"I know what you and Tricks are doing. But I'm not coming back."

Lillian stayed the course, rather than taking the bait and arguing.

"We finally got a Mayor that cares about this town."

William stopped in his tracks, placed both hands on her shoulders and swung Lillian around to face him.

"I'm serious. I can't."

Lillian forced a smile and the words just flowed from her.

"Willie Joe, you've always been so serious. Life is short. Relax."

William glanced down at the street. Seeing a crushed soda can, he kicked it and then responded to Lillian.

"You have any idea what it's like? I might as well be a Martian at Easton." Lillian snapped right back at him,

"As bad as for Baldwin and his time in Switzerland, where the kids wanted to touch his hair and skin?"

William stared off into the distance as he answered,

"Izza, what a lady…"

"She was *my* Coach," Robin retorted.

William stopped by a stone wall, gripping it with both hands. Still staring off, he answered Lillian in quiet, sincere tones,

"I don't know. You were smarter than me then and you're smarter than me now."

Lillian stood by his side, staring up at him, in an effort to command his full attention.

"I had to try harder."

William stammered.

"I'm just tryin' to say—"

Ever the intellectual, Lillian continued.

"Baldwin felt out of place, like you. And you're not alone. Many of our people that moved away still do."

William nodded, then tried another tack. He turned to face her.

"Stop showing off. You scare men that might want to marry you."

Lillian squinted, holding his gaze as she pointed at him.

"Are you scared?"

William didn't flinch. He responded instantly,

"Of you? Better believe it."

Lillian grabbed his hand.

"Don't want to marry me, then?"

"I'm married. I have a daughter. It's complicated."

His reply dissipated into silence. Finally, Lillian broke it.

"You saying you want to leave your wife and daughter and marry me?"

William squinted hard at Lillian. She playfully shoved him and laughed.

"I'm playing you."

They resumed walking and stopped in front of a sign that read "Lincoln Park Urban Center." It seemed so incongruous. Right there, in the midst of all these buildings, they stood in front of an explosion of green vegetables and plants, spilling over the sides of buckets. The only time he remembered anything remotely like it in Newark were the summers he spent working in the supermarket. He scanned the sight of the tomatoes, lettuce, cabbages and carrots, and then turned to Lillian, smiling.

"Are we in Kansas?"

Lillian continued in a serious tone.

"Remember this, the old South Park Presbyterian Church? Some graduates of Yale are giving back to Newark, their home."

William glanced sideways at Lillian. He sensed her plan. She went on with the same serious tone.

"They hired a guy with a patented hydroponic system. They plan on selling to restaurants in the area. What's left over, will go to the homeless shelters. Once we get people eating better, maybe they'll start feeling better, and... well, it' a start."

William soaked it all in, marveling at Lillian's unspoiled idealism— as well as the people with the vision and the determination to stick to their dreams. They continued their stroll through the streets. He can't help but notice that Newark has changed, for the better. The city looks cleaner, feels safer, more hopeful. Lillian stepped in front of him.

"Come back."

William furrowed his brow in confusion.

"Excuse me?"

Lillian tugged at his sleeve.

"With your wife and child, I mean. Home is home."

William shook his head, glancing at his own reflection in the tailor shop window.

"Not that simple."

"Your wife—what's her name?"

William hesitated, then responds weakly,

"Robin."

Lillian's mood kicked up as she answers, lightheartedly,

"Like the bird. Robin must be cool; maybe she'll like it."

William smothered a laugh, shaking his head as he responded,

"Cool, yeah, cool…"

Lillian continued, determined.

"Plenty of families here now. Newark is changing every day. Hell, even White folks are moving in."

William's mood became sarcastic.

"Yeah, they're all over the place."

Lillian frowned at his skepticism.

"Takes time. But it's happening."

Lillian took William's arm as they continued walking. They turned the corner, where Tricks caught up with them. William struggled to regain his composure, and then speaks.

"Look, thanks so much for everything, but I need to get back."

Tricks withdrew two tickets from his back pocket, waving them in front of William.

"Guess he's not interested in seeing Savior play."

Lillian piped up,

"Wow, Tricks; guess Newark is off the radar for Easton."

Tricks chimes in,

"I guess they like losing."

Lillian agrees.

"Guess so."

William pinged a hard glance at Tricks before replying.

"Better than Willoughby?"

Tricks glided a step, feigning a lay-up as he answers,

"Better than Cleo Hill, too."

Lillian placed her hands on her hips, shaking her head, as she addressed Tricks.

"See, Tricks, he'll stay for a high school boy and not for his high school sweetheart."

William's cell phone rang; he turned away from them to answer it. Robin's voice, although controlled, pierces through it.

"Where the hell are you?"

William tried to respond calmly.

"You know. I'll be home later."

Robin's anger escalated. She answered through gritted teeth.

"Do you even care about your daughter?"

William became alarmed, stepping further away from Lillian and Tricks.

"What's wrong with Brandi?"

Robin let him have it with both barrels. William had to hold the phone away as she screeched,

"She needs an ear operation and you don't even answer your cell phone!"

William continued to hold down his voice, replying,

"I'll be home later and we'll discuss it."

Robin launched into a rage, screaming,

"I want you home now! Get your godamn ass home where you belong!"

As William held the phone at arm's length, Tricks and Lillian shot each other a look. William answered her, contritely,

"Okay, soon."

Robin, in tears, pressed him, apologetically,

"NOW! I need you here *right now*."

Robin slammed the phone down. William turned to face Lillian and Tricks. They still have stunned looks on their faces.

"I'll call her later," William sighed.

"You better." Lillian gave him that characteristic stare over the top of her glasses.

William nodded and gestured, "Let's roll, Tricks."

CHAPTER 48

LIVING IN TWO WORLDS

Tricks and William made their way through the crowd, entering the packed gym at their old high school. Dimly lit and showing its age, the building still held inescapable memories for both of them. They cleave to it, as if they can relive their own pasts, just watching every scene like an old movie. They make their way to the bleachers. Their seats are excellent. The sights, the sounds, even the smells seem so familiar, as if time stopped, then went backwards. A small knot of men began to walk past them; then, they exchanged a glance of recognition and stopped to greet William. He felt pleased that people still remembered him.

"Clarence, Kareem, Joseph; good to see you, too," he stood and they all shook hands before taking their seats.

Then, just for a fleeting moment, William saw the scene as if he was back in his youth, on the court. Tricks gives him a nudge with his elbow and breaks his reverie. William scans the crowd in the stands, recognizing some of the coaches from the top-tiered universities. He sizes up his competition, knowing they have come to recruit talent, just as he has. He wondered if any of them recognized him—Coach K. from Duke, Coach Self from Kansas, Coach Calipari from Kentucky and Paul Hewitt from Georgia Tech. William turned to Tricks.

"It's always like this?"

"He got game", Tricks smiled and nodded back at William.

William, skeptical, fired back at him,

"C'mon; how good is he? Can't be that good."

Tricks doesn't flinch, but replies flatly,

"Michael in college—with a jumper."

William contorted his face in disbelief. Just then, the doors opened and the Weequahic High basketball team entered the gym. There is no mistaking who Savior Ruffin is. Sporting number 18 on his jersey, his sleek bearing resembles a panther, with springs in his legs. William sat back and smiled as Savior glided to the basket and rose effortlessly above the rim. That was just the beginning. Like a scene from a television sportscast, William watches Savior as he wins the tap, comes around a pick and nails a jumper. Before anyone can move, he makes a steal, spins around and dunks the ball, beats a double team and then tomahawks a dunk. Each movement more deft than the last, William watched Savior, mesmerized, as he spins, dribbles away from the defense; then jumps and slams it home to make the shot, perfectly. William's enthusiasm rises. Savior could play like a one-man team, but he doesn't. He could smoke every player on the court, but he passes and lets his teammates score, one by one. And he swelled with pride each time they did. A star with humility—that's a rare quality these days, William mused. William knows value when he sees it. He leans over to Tricks.

"I want to meet him."

"Just cause he dropped forty on Science?" Tricks queries.

"You're damn right, Tricks."

"It's already been arranged, my friend."

William slaps Tricks on the back.

"Give me some background."

"No father."

"Mother?"

"Yep."

William eyed him up.

"You know her?"

Tricks can't contain himself. His grin spread from ear to ear, as though he had waited for this moment all night long. He leaned in and whispered to William.

"You know her better than anyone."

No sooner than they turn back to the court, Savior steals the ball again and flies in for a windmill dunk. William wiped the sweat from his brow.

"Stop playing me, Tricks."

Tricks just shrugged his shoulders before responding, his eyes still fixed on the court.

"When was the last time you and her…you know…"

William dropped his head into his hands, rubbed his eyes, and then looked up just in time to see Savior slam off a breakaway. His face felt flushed as he turned to Tricks.

"Fuck…"

"Exactly", Tricks extolled, trailing off into a laugh.

For the rest of the game, William felt numb. He couldn't get Tricks' implication out of his head. At the same time, despite the complicated situation, he knew he had to have Savior on his team. How ironic that Lillian would provide the magic bullet he needed, after all these years. And he found it right back in his old high school, right in Newark.

After what seemed an eternity, William and Tricks watched the last of the crowd disperse before leaving the gym. The light in the sky had begun to fade as dusk enveloped the Newark skyline. William recalled all those evenings he spent at the Boys' Club, at the high school, at Lillian's. The Newark skyline had changed, but the spirit of his city had not. They waited patiently on the sidewalk for Savior to come out. Strutting like a celebrity, he signed a few autographs for his fans before approaching William and Tricks. William extended his hand; Savior did not shake it. An imposing, muscle-bound young Black man, L.J., moved in and confronted William.

"How many pro's your program turn out?"

William looks over at Tricks, then back at L.J.

"Sorry, who are you?"

L.J. immediately stepped right into William's space, with a menacing stare.

"Fool, I just done talking to Coach K. and he knows who I am."

Tricks approaches William and fills in the blanks for him.

"L.J. is Savior's street agent."

L.J. snapped into character, exhibiting his full bravado as he turned to Savior.

"We got no time for this fool. Ain't done his homework. Man don't even have a school jersey. Shows no respect. Let's blow, Savior."

William held his place and responded coolly to L.J.

"Look, I played here. I've been away for a long time, but I'm back. I'm Willie Joe. I'm sure you've seen my number hanging from the rafters in the gym."

Finally, Savior piped up, cocky and confident.

"I smoked all your records."

William replied flatly,

"No shit."

"As a sophomore," Savior retorted, as he and L.J. smacked fists and laughed.

William remained unfazed and responded,

"I know one you didn't break."

"Missed most three's", L.J. piped up, as he and Savior continued laughing.

"Most free throws in a row," William answered.

"That's like saying 'most fouls'," L.J. crooned.

Savior stopped laughing and asked,

"How many?"

"Seventy-three", William responded, proudly.

"Bull...shit," L.J. answered.

Savior and William locked eyes. The vibe grows stronger as the wall between them begins to crumble. Savior looked William up and down and quizzed him.

"Why you ain't never come here before?"

William sighed, shaking his head as he replied,

"Son, it's a long story."

Savior and William began to walk together, tuning in to one another's vibe. They walked past two large green fields. William pointed to one of the fields.

"Nice."

Savior nodded, then replied,

"Mother likes green; live in a park if she could."

William smiled and nodded.

"I know."

Savior eyeballed William. L.J. lagged behind, but kept close enough to hear their conversation. At that moment, they stopped in front of a well-kept three-story corner house with a flower garden. The garden showed the signs of a caring hand. L.J. began to prod William again.

"What's your record?"

Savior joined in.

"How's your point?"

"Made first team in the Humanitarian League," William replied.

"The what? Big East, ACC, Big 10, SEC; hell, we'll even consider Atlantic 10, if the coin is right," L.J. jived.

"The Human—"

"The Human what? Is this some pansy-assed Ivy League school? How does Savior go pro from this league? What's the alumni coin like? Talk to me. We one and done. Soon as he's turns nineteen, we blow," L.J. intoned.

William braced himself before responding,

"Easton can only offer grant and aid."

Both L.J. and Savior laughed so hard they could hardly breathe.

William, still unfazed, responded,

"But the education is unmatched."

L.J. and Savior continued to break out into fits of uncontrollable laughter. They approached a project, stumbling. Suddenly, L.J. turned serious and approached William with all the attitude he can muster.

"I think this Tom is disrespecting us. Comes here without perks and doesn't even know who I am."

"I assure you—" William interjected.

"You assure me nothin'," L.J. retorted, turning his back on William. Savior cooled L.J.

"Let him be, L.J. I got homework."

"He got nothin' fo' me?" L.J. drew himself up, squinting and surveying William, boring into him.

William reached for his wallet; Tricks slid in, addressing L.J. to set the record straight.

"Yo, L.J., Willie Joe is cool. He's *from* here. He meant no disrespect."

Tricks looked over at William.

"Right, Willie Joe?"

William gave a slow, tentative nod. L.J. considered both William and Tricks before responding,

"You leave my boy Savior alone, understand?"

"Yeah, you got it, L.J.," Tricks countered as he pulled William away and they hustled off.

When they were out of sight, William turned to Tricks, with conviction.

"I'm comin' back…for Savior"

Tricks slapped William on the back and replied,

"Coach will go crazy."

The faint sound of music trickled out of a bar at the end of the block. Bar patrons began to spill out onto the street, laughing. History never changes, William mused. Just get the Black man drunk so he can forget his troubles. In the morning, he has to face them all over again. Cars ambled by noisily, punctuating the scene. They reminded him of Coach's old rattletrap Chevy that carried him to Easton on his very first visit. He wondered what Lillian was doing that very moment. His cell phone rang again. He glanced down; it was Robin. He didn't answer it. He had other fish to fry at the moment. The day's events began to swirl around in his head. He knew what he had to do.

William and Tricks made their way back to Hawk's Lounge. As they approached, they saw Lillian's outline, leaning against her BMW. She slung her purse over her shoulder, thrust her leg out in that characteristic fashion and peered over her glasses.

"Have fun?"

"No," William replied, sarcastically, as Tricks just grinned.

"Somebody did," Lillian shot back.

"I need to get home," William responded, flatly.

"Let me give you a ride to your car," Lillian opened the door and motioned for him to get in.

William nodded and turned his back, as Tricks gave Lillian the "thumbs up."

William slid into the passenger seat with a sullen look. Finally, with great effort, he raised his eyes to meet Lillian's. He clamped his hand over hers before she could engage the gearshift.

"Is he my boy?"

"He's *my* boy," Lillian responded coolly.

"I mean…I'm sorry. I guess…I don't know what to say," William stammered.

"Been a long time," Lillian sighed.

"I feel like I was mugged and maybe it's just how these kids talk. L.J., man…you know him well?"

Lillian just nodded, staring straight ahead.

Then, she turned sharply around to face him.

"L.J. is here for one thing, and it's not my ass. Savior is a winning lottery ticket. And L.J. is the vetting system of the street to make sure Savior collects. You think these coaches care a lick about Savior? They care about Alumni, Boosters, Athletic Directors—and most of all, their records. L.J.'s making sure Savior gets the best deal possible. And he knows Savior will take care of him in return," Lillian just unloaded it all with that fire William knew so well, pausing briefly, then continued,

"I asked L.J. to watch over him. There's only so much a mother can do, especially on the street."

Lillian stepped on the accelerator and careened around the corner. William took the bait. Leaning back, he just let the words drop on her.

"You know how I recruit? I have dinner at four-star restaurants and talk to parents about how playing basketball will serve their sons in boardrooms or private practices.."

"And that's why you'll miss the dance again this year," Lillian shot back.

William's eyes flashed and his nostrils flared.

"I keep track of your team," she snapped, as she pulled the BMW into the parking garage and came to a stop next to William's car.

William leaned in to her, taking both of her hands in his.

"Look, I haven't stopped thinking about you either."

Lillian dropped her voice level. It's amazing how powerful one well-placed word can be.

"Stay."

She leaned in to William, kissing him square on the lips. He could not resist. In seconds, they were locked in an embrace, her tongue circling inside of his mouth. He felt her nipples harden against him. She felt his arousal. It seemed like they had never parted. Finally, Lillian pulled back. William shook his head, backing against the door.

"I can't do this," he admitted, sheepishly.

"You *are* doing it," Lillian smiled at him.

"I mean…" William began as she cut him off.

"It's late. I'm sure your wife wants you home."

Wounded, William climbed out of the car, watching Lillian speed away in her BMW. She turned away, and would not let him see the tears streaming down her face.

CHAPTER 49

WHICH WAY IS HOME?

The road trip back to Easton seemed endless. William's restlessness overwhelmed him. He wrestled with thoughts of how good it felt to touch Lillian, to how he would win over L.J. and Savior, to Coach's imminent death, to what lay ahead when he returned to Robin. As much as he wanted to please her, his life and his career lay on the line. He had to recruit Savior, but at what cost? He thought about his crumbling marriage; he thought about how much Brandi needed him. He had to find a way to make it all work out. He even toyed with the idea of having a session with Sarah the therapist, just to sort it all out. Finally, he thought better of that. Then, another thought flashed into his head. One other person might just help him make sense of it all. He would call Evan, Robin's cousin and his old college roommate. He had a glimmer of hope. Evan always remained level and calm in the face of everything. He resolved to call him and try to see him as soon as he could.

The inky sky around Clinton, New Jersey suddenly filled with stars. All the tiny towns in Western Jersey flew by; little dots on the map. Farm people, mostly. No one great ever came from these places, William thought. All the talent came from the big cities. He passed Stewartsville, remembering that Lou Ferrigno, the weight lifter who played the movie role of the comic book character The Incredible Hulk lived there. As he passed through Phillipsburg, he remembered his indiscretion with the Black woman who reminded him of Lillian. You can't escape your past. Everywhere you look, your mistakes just surround you. For the first time in a long time, William's thoughts turned to his childhood days in church. He remembered how important religion was to his mother. He recalled the incident in Beulah Baptist Church, when he thought he had seen an angel. He remembered the Reverend Pearl's sermons. There had to be a path to redemption. He felt powerless again. If he could just get his life back on track.

As he crossed the bridge into Pennsylvania, William felt some sense of relief. Odd, he thought, how two places and two lifetimes so different, could both feel like home to him. Finally, he pulled into his driveway. All the lights shone from behind the shades. All the curtains remained closed. He held his breath as he parked the car, bracing himself for whatever would happen. He put his key in the doorknob, turned it and entered. To his surprise, amid the dead silence, Robin waited for him, seated on the sofa. William treaded carefully toward her and she popped up.

"What would you like for dinner?" she asked.

"Baby, I'm sorry I'm late," he did his best to sound sincere.

"I made your three favorite meals so you can choose," Robin replied as she stood up, heading for the kitchen. He followed her close behind, her back still turned.

"Robin…"

"Since I'm more like a maid and a nanny to you than a wife. Real husbands don't hang up on their wives," Robin responded in a singsong manner.

"I'm sorry, but—"

"Or is this just a Newark thing I don't know about?" she reeled around to face him.

William's eyes flared as he became defensive.

"Shut up—"

Robin placed her hands on her hips and drew herself up to her full height, facing him.

"Or what, you're gonna bitch-slap me?" she retorted.

As they entered the kitchen, William grabbed a chair, leaned on it and steadied himself. Robin lowered her eyes and began to cry, then looked up at him.

"I'm sorry," she blurted out.

William approached her and hugged her as she continued sobbing. She nearly choked on her words. He could hear the pain in her voice.

"The last year I feel like I've been losing you."

"I'm here for you," he made every effort to soothe her.

Robin looked up at him, her eyes red and wiped the tear stains from her face.

"I have a bad feeling about Newark."

William tried to minimize her upset.

"I'm here, aren't I?"

"You hungry? I made you a steak," she motioned toward the counter top, paused, then continued,

"Or do you prefer fried chicken?"

William looked up at the ceiling, as if he sought help from above.

"Just kidding," Robin made an effort to be conciliatory.

He sank into his usual seat at the kitchen table as she served him the steak.

He dug in, ravenously.

"How's Brandi?" he asked.

Robin raised her eyebrows in surprise, then replied, flippantly,

"Glad you remembered."

"Hey…" William cut her off.

"Okay, sorry. She might need an operation soon. Something called a myringotomy, where they insert grommets to let air in," Robin explained, beginning to tear up. She made every effort to keep from crying at the thought of Brandi suffering.

"Damn. She's got the same issues as me when I was a kid," William shook his head.

"Wonder what other bad genes you passed on," Robin replied, unable to contain her newfound sarcasm, which seemed so out of character for her.

William shook his head, silently.

"That was a joke," Robin shot back.

"No more jokes tonight," William pleaded in a soft voice.

Robin sidled up to William as he ate, putting her arm around him.

"I saw a kid today that just might save my job," William confided, with a tone that belied the gravest of sincerity.

"You went to a game?" Robin inquired, quizzically.

"That's why I'm late. His name is Savior. And that's not a joke. He's the best high school player I've seen in my life. An amazing talent," William let the words flow with a renewed sense of hope and admiration.

Robin hugged him.

"I'm so happy for you," she gave him a squeeze.

"For us," William replied, returning the affectionate gesture.

"For us," Robin agreed.

"Even if I can get him for a year or two before he goes pro I can't see how we'd lose. He'd put Easton on the map," William stated emphatically.

"And Coach Cunningham," Robin beamed.

"Yeah," William agreed enthusiastically.

Suddenly, a flash of concern crossed Robin's face.

"But won't he be recruited by the big schools, like Duke and Kentucky?" she pressed.

"Sure. I have a sense about this kid. He's bright. Even a few years here would prepare him for the world he's gonna be living in," William answered.

"Save him from Newark," Robin chimed in.

William shook his head, and then confronted Robin.

"That's the other thing I wanted to mention. Newark is changing. I hardly recognize it any more. There's an energy and a vitality the city hasn't seen in years. The new mayor and his administration have done wonders for the people. Developers are coming in; beautiful buildings have gone up; people are moving back in to live there as well as work there. There are cultural events galore. Remember how you said those kids had Brandi all confused— how she was the only kid in her class from a multi-racial family, and she didn't know whether to identify herself as Black or White? The thought even crossed my mind about moving us there, so Brandi wouldn't feel so out of place," William admitted.

Robin slammed her hand on the table.

"Over my dead body will you take my daughter to Newark," she shouted, as she stormed out of the room, throwing a cup into the sink and shattering it.

William continued chewing his steak, his eyes straight ahead.

CHAPTER 50

WHERE DO WE BELONG?

Sometimes a man can only find solace when he returns to his roots—when he comes from his strengths. William, like most of us, knew this deep down. He often felt as if he had to constantly break down walls to get where he wanted to go—race walls, gender walls, class walls... it seemed like the walls confronting him and blocking his path just never ended. When he walked onto the basketball court, there were no walls—a clear path lay in front of him. It didn't matter in the least to William that he never went pro; it mattered that his coaching career had hit a wall.

Night had set in. William finished another painfully quiet dinner with Robin. He felt worse for Brandi than he did for himself. He could feel her tension as he tucked her in. He stood in the kitchen doorway, watching Robin finish the dishes. He didn't even know how to approach her any more. He simply stood in the doorway and announced,

"I'm going out", and left.

William pulled into the campus, parked in his usual spot, walked into the gym and suited up in an Easton jersey. He heard a few girls laughing in the pool down the hall. Otherwise, he saw and heard no one. He took to the court and began the same drills he put his team through at practice. He never lost his touch. Lay up after lay up, he kept sinking baskets. He grabbed the rebound, spun around and came face to face with Gordon, who questioned why he was here now. Without answering, William went for the three-pointer and made it. As he retrieved the ball, without breaking the intensity of his concentration, he replied,

"The gym always feels like home."

"Is that why you were so good?" Gordon queried.

"That's only part of it. *Needing to be good* is another part. You have that. I'm not sure about the rest," William replied, turning away and sinking another foul shot, seemingly effortlessly.

"They try, but they don't need it," Gordon confided, referring to his teammates.

"Neither do you," William responded, dribbling past Gordon and sinking a jump shot.

"Yeah, I've been making a habit of not doing what is expected of me," Gordon acknowledged.

"That's why you're my captain," William offered, passing the ball to Gordon.

Gordon took the shot and missed.

"Maybe I should be spending more time here," Gordon admitted.

William set the ball down, dropped onto the bottom row of the bleachers and mopped his brow with a towel. Gordon joined him. Without meeting his eyes, William stared across the court as he spoke.

"Sometimes I wonder if I'm not just spinning my wheels here. Easton isn't exactly—"

"Duke, I know. But...never mind," Gordon cut himself off.

"Go ahead," insisted William, eyeing him.

"I don't know. Like you, Coach, you had a tryout with the Celtics. The chances of me going pro are slim. But I love basketball, this team..." Gordon urged, holding William's gaze.

"I guess I just take pride in it," he continued.

"You're gonna go far in life, Gordon," William nodded and patted him on the shoulder.

"Coach, don't give up on us," Gordon implored.

William nodded, then extended his fist and Gordon met it with his own fist.

"Come on; I need a Sundae," William rose up from the bleachers.

"Really?" Gordon answered.

"Really," William replied, smiling.

The two of them slapped one another on the back and walked off the court together.

The next few days passed as uneventfully as ever. Before practice, William found a quiet moment and dialed his old friend Evan. He needed that steadiness, that voice of reason. It seemed like time stopped whenever they spoke. Evan's demeanor never changed. Best of all, William knew he could count on him.

"Ev, William. You in the middle of a deal? If you are, I'll talk to you later."

"It wouldn't matter if I was, if you needed to talk to me," Evan replied.

"Well, it happens I do. Listen, things have not been so good here lately. I wish you and I weren't so far apart. I would come and see you. This feels awkward on the phone. Any way, this gig is getting tired here at Easton, and the powers that be—well, they would like to can my ass. I can deal with that…it's your cousin I don't know how to deal with. Robin and I have not been getting along well lately. I'm sure we can get through it, but I'm afraid it's really taking a toll on Brandi," William blurted out.

"William, now hear me out. A job is a job; it's not the end of your career. You can always get another job. Nobody can take your talent away from you. Now, let's keep our balance and let's keep our perspective here. So you and Robin have had some disagreements; that doesn't mean you're headed for divorce court. Everyone has a fight every now and then. Nobody has gotten violent; neither of you has left the other; you're not having an affair and neither is she, so it's not really that bad now, is it?" Evan prodded.

"I suppose not," William admitted.

"Look, here's what I want you to do, and I mean this. The next time Robin gets upset with you, just don't let her push your buttons. Instead of thinking of how you'll come back at her, think of yourself on the basketball court. Imagine yourself going for a jump shot. You'll be amazed at the difference in what happens. Look, right now, it's action-reaction, action-reaction with the two of you. I know my cousin. If you come at her with empathy and acknowledge her hurt, she won't over-react. If you come at her with anger, she'll just get defensive, like a lioness defending her cubs," Evan continued.

"So you really don't think I have anything to worry about with her?" William probed.

"William, it's all in how you handle it. You know this. You teach this on the basketball court. It's the same in life. It's not about what *happens* to you; it's about what you *do* about what happens to you. Look, you can't entirely separate what's going on with your job from what's going on in your home life. Robin feels you pulling away from her, too," Evan asserted.

"Thank you, my friend; thank you. I always feel better after I talk to you, Evan."

"Now, just go and get on with your life, William," Evan replied.

William knew Evan had his head on straight. But it's one thing to know something intellectually; it's yet another to know it emotionally—and to put it into practice. He vowed to do it.

After a long, hard day of practice, William felt the usual frustration. He knew the team had given him what they had. But it wasn't enough to create a win. He needed the missing element. He needed a savior, literally. He needed Savior Ruffin. He avoided any unnecessary confrontations with Chamber Higgins. He sat in his office long after everyone had gone home, reviewing the season's stat's. He pulled out every news clip he could. He even reviewed the videotapes of the team's games and their practices. Finally, William pulled his watch out of his pants pocket where he had stashed it. The hour grew late. He called Robin to let her know he was on his way home. He just felt drained.

As much as he tried to soothe Robin, he felt powerless to stop the chasm from widening between them. Each felt the other slipping away. After dinner, Robin put Brandi to bed. Then, she quietly put herself to bed without even saying a word to William. He felt like confronting her and shattering the silence, but he thought better of it. Evan's words echoed in his head. Instead, he slumped into the living room couch and began flipping through the TV channels. He intently watched a college basketball game until he could no longer keep his eyes open. Finally, he drifted off to sleep on the couch. It was a restful sleep and he needed it desperately.

Finally, William arose and glanced at the cable TV box, trying to focus his eyes on the clock. It read 4 A.M. He shook his head, went into the downstairs bathroom and doused his face with cold water. He climbed the stairs, peering into the open door of Brandi's room. She stirred, and seeing him, sat up.

"Hey, daddy."

"Hey pumpkin. How are you feeling?"

"It doesn't hurt as much today," she admitted.

"The antibiotics are working. That's good," William smiled at her, sitting on the edge of the bed.

"I don't want an operation, daddy," Brandi implored.

"Let's not worry about that for now," William put his arm around her to reassure her.

"You think I can stay home from school today?" Brandi looked at him, wide-eyed.

"I thought you said it feels better," William responded.

Brandi wrinkled her nose and furrowed her brow, as she often did.

"It's not *that much* better," she offered.

"Let's wait until mommy wakes up. She knows what's best," William assured her, as Robin entered the room and sat next to Brandi.

"I think we better give it one more day before you go back to school," she replied, and Brandi hugged her. William leaned over and sneaked a kiss on Robin's cheek. She pretended not to notice.

"Have daddy help you dress while I make breakfast," Robin said as she left the room. Brandi jumped up out of bed and began to rifle through her drawers for the perfect stay-at-home outfit.

After an early, leisurely breakfast, William left the house and headed for work, leaving Robin to care for Brandi. He sensed his old confidence returning as he reviewed Evan's advice. After all, "It's just a job; it's not your whole career. You can always get another job." He deposited his attaché case under the desk and trotted right into Chamber Higgins' office. Chamber looked up at him, mildly surprised.

"You want to win?" William asked him.

Chamber laughed before responding.

"Is that a trick question, Cunningham?" Chamber pursed his lips.

"I need you to have my back," William confronted him, staring him down.

"What's up?" Chamber quizzed.

"Savior Ruffin. I've seen him in action. He's the best thing out of Newark since Cleo Hill," William held his ground. Chamber leaned back in his chair.

"Come on, " Chamber exhaled.

William banged on Chamber's desk.

"Listen to me. We get this kid and I guarantee a championship," William asserted.

"Great! Get him," Chamber replied, flatly.

"He needs a full grant and no loans," William insisted.

"Do I look like Houdini?" Chamber waved his arms at William.

"High major schools are throwing the kitchen sink at this kid," William countered.

"Breezy Smith plays by our rules and he gets them," Chamber flexed his arms and locked his hands behind his head.

"You don't get it! This kid is going pro in a year or two from anywhere. But after we win, I'll have the street cred to get more players—the best players you ever saw," William railed.

"My hands are tied; you know the rules," Chamber snorted at him.

"If you can't jump, you can't dunk. And these kids on this team can't. And if I hear one more thing about Breezy Smith…" William fumed, clenching his fists on Chamber's desk.

Chamber rose to his feet, drawing himself up, his veins popping as he attacked William.

"I don't like your tone."

"I don't like—"

"Give me a reason," Chamber turned and went back to his desk.

William caught himself, sat back down opposite Chamber and took a deep breath.

"I'll get him—with these rules," William coolly responded, dropping his voice level.

Chamber poured himself a glass of water, paused, and then leaned across the desk to William.

"You think Savior is gonna run a Princeton offense?"

"If teams can run it in the NBA, why can't this kid do it here? He will if I tell him to; a PRO is a PRO," William assured Chamber, before leaving the office.

CHAPTER 51

SOMETHING ABOUT A HOME

The pace of life quickens. Not much else really changed since William studied at Easton. Now the students spent more time on their computers than they did watching television. The Easton basketball team members were no exception. This internet thing became the real game changer, when all was said and done. Everyone knew everything about everyone else now. And once it was out there, it stayed there. Gordon leaned in to read the text on his screen and did not look happy. He ran out and brought Ritchie in, urging him to read it, too.

"I don't believe it. Its' just a stupid blog," Ritchie asserted.

"Blogs tell the truth or else no one will listen to them," Gordon countered.

"Breezy Smith wins every year. Easton would be a step down," Ritchie shook his head in disbelief.

"Unless Easton is throwing serious cash his way," Gordon replied, flatly.

"Well, even if it's true, what can we do about it?" Ritchie threw his hands up in frustration.

"I just feel bad for Coach Cunningham," Gordon brooded, looking out the dormitory window.

"He is a good guy. It's not his fault you can't hit a three," Ritchie shot back at him.

Gordon flashed Ritchie a look of annoyance.

"Look Gordon, we're seniors. Let's stop pretending basketball is in our futures and worry more about the front page of the "Wall Street Journal", Ritchie offered, as he exited the blog and pulled up the famed business journal's website.

"Right, and when your company is being leveraged out, and the stockholders are screaming, and you need to stand in front of the board and show nerve—nerve that you learned right here when the game is on the line because you care—basketball will prepare you for that moment. And it's gonna come, just like Coach Cunningham is gonna have to man up and find another job, another coaching job, after the record we gave him," Gordon fired back at Ritchie, his face flushed.

Ritchie grew silent, picked up a basketball and twirled it in his hands, then thrust it into Gordon's chest. Gordon grabbed the pass, never taking his eyes off of Ritchie.

"It's not my fault. It's not your fault either. It's his life. And there's nothing we can do about it. It's not like we're gonna turn Black over night and learn to jump," Ritchie replied, sullenly.

"Speak for yourself," Gordon let the words roll off his tongue slowly and deliberately.

"I speak for the team. You can't jump," Ritchie asserted.

Gordon held his gaze, and then spoke.

"There *is* something we can do."

Ritchie glared back at him, stood up and declared,

"I'll tell you one thing I won't do—something stupid. I won't screw up graduation. Let's not go there."

Gordon rose up, got in his face and let Ritchie have it right back.

"Do me a favor and reach down your pants. Do you feel balls or Milk Duds?"

Gordon shook his head and knocked into Ritchie's shoulder as he headed out the door, still seething.

The Cunningham household still had a pall hanging over it—the kind you can almost see. Robin continued her coldness; William kept a safe distance; and Brandi just rolled along with it all, more worried about her ear infections than her parents' petty squabbles. William arose from his sleep on the living room couch and squinted to read the time on the cable TV box—5 A.M. He had become accustomed to this; so much so, he now kept his clothes in the downstairs guest closet, avoiding any unnecessary confrontations with Robin. He got dressed and quietly climbed the stairs. He peered in to Brandi's room, watching her sleep. William silently entered the room, kissed his two fingers and put them on her heart. He left the house without incident.

The Subaru lurched as William peeled out of the driveway in reverse, then shifted and rumbled down the street. He never did replace that noisy muffler. He pulled onto the crowded highway, impatient. Sitting in traffic, he began anxiously punching the buttons on his radio dial. Finally, he stopped on a station playing rap music, then turned up the volume, blasted the radio and lowered his windows. He turned and noticed a conservative looking White couple stealing glances at him. He turned up the volume even more. The traffic finally broke and William practically floored the accelerator on the Subaru. The rest of the trip turned into a blur. William pulled into the hospital parking lot, searched for a space and turned the key. The sounds of the city enveloped him. He felt at home as he made his way through the all too familiar doors of the Beth Israel Medical Center. Like so many hospitals, Newark's pride and joy had been taken over, now part of the St. Barnabas system—all in the name of progress, of course. William wondered about that. Who had more money? The powerful Catholic Church, or the Jews? It didn't really matter.

He stopped in to the cafeteria, ordered a cup of coffee and a bagel and took a table by the doorway. No sooner than he began to chow down on his breakfast, Lillian walked in, dressed for work. Surprised to see William, she stopped in her tracks, put her hands on her hips and addressed him.

"Don't you have a job?"

William smiled, rose up from his seat, and much to her surprise, kissed her.

Lillian stood her ground, slung her shoulder bag over and circled him.

"I'm a tough city girl, but there's only so much I can take."

William, unfazed by her answer, folded his newspaper under his arm, extended his other arm to her and replied,

"I know. Let's go see Coach."

Lillian accepted the offer, took his arm and they headed for the elevator. They shared the ride in silence, with one older couple in front of them, leaning on canes. They entered Coach's room in silence, holding onto one another as a small Filipino nurse's aid and a large Black nurse checked his machines, adjusting his intravenous drip. He did not appear to be doing well at all. The nurse, who had been oblivious to their entrance, turned to William and Lillian.

"I'm sorry; there won't be visiting hours today. He needs rest."

William and Lillian both felt drained at the sight of Coach, who did not so much as open his eyes, even as they left the room. They descended the floors in the elevator, Lillian holding William's arm. They left the building and William spun Lillian around to face him.

"You have time before work? I'd like to see the Boys and Girls Club."

"You remember where it is?" Lillian teased him, peaking over the top of her tinted glasses, as she always did.

"Come with me," William pressed her hand.

"I got a job," Lillian released his grip.

"I saw your house," William confided.

"Savior told me," Lillian responded.

"Ruffin?" William quizzed her.

Lillian couldn't hide her pleasure.

"You remember; our favorite singer. I got my reasons. Some things haven't changed in Newark. And I thought, if you heard the name, maybe... forget it."

Lillian moved away from William, overcome by a sea of emotion.

"Is he—" William queried.

"Would you be here, talking to me if he was just some kid dreaming of college? If his talent was in his head and not in his leg?" Lillian answered, sorely.

"Hey—" William retorted.

"Hey, nothing. You know what it took for me to get him to this point. Fact is he don't need basketball. I made sure of that," Lillian shot back.

William raised his palms in a gesture of surrender and took a step back before answering.

"I want the same for Brandi," he insisted.

"And so does your wife, I'm sure," Lillian added.

Lillian went to cover her face as William leaned in to kiss her gently on the cheek, before responding,

"Come by tomorrow. Sorry, I'm confused."

William smiled, buttoning his jacket, as he replied,

"Like I said, it's complicated."

The neighborhood surrounding the Boys and Girls Club had not yet been blessed with urban renewal. It still looked like it did in William's day—like a bombed out ghetto. William pushed his way through the

270

graffiti-covered exterior door and stood in the vestibule. It even smelled the same. He gazed through the gym doors, and then entered. Peeling off his jacket and dropping it on the bleachers, he picked up a basketball. As he dribbled it toward the basket, he felt transported back twenty years. Unnoticed, Tricks walked out onto the court carrying a beer bottle wrapped in a paper bag. Drunk, he looked like a mess. When he saw William, he put the beer down and tried to hug him. William drew back and confronted him.

"Man, I just had breakfast and you smell like beer."

William's statement sobered up Tricks.

"What the hell are you doing here? Go back to your suburb and your fancy-assed Whole foods market. We don't need you."

"Easy, Tricks. I'm just worried about you," William replied, sincerely.

"You don't care about nothing but your own ass. Always been like that. Ran the first chance you got and never looked back. This was a bad idea," Tricks lashed out at him as William swished the ball into the basket from the foul line.

"That's an 'H' for you," William responded, never taking his eyes off the ball.

Tricks considered William, then broke into a smile and said,

"Make it Cat. Too early for Horse," as he missed the shot from the foul line. But his face hardened; he's ready now.

William shot from the corner and missed; Tricks made a lefty hook from the key; William missed; Tricks banked in a lefty lay-up that William missed.

Tricks steadied himself from the foul line and nailed a lefty free throw. William remained at the foul line, bounced the ball three times, and then missed the lefty free throw.

Tricks grinned.

"You still got no left."

Tricks and William embraced each other with the conviction that only comes from true friendship.

William drew a deep sigh, and then exhaled.

"This place doesn't look half bad."

Tricks mopped his brow, dropped down on the bleachers, catching his breath.

"I try. Not been easy. Since Coach got sick, the city is cutting the funds. Said unless we get…"

William nodded, then answered,

"Let's see what we can do."

Tricks slapped the ball between his hands, looked up at William quizzically and inquired,

"What you doing here so early?"

"I'd like to see Savior before L.J. wakes up," he replied, taking a seat beside Tricks.

Tricks nodded, turned to William and replied,

"You got to see him sometime."

"I know. Savior first," William replied.

CHAPTER 52

WHAT MAKES A HOME?

When they say you can choose your friends but you can't choose your family, nothing rings truer. One quick phone call from the highway rest stop, and much to her surprise, Robin greeted her sister Christine at the door. Christine had a way of just settling in—no, make that taking over. She hadn't shown her face at the Cunningham household since William and Robin's anniversary party four years ago. Now, she made herself at home, sipping tea in William's easy chair, as Brandi ran around the house in her usual high-energy fashion. Christine eyed Brandi with that holier-than-thou attitude which accompanied her everywhere she went.

"You don't look sick to me," Christine pronounced.

"I love you, Auntie," Brandi assured her as she flitted past Christine and left the room.

Christine stared Robin down with an accusatory look.

"You need to protect that girl."

"She's fine," Robin asserted, as she folded her freshly washed laundry.

Christine sipped her tea, inhaled and let her words drop like bombs on Robin.

"Here. Not in Newark. I mean, what the hell is he thinking?"

Robin continued folding the laundry, not even looking up as she replied,

"I don't know. He gets like this every few years. When things get tough he wants to run home."

Christine practically slammed her teacup into the saucer to emphasize her words.

"Home? Excuse me, but a crack den is hardly a home."

Robin stood up, lifting the pile of neatly folded sheets and towels and flatly replied,

"William has never done drugs."

Christine rolled her eyes. This time, Robin returned her stare.

"Hey..."

"Come on, Robin..."

Christine waved her hands, as if to say, "Forget it." Robin dug her heels in.

"Black and Newark equals drugs?"

Christine ran her index finger around the rim of the coffee cup, flipped her hair back in a haughty gesture, sighed and continued.

"No...look. I—our family, just wants you back in Holyoke. Brandi will go to Middlesex Academy, like you did. Back home."

Robin leaned across the table to Christine and took hold of her hand as she confronted her.

"*This* is home now; Brandi and William *are* home."

Christine's stare grew icy as she gripped Robin's hand harder.

"He wants you to take Brandi back to Newark—enough said."

Robin straightened up and gritted her teeth as she responded,

"You don't like him because he's what—too Black for you? Got a basketball assistance instead of an academic scholarship—"

"Like you did for pre-med and quit that after you got—"

"He could never have gotten in without his intellect," Robin insisted.

"Grow up, Robin. He's from a broken home. He was raised in a gym. We're worried about Brandi," Christine withdrew her compact from her purse and checked her make-up.

"Excuse me?" Robin swung around, placing the stack of linens on the coffee table.

"This is not late breaking news. Ask Bill Cosby. He's begging African-American fathers to raise their kids," Christine pontificated as she re-applied her lipstick with a deliberate motion.

Robin felt the anger well up inside of her.

"He's never left me or Brandi. He's a good father."

"Newark?" Christine gloated.

"How dare you?" Robin's temper flared as she gritted her teeth.

Christine continued in her usual condescending tone,

"You're my sister, Robin. I love you and Brandi. Come home; we'll take care of you."

"This *is* my home," Robin asserted, as she began to tear up.

Christine continued to casually re-apply her make-up as she went on with her diatribe.

"Don't you see the writing on the wall? He's taking his first steps back to his old life."

Robin stopped in her tracks at Christine's words, just as Brandi re-entered the room. Brandi took "center stage" between her mother and her aunt, commanding both women's attention.

"Watch this," she implored them, as she twirled a cheerleader's baton.

Christine, oblivious to Brandi, continued on.

"Look, Robin, our family asked me to come here for you and Brandi."

Robin folded her arms across her chest and held her position.

"You've been looking for an excuse for me to leave him ever since we got married."

"And here it is," Christine intoned, as she stood up, slipping her shoes back on.

Robin picked up a magazine from the coffee table and hurled it at her, responding,

"He wouldn't leave us."

"Then why did you call me?" Christine responded, buttoning and belting her sweater.

Robin's confusion showed, along with her anger. She began to circle the living room, slapping her leg in frustration.

"We love you. Come home," Christine announced, mechanically.

Robin continued circling the room as Christine repeated herself.

"We love you; come home. *Please* come home."

Robin stopped and screamed,

"*This* is my home. Now leave it and never return."

Brandi returned to the room without her baton and hugged Robin. Christine composed herself, then left without saying a word to Robin or Brandi. After the door closed, Robin began to sob. Although she tried, she could not restrain herself. Brandi approached her, worried.

"Mommy, I'm scared. Is everything Okay? Is it okay? I have to know."

"Don't worry; we'll be okay," Robin assured Brandi as she hugged her, dried her tears with the back of her hand and stroked Brandi's cheek.

"When's daddy coming home?" Brandi urged Robin for an answer.

"Soon, sweetheart, soon," Robin replied, as the question burned into her consciousness. She wished she knew the answer herself.

At that very moment, William found himself walking with Tricks through one of Newark's toughest neighborhoods. The hardened faces of the hopeless peered back at them from alleyways and front stoops. Even the beat up cars and graffiti seemed to grimace back at them with menacing looks. The scene resembled a war zone. Finally, they arrived at a fenced-in, worn out looking basketball court. Faded paint marked the key and the barely discernible foul lines. Remnants of the basket hung from a weathered hoop; the backboard pummeled from thousands of slaps.

As they approached, William and Tricks noticed L.J. intently watching Savior play his game. They can't help but notice the players, as they engage in a hard, fast, tough game of street ball—not the genteel brand of prep school ball played on most college campuses. Tricks leaned in to William.

"You call a foul here and you might as well be calling for your momma."

William acknowledged, responding to Tricks under his breath,

"I need to bring my team here to see this."

As swift as he is, Savior finds himself pushed off the blocks by Keyshawn, who is bigger, older, stronger and meaner. Then, without hesitation, Savior spun and dunked right in Keyshawn's face, gloating and laughing as he completed his moves. William, impressed, reacted, confiding in Tricks.

"I can't believe Michael was even this good at his age."

"He's Newark's proud son," Tricks replied.

Just then, Keyshawn pushed Savior and L.J. planted himself on the court squarely between them.

"That's enough bustin' ass for today, Savior. Go home now," L.J. commanded, as he got in Keyshawn's face.

"Don't worry; I ain't gonna hurt your meal ticket," Keyshawn insisted to L.J.

Before Keyshawn can react, L.J. landed a punch. Keyshawn, in turn, lunged at L.J., taking him to the pavement. As they struggled, L.J. wrestled, landed on top of Keyshawn and whipped out a handgun.

"You damn right you're not gonna hurt him," L.J. shouted.

Keyshawn stared down the barrel of the cold steel weapon in silence.

"You play nice, you keep your head. Got it?" L.J. continued, his nostrils flaring.

Keyshawn nodded slowly; L.J. let him up and Keyshawn sauntered off, leaving the court. L.J. shot a glance at William.

"Didn't I tell you to leave my boy alone?" L.J. pressed William. "I just—"

"It's cool, L.J. He knows I ain't going to Easton. Just talking," Savior put a hand on L.J.'s shoulder.

L.J. eyed William for what seemed like an awfully long moment.

"About what, then?" L.J. inquired.

"It's cool, L.J.," Savior assured him.

"Just sharing some of my experiences in high school," William added in a conciliatory tone.

L.J. continued with another long stare, then laughed again.

"Shit, you whiter than paint now. Share, just sharing. Man, go share your shit," L.J. prodded.

L.J. and Buzzy slapped hands and strolled away, mocking William. Savior, William and Tricks walked off in the opposite direction.

"Man, he's worse than my mother sometimes," Savior shook his head.

"And more dangerous," William acknowledged.

"I don't know about that," Savior replied.

William smiled at that last exchange.

"I do want to talk about Easton," William confided.

"I mean no disrespect, but I need to show what I can do against real competition. The Human…" Savior replied.

"Humanitarian League," William answered.

Savior nodded, grinning.

"Too easy," Savior responded.

"Take an official school visit; see why maybe Easton *would* be a great place for you," William urged Savior.

"I only get five of them," Savior replied, not moving. "I'll talk to my mother."

William looked Savior over, as if he was inspecting him."

"I'll talk to my mother," Savior repeated.

"Son, when I was growing up and in your shoes, my coach told me something I never forgot. Basketball is the bait, but academics are the hook. One day you'll be my age and you won't be jumping out of the gym any more. Understand?" William offered.

Savior took in William's every word, but did not answer.

William and Tricks made their way back to William's car. The two men exchanged glances that told the whole story. No words required. William knew he had just taken an important step. Tricks knew it, too.

William returned home tired. He did not share the day's events with Robin.

Nor did she confide in him about her sister's visit. They both just sat quietly together until Brandi's bedtime. When she was settled, Robin encouraged him to come to bed with her for the first time in two weeks. Both of them slept soundly.

The next day, William's resolve grew stronger, along with his determination. The team suited up for practice. He began to work them hard. Jason failed to go up for a rebound that he should have gone for. William blew the whistle.

"Are you guys trying NOT to make the dance? March Madness not in your schedule? Animal drill," William barked at them, pointing to Gordon, Ritchie and Jason.

Jason confronted Gordon.

"What happened to the Princeton offense?"

The two of them moved under the basket and began boxing. William shot and missed on purpose. Ritchie hip checked Gordon and Jason grabbed the rebound. Gordon and Ritchie eyed one another. At that moment, Chamber Higgins entered the gym, checking in on the practice. Another shot missed and Gordon nailed Ritchie with an elbow to the nose, drawing blood. Ritchie and Gordon began to go at each other, both furious.

"Is this what you want? Is this gonna make us win?" Gordon snarled at William.

"It just might," William shot back at him.

Ritchie took a towel from one of the student assistants and slowed the bleeding down to a trickle.

"More," Ritchie announced.

Reluctantly, Gordon got under the basket with Jason and Ritchie as they fought for the rebound. This time, Ritchie fought off both Jason and Gordon and made a nice reverse lay-up after the rebound. Ritchie eyed Gordon, who extended his fist; Ritchie smacked it.

The whistle blew. William motioned to the team.

"That's enough; circle to me," William shouted.

The players circled around William as he scanned each of their faces. He looked over to Benny, a scrawny kid whose chances of getting into the next game were zero. Benny looked at his teammates as William addressed him.

"Benny, how's your father doing?" William inquired.

"He's okay. They think they got all of the tumor," he answered.

"You ready?" William asked him.

"Yes, sir," Ben replied.

William nodded.

"Sid, I like your defense the last three practices. Be ready in case their point gets hot," William cautioned.

Sid, a twelfth man if there ever was one, flicked glances to his teammates and nodded to William.

"Win, win, we're in. We lose, strippers, Atlantic City, on me," William announced, his face revealing nothing.

The boys pinged looks at one another, waiting for somebody to react.

Gordon cracked first, with a big grin. William spun around, facing him.

"That was a joke."

The boys all exploded into laughter. William and Gordon nodded, as William stopped in front of Sid.

"I think Sid still wants to lose," William surveyed him.

"He's got something to do under his sheets tonight besides study," Ben piped up.

The boys slapped Sid playfully. William motioned for the boys to huddle.

William nodded to Sid, who raised his fist.

"We win as one; we lose as one," Sid affirmed.

"Win!" the shout went up from all of the team members in unison.

Chamber motioned to William to come into his office. Chamber closed the door behind them and launched into his diatribe.

"What the hell do you think you're doing?" Chamber glared at William.

"Trying to win," William replied, holding his gaze.

"All we need is a lawsuit," Chamber retorted.

William waited for the proverbial other shoe to drop, then responded.

"Atlantic City was just—"

"Animal drills?" Chamber shot back at William, leaning across his desk.

William threw up his arms in protest before responding.

"You did. I did. Anyone that's played organized basketball has done animal drills."

"Don't lecture me," Chamber admonished.

"I guarantee Breezy does it," William answered in a cavalier tone.

"Why, because he's Black?" Chamber nearly blew up at William.

"Damn right. These boys are soft. You know it and I know it," William fired back.

"We don't need to draw blood," Chamber pointed his finger at William.

"That's exactly what we need. I was in Newark yesterday. If you call a foul you might as well be calling your momma," William asserted.

"This isn't Newark," Chamber gritted his teeth at William.

"A little bit of Newark is just what we need here," William countered.

Chamber stepped out from behind his desk and slumped down on the sofa as William continued.

"I think we can get this kid Savior. I'm bringing him here for a visit," William insisted.

"If he's as good as you say, why would he come here?" Chamber offered, downing a cup of water from the water cooler.

"Me," William replied confidently.

Chamber nodded his head, the veins in his forehead still popping from the confrontation.

"Let's see the kid first," Chamber answered.

"Fair enough," William responded, feeling the sweat bead up on his forehead.

"Maybe I underestimated you," Chamber offered.

"You're not the first," William stated, flatly.

"Granted. But there is the matter of Wilma Kraut," Chamber looked like the poker player that had just revealed his hidden cards.

"That bitch. Look, I don't know what you heard, but let's set the record straight right here and now. I attended that Faculty Senate Promotions Committee meeting just like you asked me to, when you had to take your wife for those medical tests. Associate Dean Kraut had it in for me the minute I walked in the door. She fought me on every suggestion I made. I remained a gentleman; I kept my cool and I approached her after the meeting. I told her we were on the same side, and that we were both fighting a common battle of discrimination. She insisted that we had no racism at Easton, only sexism. Then she accused me of being part of the problem instead of part of the solution. That's when she got my back up. I asked her if everyone with a dick was part of the problem. That's when she stormed away—and that was the end of it. I swear. Ask anyone who was there," William insisted.

Chamber just nodded.

CHAPTER 53

STRAIGHT TO THE HEART

William's strength had always come from that deepest part of him—the part that Coach recognized and awakened when William's uncle Ben first introduced him to his future mentor. When a man—or a woman, reaches down into that place where he or she stores the darkest fears—that's where talent comes from. Sometimes we lose touch with our strength. We need to rediscover it all over again. For so many men, that's the role a woman plays in their lives. For couples who are soul mates, that's the role each plays for the other. For some, it's their faith.

William had become rudderless—adrift in a sea of pain, blinded by the pounding surf—and unwilling to reach for a helping hand. Without Robin's support, completely out of touch with religion, where would he find guidance, strength or solace? Secretly, he sometimes wished he would find it in Lillian. He knew he could not take much more of Robin's coldness, of Chamber's threats...and his team's shortfalls. Where could he turn?

Basketball is a funny sport. Not because of the players or the fans; it just has a different and almost unexplainable dynamic. Teams function like well-oiled machines, but they malfunction when the big gears don't engage. William always knew how to lubricate the gears to get them moving and to build momentum. He knew whom he needed to talk to. Very quietly and very discreetly, he waited for the right moment—when Chamber locked his office and left for lunch. William approached Binky Hall, a short hulking man with the aspect of a professional body builder. How he ever got the nickname Binky, no one could ever figure out. Maybe he just didn't like the name Bill. Binky had been the Equipment Manager at Easton for several years. He knew things. William approached him, extended his hand and offered a bottle of water. The two men slid down the wall and sat on the hallway floor.

"Ain't seen much of you around here lately, Coach Cunningham," Binky took a long draught, sucking down the cool water.

"Likewise. Been busy, my man. I need a favor. Binky, you've always had my back and I appreciate that. It means a great deal to me," William confided.

Binky studied William intently, waiting to find out how he could help. He never asked for anything in return. That was his nature. William continued, twirling his water bottle like a basketball.

"Bink, you've got the pulse of the school at your fingertips and in your head; not just the gym and the athletic department, but the whole power structure here at Easton. When Wilma Kraut attacked me and tried to get me canned, you knew what to tell me to do. It ain't over yet, I can tell you that. Chamber's gunning for me; I know it. I feel like the walls are closing in. Tell me what I need to do," William urged him for an answer.

Binky leaned his head back against the wall, his massive bull neck flush against it. He closed his eyes for a few seconds, opened them and looked down at the water bottle. Then, he blurted out the answer, much to William's surprise.

"Make a peace offering. Go the extra mile for Dean Kraut's cause; do her a solid. Do something tangible and visible for the women on campus. You'll see; it will come back to you big time," Binky offered.

William, at first incredulous, took in his words, considering the outcome and the effect. It made perfect sense to him. He felt re-energized. Both men stood up, locked their hands in a powerful grip and each went his separate way. Binky's words echoed in William's head. Why fight someone when you can become his or her ally? As the day went on, he began to formulate a plan to deal with L.J., using the Binky theory, as he began to call it. Now, if he could just apply the same strategy to his marriage, his life's journey would go a lot smoother.

That night, William tucked Brandi in after dinner. He felt bad knowing he planned to leave again, even for just a day, when she still had severe discomfort from the earaches. Robin turned in early. Much to his surprise, she did not question him when he said he needed to leave early the next morning. For the first time that week, he felt full of resolve—and he slept soundly.

William peeled out of the driveway just after daybreak, stopped in to the campus, checked in to his office and set up one of the student assistants to cover his daytime duties. In minutes, he flew out the door, stopped at the convenience store, filled the tank of the Subaru, filled his coffee thermos and headed onto Route 78 East. The sun glare and the traffic proved relentless. He hit the button on the radio and pulled in Allentown's classic rock station. Enough of that. Headed for Newark, he needed to get in the groove. He punched the seek and scan buttons until he found a rap song. Although he felt strong, he would need to put himself in the zone for what lay ahead. He reached back and slung the bag he had stashed onto the front seat. Like a warrior, he had his armor and his weapons at the ready.

William glided off the ramp onto McCarter Highway in Newark. He passed through the Ironbound section and headed for the old neighborhood. Glimpses of discount tire stores and bodegas flashed by. He turned off of Broad Street onto the cobble stone side street, crossing over the tracks of the still active Newark subway system. Broken glass sparkled from the sidewalk; gang graffiti in day glow colors assaulted his eyes. Razor wire topped an empty lot with a burned out foundation. He parked on the sidewalk and walked around the corner to the basketball court, the bag over his shoulder. He spied L.J. and two of his thugs, Koby and Sleeper-Z, cutting up. L.J. turned, spotted William and assumed his scowling mask.

"I'm getting' pretty tired of seein' y'all. Pretty soon, I'll be treatin' you like any other White man or cop that comes down here."

William reached in the bag and withdrew five tickets, slapping them into Koby's hand.

"Yo, man, Nike town? Keep it comin'," Koby wailed.

"Size twelve next time, ya dig?" Sleeper-Z peered over William's shoulder, into the bag.

L.J. stood off to the side, arms folded over his chest, disinterested. William handed two tickets to him.

"Court side; Nets, Knicks," William proudly announced.

Finally, L.J. broke into a smile. William addressed him, toe to toe.

"I'd like to take Savior to Easton for a visit."

"No problem. He ain't goin' anyhow," L.J. responded, tucking the tickets into his jacket pocket.

"Right," William answered as he strutted away.

"Yo, White boy!" L.J. shouted after him. William stopped and turned around to face him.

"Next time I want kicks, size thirteen," L.J. instructed him.

"Pardon me?" William inquired.

"Pardon me?" L.J. mocked him.

"Leave that White shit at home when you come here. You been in the House, right?"

L.J., Koby and Sleeper-Z surrounded William, waiting for his answer.

"House? Prison? Never," William replied.

"Nah, White folks don't go to the House," L.J. insisted, as he and his thugs all shook their heads.

"Hey, L.J.," William began to interject, as L.J. cut him off.

"This is how it works. Every time y'all come here, you bring a present. Then, if I feel like it, I give you a sniff. Only, since y'all are my bitch, it depends on how I feel. I owe you nothing, but you need to keep payin' every damn time," L.J. crooned as his thugs sneered.

"Them's the rules," L.J. spun around as Koby and Sleeper-Z continued laughing and high-fiving one another. William drifted away.

A few minutes later, William planted himself on a car, staring at Lillian's door. Finally, he mustered up his courage as the front door opened and Lillian appeared. He couldn't help but notice how well she filled out her pantsuit.

"I don't bite," she said, over the top of her tinted glasses.

"Just admiring the flowers," William played along.

"I don't see any chocolate, so I guess you're here for my son," Lillian responded, tossing her key ring from one hand to the other.

William shrugged, feigning disinterest.

"It seems I'll always enjoy the company of men as long as Savior stays in high school," Lillian sighed, wagging her finger at William.

"Come on. Let's get this show under way," she motioned William to enter.

He nodded and followed her inside, taking in all of her accoutrements. Lillian's condo bore all the trappings of success—iMac, Plasma TV, expensive Herman Miller furniture. Savior looked bored as he sauntered into the living room to join William and Lillian.

"Can I get you something to drink?" Lillian offered.

"It's ain't nowhere," Savior piped up.

"Leave the street language in the street, please. What is nowhere?" Lillian snapped back at him and Savior turned away.

"Diet anything is fine," William answered, settling into an overstuffed leather wing chair.

Lillian glared at Savior on her way to the kitchen.

"I can't believe I'm wasting a visit on a school I already know I ain't goin' to," Savior steamed.

"You just might be surprised at what you find there," William replied.

"What, White boys that can pass the ball? Hit an open J?" Savior railed on.

"I'm asking you to trust me," William asserted.

"Shit; all you coaches want the same thing—to win. That's all I trust," Savior snarled back at him.

William paused for a moment, falling silent. He waited for a way in, and then proceeded.

"Those schools that want you are factories. Their recruiting list is the McDonalds of 'All Americans.' If something happens to you, they get another all American next year. At Easton, we care about our players. I care about you," William assured him.

Savior went quiet as Lillian listened from the kitchen, holding back her tears. Then, she swept into the room carrying a tray filled with glasses of soda. William continued his speech.

"I understand why you might think Easton is not right—"

"Is Savior expressing doubts about Easton? We are not signing a letter of intent, are we?" Lillian leaned in anxiously, awaiting an answer.

"I only get five visits—" Savior piped up.

"And Easton will be one of them," Lillian insisted, as Savior quieted down.

"Lillian, Savior is right to be upset. Five is a small number for someone with his talent. Every coach in the land wants him. Even if it's just for a year," William affirmed.

"I want him to have an education," Lillian delivered each word with a certitude and a conviction level that meant business.

"We have time to discuss that," William assured her.

Lillian unconsciously grabbed William's arm. Savior followed the gesture with his eyes, studying her.

"But what they can't offer is me. Your mother and I...we knew each other in high school. It's personal to me that you get the best advice and guidance," William mustered all the sincerity he could as he nodded to Savior and gestured to Lillian.

Savior took a long hard look at the two adults in the room.

CHAPTER 54

OTHER WORLDS

William felt as if he had gotten a reprieve. He wondered whether Savior only agreed to come to Easton to placate his mother—or if his curiosity had gotten the better of him. Still, William was just as curious—partly because Savior had such a great talent and partly because he felt close to him, knowing Lillian had raised him. Then there was still that other thing in the back of his mind. That little voice kept William wondering. Even if Savior wasn't his son, he was the son he would have had if he and Lillian had remained together.

Finally, the day had come. William pulled the Subaru up to the curb. Before he could get out, Lillian greeted him with a big hug and a look that said, "Take good care of my baby." William knew that look. He had seen it many times before on his recruitment calls. But this time was different. Savior followed Lillian out of the house, kissed his mother goodbye and slid into the passenger seat, silent.

William decided to just let it happen, rather than trying to engineer the outcome. He kept the car radio off and just watched Savior as they whizzed out of Newark onto the highway. William felt the tension begin to dissolve. From time to time, he glanced over at Savior, noticing the youth's eyes widening at the sights. Evidently he had not seen that much of the world outside of Newark yet. William knew that feeling of amazement; he had experienced it himself. In fact, he felt like he had stared into a mirror when he looked at Savior. He saw his own history in him.

After very few casual exchanges, they finally pulled into the Easton campus. William parked in his reserved space; Savior nodded and climbed out of the car, surveying the scene. Bright morning rays of sun glared from the gleaming glass and steel buildings. As they approached the gym, William felt that quiet bond of understanding forming. The two men had entered that space where neither rank nor privilege rein; where all are equals. Savior spoke first.

"Feels like a park."

"That's the idea. They feel a calm environment promotes study," William offered.

Savior turned to him.

"You like it?"

"Took me a while. It's a shock from Newark. But I love it now," William assured him, as Savior nodded before replying.

"Syracuse had all these parties where I met alumni and stuff."

"Easton doesn't feel the need to sell the college. You need to buy into it.

You need to want it," William asserted, exuding confidence.

As they entered the gym, Savior looked around curiously at the squash courts.

"What are they?"

"Squash courts. Don't worry; I never heard of squash either before I came here," William confided.

"It's small," Savior remarked, surveying the courts.

"And fast. White folks' sport," William responded matter-of-factly.

William and Savior smiled at one another, knowingly.

"Can't be that fast," Savior replied.

"You'd be surprised," William answered, placing a hand on Savior's shoulder as he guided him toward the basketball courts.

William and Savior joined Gordon as he practiced his shots. Savior turned to William.

"Man, this is like one of Kentucky's practice gyms," Savior said, flippantly.

Gordon approached them.

"What's up?" he asked them quizzically.

Savior gave a nonchalant shrug.

"You dropped 40 on Science," Gordon acknowledged.

"Can't zone me up," Savior replied.

"Show me," Gordon challenged him, flinging the ball to Savior.

"Not now; I'm showing Savior around," William shot Gordon a look.

"No problem," Savior piped up.

"Yeah, shooting is different than dunking," Gordon needled him.

Savior rose to the challenge, grabbing the ball and nailed a three point shot. Game on. William took a seat on the bleachers. He knew to stand back and let it happen. At that moment, Jason peered in through the door, ran back to the dorm and told Ritchie to come watch Gordon play the Black kid in the gym. Savior laced up his sneakers, continued his moves and did a 360 jam. The gym began to fill with curious onlookers. About twenty students watched the action and applauded as Ritchie and the other teammates ran in. William had slipped out, joining Chamber above the gym as they observed from behind a glass partition in the rotunda.

"This is a borderline violation," Chamber quipped.

"You are looking at Easton's future revenue and credibility in this basketball league," William replied, feeling in control.

Chamber nearly stepped into the glass as he watched Savior move. Gordon, although out-matched, remained tenacious. He stole the ball from Savior, faked a drive and nailed a three point shot. Savior wasn't about to let Gordon gain any ground. He stared him down and moved in for the kill like a pool shark playing his best billiard game.

"I'm gonna tell you exactly what I'm gonna do now," he put Gordon on notice, as he backed toward the basket. Then Gordon nailed him with an elbow into the small of his back.

"I'm gonna fake left, then spin right and jam it in your face," Savior announced to Gordon

Just then, Gordon jabbed his elbow sharply into Savior's kidney.

"Keep pushing, 'cause you can't shoot," Gordon goaded Savior.

Savior faked left, spun right and jammed, nailing Gordon with an elbow to Gordon's head—delivered as promised. Then Savior spun and rocked the basket with a jam.

"All girls can shoot," Savior replied as he dropped back onto the court with a thud.

Gordon felt the impact but resisted the urge to rub his head, refusing to show any sign of weakness. William hustled into the gym, approaching Gordon first.

"You okay?" he queried.

Gordon nodded. William rubbed Gordon's head where Savior's elbow hit, bringing him close and whispering,

"Good D", as he slapped Gordon on the butt. Savior came over and extended his hand to Gordon, much to William's surprise. Gordon shook Savior's hand.

"C'mon. Let's take a walk," Gordon invited Savior.

Chamber and William watched as Gordon and Ritchie lead Savior out of the gym.

"That's the quality of an Easton ball player we expect," Chamber announced proudly.

"Gordon is the best we have," William agreed with him.

"I meant Savior," Chamber replied, to William's surprise.

William, about to reply, hesitated as his cell phone rang. Keeping his eyes on Chamber, he answered the call. He could discern the sound of a hospital paging system in the background. His face fell. He could hear Lillian's voice breaking as she spoke.

"Coach has passed. Come home, Willie Joe, come home," was all she could say through her tears.

William averted his eyes from Chamber as he inquired,

"When is the wake?"

He listened, nodding his head and replied,

"Wait for me at the hospital."

William stared at Chamber. Without a word, he left.

Outside, Savior walked the lush grounds of the Easton campus with Gordon and Ritchie.

"Are you gonna win the States again?" Gordon pressed Savior.

"St. Anthony's is always tough and my guard twisted his ankle. But no biggie; I'll just shoot more," Savior replied confidently.

"Just like that?" Ritchie quizzed him.

Savior just shrugged.

"You seriously thinking about coming here?" Ritchie's excitement level rose as he posed the question.

Savior shrugged again, then answered,

"Either that or I turn Pro."

Just then, two pretty coeds, Brooke and Avery, stopped Ritchie and Gordon.

"Hey guys, you coming tonight?" Brooke asked.

"Wouldn't miss it," Gordon flashed her a smile.

"Meet Savior," Ritchie interrupted.

Both girls extended their hands and Savior shook them both.

"Do you have a last name or are you a spy?" Avery teased.

"Ruffin," Savior replied.

"Oh, please tell me your father was David," Brooke pleaded.

"Oh, no, music class—" Avery nearly sung the words.

"Talking about my girl…" Brooke offered up the familiar lyric, and then proceeded to sing a few lines of the Temptations' song.

"Tell me, is that about your mother?" Brooke asked, playfully.

Savior, stunned, remained silent. Gordon came to his rescue.

"Savior is a basketball recruit," Gordon interjected.

"So, does that preclude him from being related to David Ruffin?" Brooke continued.

"I don't get that either, Gordon," Avery stated.

"No, I don't…I'm not related," Savior replied.

"Too bad," Brooke answered.

"Stay and come to the party, Savior. We'll get rid of those jocks and we'll talk about literature," Avery cooed.

"Okay," Savior nodded.

Brooke and Avery waved goodbye and continued ambling across the campus, chatting endlessly.

"Do these girls mean they want…you know…" Savior inquired.

"No, they mean talk about literature. They make you work around here for sex," Gordon replied.

"A little different than what you're used to?" Ritchie shot back at Savior.

"At Syracuse they had a party for me and the girls just asked me about basketball and then…"

"Then sex?" Gordon asked.

"If I wanted it," Savior responded, unable to contain his smile any longer.

"Bet you wish you were a great basketball player, Gordon," Ritchie nudged him.

"No shit," Gordon replied, smiling, yet unable to hide his envy.

Savior slapped hands with both Gordon and Ritchie.

"But these girls here like to talk. That's nice, too," Savior asserted.

Gordon and Ritchie eyed each other, shaking their heads "no."

"And talk and talk and—" Gordon offered.

"And talk some more," Ritchie interrupted.

"Let's show Savior the Bitter End," Gordon suggested.

"The café on campus," Ritchie explained.

"Cool," Savior responded, following their lead.

CHAPTER 55

THE GREAT DIVIDE

Every day William woke up feeling the tension kick in like a tightly wound spring. He felt as if the quintessential sword of Damocles hung over his head by a delicate thread. He felt the tension from Chamber looking over his shoulder; the tension of his job hanging in the balance; the tension from the team trying but falling short; the tension between himself and Robin trying to hold it together; the tension of wanting to do right for Brandi—and other tensions. The other tensions trickled inside of him; the undercurrent that pulled him down. Occasionally he allowed them to poke through into his consciousness. The tension of his two worlds colliding—Newark and Easton; the tension of his old life and his new. Underneath it all, he could feel the magnetic pull of his past, drawing him to Lillian. He tried to bury it, but it just kept resurfacing. He even considered a visit to Sarah the therapist, but he did not have the confidence in her to help him sort it out.

Friday morning rolled around; William, Robin and Brandi enjoyed one of their more pleasant breakfasts together, but William felt himself drifting away. Robin felt it, too. He saw Savior's face in front of him, then Lillian's. Finally, Brandi pulled him back to the breakfast table.

"Daddy, we have no school today. It's teacher's convention, or something like that. Can I come visit you at work today? Please, can I?"

"Sure, sure; if mommy wants to bring you. That'll be fine," William stroked her chin and put his finger to her lips. Brandi kissed it, turning to Robin.

"Please mommy, can we visit daddy at work later? We can have lunch at the college cafeteria, okay?"

Robin curled her arm around Brandi, patting her shoulder.

"That sounds like a good idea. Now, give daddy a big hug and a kiss before he leaves for work."

Brandi jumped on William's lap and kissed his cheek. He winked at Robin, stood up and lowered Brandi to the floor.

"See you later girls," William kissed Robin and left the house.

He had planned to drill the team hard that day, but sometimes plans have to change. After sorting through the pile of mail on his desk, he reviewed the videotapes of the season's games. Diligently, he went back over every play, reversing the tape, freezing it and analyzing each player's every move. He hardly noticed the time. Suddenly, the phone on his desk rang with a harsh sound, interrupting his note taking. He lifted the receiver. He recognized the voice, as broken up as it was. He felt a pall come over him. Hunched over his desk, he didn't even notice Robin and Brandi at first, as they entered his office.

"Okay, I'll see you tomorrow," the words fell out of his mouth with great effort and sadness.

The phone still glued to his ear, William stared at Robin; she stared back at him as he continued his conversation.

"Okay; me, too."

He let the receiver drop onto the cradle of his office phone.

"Me, too what?" Robin demanded, glaring at William.

"Robin, Coach has died," William replied, his voice flat.

"Who was that?" Robin pursed her lips, her hands on her hips defensively.

"Did you hear what I just said?" William furrowed his brow, annoyed at her.

"Brandi, go to the pool; I'll meet you there soon," Robin commanded.

"Can I go swimming?" Brandi's eyes lit up.

"No!" Robin and William retorted in unison, sharing a moment of unity.

"Okay, okay," Brandi acknowledged, skipping out in her usual fashion.

"I want you to come with me tomorrow to the wake," William looked up from his desk at Robin.

Robin relaxed her posture, drew a breath, but continued to fight something inside of herself as she spoke.

"Who was that on the phone?"

"A friend," William responded coolly.

"An old girlfriend?" Robin could not hold back her suspicions.

"Is this where you want to go? I just found out Chamber can't get a penny more for Savior," William scowled at Robin.

"Yes, this is more important," Robin leaned over the desk, confronting William.

William threw his arms up in frustration. Robin walked around the desk, standing over him and leaned against his shoulder. She dropped her voice and spoke softly, struggling to get the words out.

"I love you. Don't you understand? And I'm scared if you go…"

Robin turned away, fighting off her tears.

"That's why I want you to come with me. And Brandi," William implored.

"Lillian is an old girlfriend?" Robin inquired, wiping a solitary tear.

"So what? That was twenty years ago," William shook his head, sighing.

"Just be honest with me," Robin straightened up.

William banged on his desk.

"If I can't get Savior I'm toast here. I'm gone," William stammered, frustrated.

"I don't care," Robin grabbed his hand and stared into his eyes.

"I care," William shot back, rising from his chair to comfort her with a hug.

"You need to trust me," William urged.

"Just don't ask me to move to Newark," Robin begged him.

Just then Savior stuck his head in.

"I can come back later," he darted a glance from William to Robin.

"Come meet my wife, Robin," William beckoned him in.

Savior politely extended his hand and Robin clasped it between both of her hands, feeling the massiveness of it. She smiled at him warmly.

"I hope to see you here next year," Robin said.

"Me, too. It's really nice to meet you, Mrs. Cunningham," Savior replied sincerely.

William, surprised, nodded at Savior as he left the office.

"Polite young man," Robin remarked to William.

"He's our future," William stated.

"*We're* our future," Robin responded, holding both of William's hands in her own.

"I've got to get this kid home. I'll see you and Brandi at dinner tonight," William embraced Robin, reassuring her.

William found Savior with Ritchie and Gordon in the parking lot outside the gym, waiting by his Subaru. They took off, whizzing down Route 78, headed for Newark. This time, William left the car radio off again. He searched Savior for any sign at all. He knew something happened during that visit. He somehow felt just that much closer to Savior. Finally, they came down the ramp onto McCarter Highway and began to wind down the streets of Newark. The city seemed very much alive at that moment. William felt its pulse—and its draw. He pulled up in front of Savior's house. Savior appeared deep in thought.

"You coming, Coach?" he asked as he unbuckled his seatbelt.

"I'll come by later this week," William answered.

"Okay," Savior replied.

William waited a moment.

"What do you think?" William asked nervously.

"It's not what I expected," Savior responded.

"Yeah, it's not Syracuse or Kentucky," William acknowledged.

"It's better," Savior answered, to William's amazement.

"I think so, " William nodded.

"Yeah," Savior smiled back at him.

After a moment of silence, Savior opened the door.

"Later," Savior waved back at William as he headed up the walkway to the house.

William watched him enter the house, then drove off.

William returned to Easton, ran the team through a practice, but decided against running them too hard. After practice, he finished reviewing the videotapes for the season, packed up his briefcase and headed home to a quiet, but somewhat tense dinner with Robin and Brandi. He left Robin to getting Brandi ready for bed. Somehow he still felt the wall between himself and Robin, even though they had both communicated their deepest concerns and fears honestly and openly. He just didn't have it in him to face another confrontation. He felt the love, but not the understanding he needed. He wondered if he had gotten back what he put out—love without understanding. The laws of the universe always prevail, he thought, in a rare philosophical moment. Robin just didn't understand his world. Maybe he didn't understand hers. Somewhere, there had to be a place that was their world. He felt as if he had lost that place.

William sank into the living room couch, oblivious to whatever Robin and Brandi were doing upstairs. He picked up the TV remote, began to flip through the channels and quickly felt the tension of the day overwhelm him, as it turned to fatigue. He turned the TV off, put down the remote and lay down on the couch, still fully dressed. In seconds, he drifted off to sleep. He quickly slipped into a dream landscape of his own making. All the issues of the day appeared, as if they comprised a newscast. He saw himself visiting Izza Morgan, the wise, influential teacher who had always challenged his intellect. Now, each newscast in his dreamscape mirrored the classic conflicts. He saw himself in full gladiator dress, battling Chamber Higgins. He could practically feel the blood flowing from him as Chamber cut him with his sword. Izza, dressed Elizabethan style, gave the commentary, like a play-by-play announcer, citing this scene as "man versus man." Suddenly, L.J. appeared, battering William's shield with powerful blows. Next, the scene changed and William found himself in a rumbling earthquake. The ground beneath him shook and split. He had one leg in Easton, the other leg in Newark. The chasm widened. Izza, still appearing Shakespearian, proclaimed this as "man versus nature." Instantly, William found himself alone in an arid desert. The sands whirled around him. He could not see her, but he could hear Izza's voice as he struggled with himself—whether he could coach in "the hood" of Newark, live in the White world, coaching in Easton and doing right by his family. Then, he saw Lillian coming toward him, appearing as a Nubian princess. As she approached, he reached for her and she dissipated into desert sand.

William awoke to Robin's hand gently shaking his shoulder. She put her finger to her lips to let him know that Brandi was asleep and led him upstairs.

CHAPTER 56

THE DEVIL AND THE ANGEL WITHIN US

Sometimes the most somber occasions bring out the best in us. Sometimes they bring out the beast in us. William knew he had to return to Newark to pay his respects to Coach, one of the first people who believed in him enough to show him how to rise above his circumstances. There was no separating Newark from Lillian. William knew this. He knocked on her door. In minutes, they walked the street, arm in arm, reminiscing.

"Remember when he caught us in the Boys Club?" Lillian mused.

"Coach, he thought they were gonna lynch me," William chuckled at the memory.

"He was gonna do it himself," Lillian couldn't hold back her laughter.

"It's gotten better," William confided.

"But still easier to marry a Black girl. You love her?" Lillian queried.

A silent moment passed between them.

"If you thought much in Izza's class you would have gotten an "A,"" Lillian offered.

"You confuse me; you always did," William shook his head.

"Want to make it easy?" Lillian challenged him.

They stopped walking outside Saint Benedict's abbey.

"Catch me first," Lillian threw down the gauntlet, as she scooted behind the abbey.

William sprinted after her as she headed toward a soccer field. William could not close the gap. He squeezed his knees and gasped for breath. Lillian kicked off her shoes, prancing across the grass—an oasis in the midst of an urban desert. Finally, William joined her, catching his breath.

"Making it easy, are you?" he asked.

"You're too old for me," she responded playfully.

William surprised her, tackling her to the grass. They both rolled around, laughing. As their eyes met, they kissed.

"This feels good," William acknowledged.

"This feels right," Lillian added.

"Tell me what I already know," William answered.

Lillian rolled away from him, still lying on the grass.

"So you'll stay for him?" Lillian caught him with her gaze, wide-eyed.

"Lillian…I have a wife and a child," William responded.

"Oh, you need a family to care for; I can give you that. Want a guarantee? I can do that, too. I love you, always have. And I'll love you forever. Twenty years has not dimmed that light one bit," Lillian proclaimed.

"Is he—"

"It's not about him! It's about *me*! And what *I* need…" Lillian nearly shouted the words at William.

Lillian buried her head in her hands. He had never seen this vulnerable side of her. The façade had broken and revealed her raw emotions. He felt compelled to respond.

"My feelings for you have never changed from the first time I kissed you at the freshman formal," William admitted.

They held each other for what seemed like a long time before leaving the soccer field. Both Lillian and William felt the strain from the weight of their emotions bearing down on them as they headed down the street.

The crowd packed the McCabe Funeral home. Several of the high powered college basketball coaches stood on line to pay their respects— Bob Hurley, Pete Carril, Bob Farrell and Milt Gaylord. William led Robin and Brandi inside. As soon as they entered, Tricks approached William and hugged him. Distraught, he could barely keep his composure as he turned to Robin.

"You must be Robin. Thank you so much for coming," he said, then turned his attention to Brandi, studying her closely.

"I see your mother in her," Tricks asserted.

"I was hoping. I look at her sometimes and see that look," William confided as Tricks smiled.

"I know that look; it's nice to see it again," Tricks replied.

William flashed Tricks a look telegraphing a message that this would be brutal as Lillian entered the room, stunning, dressed all in black. She held the hand of her ten year-old niece Sophia. Passing right by Robin and William, she squatted down to Brandi and gave her a white rose.

"Just because the grown-ups are sad doesn't mean a sweet young girl needs to be," Lillian offered.

"Come with me. There are other kids here, too," Sophia urged Brandi.

Sophia and Brandi ran off, leaving the room full of mourners. Just then Lillian faced Robin and extend her hand in a formal manner, almost coldly.

"Thank you for coming," Lillian said.

"And you are?" Robin responded, equally coolly.

"I'm sorry; Lillian. I thought Willie Joe might have mentioned—"

"Willie Joe? You mean William," Robin responded as if she had to protect her territory.

Lillian forced a tight-lipped smile.

"You're lucky to have one of Newark's best sons," Lillian answered.

"I know," Robin asserted.

Lillian nearly smirked at Robin, sauntered over to William and hugged him tightly. She then led him by the arm into the wake. Robin fumed, ready to scream, but Tricks intervened.

"Coach asked that William and Lillian receive the mourners. It was his wish," Tricks appealed to her.

Everyone crowded into the chapel as little Sophia walked up to the podium next to Coach's casket and sang "Amazing Grace." William and Lillian stood in front of the casket as the long line of mourners filed past, offering their condolences. Robin sat a few rows back, still fuming. Brandi rejoined her, hiding her eyes from the dead body in the open casket at the front of the room. One of the mourners, an elderly woman, stopped to spend a moment with William and Lillian.

"It's so nice to see you two together after all these years," she stated.

As she left, Lillian put her arm around William and ran her nails over his back. Seeing this, Robin bolted up, pulling Brandi to her side. They both shouldered their way out of the wake. The sound of Robin's heels pounding the tile floor broke the momentary silence as heads turned to see them disappear from the room.

Walter Townes

William slipped out, catching up to Robin and Brandi as they rushed down the block.

"How dare you insult me like that?" Robin choked on the words.

"What did I do?" William confronted her.

"You know what *she* did," Robin snarled back at him.

"We are all very upset," William tried to console her as Brandi cried.

"Come here sweetheart," William implored, as Robin caught a cab.

"It's okay; I'll be home soon," William assured her as Robin forced Brandi into the taxi.

"Don't call that home. This is your home. Always was, always will be," Robin asserted.

"Stop it, Robin," William replied.

"Go. Don't keep your girlfriend waiting too long, Willie Joe. She's upset —your Black girlfriend...how could you do this to me?" Robin shouted as she slammed the taxi door and it pulled away.

CHAPTER 57

DRAWING BACK THE CURTAIN

The strain of losing Coach played upon William. Heaped on top of it, the prospect of losing Robin weighed heavily upon him. Add to that his conflicted feelings between the two worlds of Newark and Easton, along with his smoldering love for Lillian, and William felt like collapsing. But he didn't. Something deep down inside of him kept him going—perhaps the compulsion to see it all through. He felt he needed to go down the road and discover where it would take him. The gnawing question always boiled down to this—did he learn anything from his journey, from his experiences? He could not shake the picture from his mind of Robin leaving him behind.

Finally, William mustered up the resolve to do what he knew he needed to do. All the mourners had long since departed when he pulled past the gates of Calvary Cemetery. William looked around. Dusk had begun to fall. He approached Coach's grave, bowed his head and folded his hands in front of him. Slowly, he lifted his head and addressed his fallen mentor.

"What should I do, Coach? I don't belong there. Who am I kidding? I'm not a White man," he shook his head.

Just then, a White man about seventy years old, dressed in a trench coat, stood next to William. Although he felt the man's presence, William remained silent for a while. Finally, he spoke up.

"You know Coach?" he turned to the man.

"What do you expect him to say, he's dead?" The man chided William.

"Excuse me?" William inquired, quizzically.

"If he were alive, he might say to you, 'Open your eyes, see things as they are. Embrace what you have,'" the man spoke in an almost consoling tone.

"Been doing that all my life," William responded in a loud whisper, his voice cracking.

"Have you?" the man queried, not convinced.

"Who are you?" William finally demanded, insistently.

"You are provoked by the situation you are in. But the situation can't hurt you. It's your interpretation of the situation that matters. *That* you can control," he pronounced each word slowly, with a steady assurance that confirmed he knew a truth.

Finally, his words struck a chord in William, who now paid rapt attention to the man.

"You sound like Coach," William admitted in hushed tones.

"I should. I'm his brother, Vernon," the man conceded.

William slid him a look of extreme surprise.

"My family adopted him as a little boy. Not easy on us or on him. But he always wanted to give something back to his roots," Vernon confided to William.

William extended his hand in gratitude, now with a newfound respect for this stranger, and Vernon clasped his hand firmly. William instantly felt the warmth emanating from Vernon as he addressed him.

"Pleasure to meet you."

"He mentioned you. Had quite a liking for you," Vernon smiled gently, digging his hands into his coat pockets.

"Feeling was mutual. He wanted me to take over for him," William replied, staring down at Coach's grave.

"Maybe, maybe not," Vernon responded.

"I don't follow," William searched Vernon's face for an explanation.

"What's right for him might not be right for you. This place defined him.

What defines you?" Vernon queried.

"Father, husband, Coach," William replied sullenly after a long, contemplative pause.

"You are a happy man, then," Vernon asserted, smiling.

"But it's at a —"

"White school? How does that void who you are?" Vernon pressed William.

"It doesn't," William agreed after another long, thoughtful pause.

Vernon extended his hand again and shook William's hand firmly, with the same conviction his words carried.

"Then enjoy your life. It goes quicker than you think," Vernon affirmed.

Once more, Vernon approached his brother's grave, stopped, kissed his hand and patted the tombstone. He then shuffled away slowly, leaving William alone in the dark.

Where to now? William backed the Subaru out of the cemetery gates and headed to the one place he knew he would feel welcome. Lillian greeted him at the door of her condo, smiled and beckoned him in. They did not need to exchange words. She quietly slipped into the kitchen, returning with two cold bottles of beer. They both sank into the sofa and cracked open the beers in unison. William stretched his legs out. Lillian gently patted his shoulder.

"Glad you came," she confided.

"Where was Savior today?" William inquired, still not seeing any sign of him.

"Basketball tournament. Where else?" Lillian responded.

William nodded, pleased that Savior had not avoided Coach's funeral.

They both sipped their beers silently. Then Lillian spoke.

"Where will you go tonight?" she asked, leaning her chin on William's shoulder.

"I was just wondering about that," William admitted, exhaling with a long breath.

"Stay here," Lillian urged, reaching out her hand to William.

"Love me, Willie Joe," she begged.

Instinctively, he slid closer to her, his hands raking over her breasts as he kissed her passionately. Suddenly, he jumped up from the sofa.

"Love me. We both need it," Lillian pressed him, grabbing his hand.

"I know. I'm..."

Lillian stood up, knowing the moment had passed. She strode into the kitchen, laying her beer on the counter. She rejoined him. Perched on the arm of the sofa, she spoke to William.

"I'm okay now. You've been through more than me today."

Lillian pointed to the room at the end of the hallway.

"That's your room for tonight. We'll evaluate again tomorrow or the next day. You're welcome to stay as long as you like," she said matter-of-factly.

"Lillian…" William called to her as she turned, reached into the kitchen and picked up her beer, then left the room and disappeared into her bedroom.

William nodded, confused and withdrew two more beers from the refrigerator. He slumped down on the sofa, cracked open one of the beers and took a long draught. He debated with himself, conflicted over whether to go to sleep at that moment or not. Finally, he picked up the remote control and began flipping through the channels of Lillian's TV. Something stopped him. His favorite movie, "The Godfather," was playing. William sat back and let the familiar scenes unfold. His eyes grew heavy once again, but he did not succumb to the temptation to sleep. As the film drew to a close, he once again viewed the scene with Michael in the church. He knew at that moment, like this character, and exactly as Coach's brother Vernon told him, he must also face each of his challenges with each of the people in his life. Then, peacefully, he fell into a deep sleep.

Life always goes on, whether you're there to participate in it or not. So, too, with college. Gordon committed himself to the team, to his studies and to the all-American past time of pursuing the women on the Easton Campus. He and Avery had begun to spend a lot of time together. They began a leisurely stroll across campus, his arm wrapped tightly around her waist, when he noticed Chamber Higgins walking side by side with a Black man he had never seen before. It grabbed his attention as he observed them entering the gym. He spun Avery around to face him.

"I need to go in there," he insisted.

"I'm going with you," she tossed her hair back in a gesture of defiance.

"You can't. I might get in trouble," Gordon twirled a lock of her hair as he looked into her eyes.

"We're in college. Now is the time to get in trouble," Avery dared him, sliding his hand across her breast.

Gordon knew there was no winning with her, so they entered the building through the side door. The entire building looked empty until Chamber and the stranger walked onto the gym floor, stopped in mid-court and looked around. Gordon and Avery peered through the door as soon as the two men turned their backs.

"We are looking to double the size to seventy-five hundred," Chamber announced, his voice echoing.

"You better have a good team," the other man asserted.

"That's where you come in," Chamber assured him.

"That's what I do..." the man replied confidently, as he walked to the sideline.

Gordon and Avery had slipped into the gym and hidden beneath the bleachers. They whispered to one another, barely able to conceal their amazement at what they had heard.

"They're getting rid of your coach?" Avery asked.

"Sure looks like it," Gordon acknowledged.

Chamber approached the man, standing at the sidelines.

"How does it feel, Breezy?"

"It will feel better when it's mine," Breezy replied.

"When we don't make the dance this year, William is gone," Chamber assured Breezy.

"You still have a chance," Breezy turned to face Chamber.

"Trust me, he's lost them," Chamber remarked.

"He can coach. And even *I* can't win without players," Breezy acknowledged.

Chamber chuckled, then answered him.

"He brought Savior Ruffin for a visit."

Breezy cut Chamber with a sharp look.

"Savior Ruffin? He got Savior Ruffin to burn a visit on Easton?" Breezy's nostrils flared as he spoke.

"If he could interest a kid like Savior, I expect no less of you," Chamber challenged Breezy.

"Savior Ruffin will be a lottery pick if he goes to college or not," Breezy asserted.

"I told him Easton doesn't offer full rides," Chamber replied.

"If I could get Savior Ruffin, I'd pay him out of my own pocket," Breezy replied.

"Let's not worry about what's not gonna happen," Chamber bellowed.

"If I do come here, I can't win without players," Breezy confronted Chamber.

"With your reputation, I'll have more leverage convincing the powers that be to do what it takes for you to build Easton into a powerhouse," Chamber barked with all the bravado he could muster.

"Right," Breezy laughed.

Gordon and Avery watched the two men exit the gym, waited and then quietly slid out the side door. They hoofed across campus until they were out of breath. As they entered the quad of dormitories, Avery stopped Gordon in his tracks, spun him around to face her and confronted him.

"What are you gonna do?"

"Don't know," Gordon shook his head, shifting his weight from one leg to the other, confused.

"I mean, let's not overreact. Schools change coaches all the time. So what?" Avery asked.

"He's my coach. You wouldn't understand what that means," Gordon answered, excitedly.

"Excuse *me*," Avery dug her heels in, hands on her hips.

"Whatever," Gordon responded, frustrated.

"You're not gonna do something *stupid*, are you?" Avery grabbed Gordon's shirtsleeve.

"If not now, when?" Gordon shot back at her.

CHAPTER 58

TIME TO CHOOSE

William awoke with a start, taking in the unfamiliar surroundings of Lillian's guest room. A single shaft of light penetrated the half-open curtains. He struggled to focus his eyes as he rolled out of bed and stepped into the pants he had left on the side chair. Shuffling into the kitchen, he found coffee and bagels awaiting him, topped by a hand-written note. The note brought a smile to his face.

"Help yourself to everything. Dinner at seven? Love, Lillian."

Just then Savior shuffled out of his bedroom, eying William.

"This is a first," he remarked flatly.

"Your mother and I…" William began.

"Yeah…" Savior cut him off, grabbing a bagel.

"I heard good things about Coach McLeod," William offered.

"Whatever," Savior grumbled.

"Is that a sentence?" William shot back at him.

Savior snapped a defiant look at William.

"Only my mother tells me how to talk and she ain't here."

"You listen to your coach," William admonished him.

"And he ain't my father," Savior responded coolly.

"Not a morning person?" William fired back at Savior.

"What you doing here? She's gonna *make* me play for you," Savior responded, deeply annoyed.

William softened as he poured his coffee.

"Look, son—"

"I ain't your son. You can start telling me what to do October fifteen. You can go home to your white-ass neighborhood now. You got what you came for last night," Savior snarled.

William pounced, slamming Savior against the wall, holding him there with a forearm under his neck.

"I don't like what you are implying. We are only thinking about your future and what's best for you," William growled at Savior.

Savior showed no sign of fear or hurt, only boredom, as William released his vice-like grip on him. Savior ambled over to the kitchen counter, grabbed another bagel and left the house. William sank into a kitchen chair, burying his head in his hands for a long moment. He looked at his watch and knew he had to head back to Easton. The trip seemed endless. He didn't even turn on the car radio once.

Back on the Easton campus, Gordon had gathered his team in the gym. Avery sat on the bleachers, watching intently. Gordon stood center court as Chamber Higgins approached him with his usual swagger.

"Where's your coach?" Chamber queried.

Gordon just stared at Chamber for a moment, and then sprinted back to mid-court, addressing his teammates.

"Those who want to join me, do it now."

The rest of the team sprinted over to Gordon, surrounding him in a circle. He held his place and continued,

"All those in the circle are a family. All those in the circle are ready to fight. All those outside the circle will never be admitted."

Gordon leveled his gaze at Chamber and raised his clenched fist in the air. One by one the other players followed suit, raising their clenched fists in the air. Just then, William entered the gym. Witnessing the team's actions, he immediately comprehended and embraced the show of loyalty. He sprinted over to the circle, standing next to Gordon and raised his own clenched fist.

"This is a closed practice; only family allowed," William asserted.

"You can close it, but I'll tell you something..." Chamber began, but the players started to whoop it up while jogging in place, drowning Chamber out. Chamber managed a nod, the only gesture he could make, and left the gym.

William proudly walked up to each player as the noise died down, touching his forehead to theirs. Finally, he approached Gordon. Before he could make a move, Gordon hugged him tightly. We all experience defining moments in our lives. William would hold this one in his memory for as long as he lived. Nobody could have paid him a greater tribute than these young men did. He just stood there taking it in as his team members dispersed, leaving him alone to ponder his future.

Still living in two worlds, the clouds of confusion had begun to disperse. William wondered if he could ever really bridge the two worlds of Newark and Easton. No matter. He knew what he needed to do next. He turned the Subaru around and headed back to Newark. Parking the car, he walked through the doorway of his old home away from home, remembering all of the familiar sights, sounds and smells of the Boys and Girls Club. He saw no one. Pushing open the gym door, he found Tricks sleeping off a drunken stupor at mid-court. Approaching him with disdain, he kicked his old friend in an effort to wake him. Tricks awoke, angry and disoriented.

"Don't you have a home any more?" William chided him.

"What? How'd you get in? What are you doin' here?" Tricks grumbled at William.

"It's time for you to do something with your life," William reproached him.

"I just woke up," Tricks replied, stretching his arms over his head and attempting to stand up without wobbling.

"You've been sleeping all your life," William stated.

"Look at yourself. Who the hell are you to talk?" Tricks lazily replied, still in slow motion.

"Someone that is not gonna take over this club. You are. So start acting like it," William affirmed.

Tricks rubbed the sleep out of his eyes, let out a final yawn and looked William in the eye as he replied,

"What? I can't—"

"Yes you can. Coach even said so," William glared at him.

"Now I know you're lying," Tricks grinned at William, shifting his weight from one leg to the other like a petulant child.

William slowly shook his head, signifying "no."

"C'mon. Look at me," Tricks insisted, incredulous.

William leaned over and shook Tricks as he confronted him.

"That's right, look at you. I'm leaving and never coming back. It's on you to make this club work; make it become what it once was. You can do it. You're too good of a man to fail. These kids need you like I needed Coach."

Tricks turned and picked up a ball, began to dribble and challenged William.

"One more game."

Holding his place, William shook his head, "no." Then he walked over to Tricks and hugged him for what they both knew would be the last time ever.

The afternoon sun poked its way through the buildings as William drove back to the projects. He braved the foreboding neighborhood, with its gang graffiti, broken glass and impending air of hopelessness. Finding his way to the tiny fenced-in, concrete court where Savior played his game of street ball, he spied L.J. and went right up to him. L.J.'s thugs laughed.

"Man is in my face," L.J. piped up.

"I'm not playing that game," William stared him down.

"I'm the only game that matters," L.J. adjusted his shades.

"I love that boy. I *was* that boy. And because of guys like you our kids are in trouble," William sneered at him.

"You still trying to get Savior to Easton. It's coaches like you that are killing our kids. You don't care about them. You only care about the record they bring you," L.J. snorted back, spinning around and slamming fists with one of his thugs.

"Savior can go pro right now. It don't matter where he goes. So tell me, what are *you* doing for him?" William challenged L.J.

"Protecting him," L.J. responded coolly, placing his hands in his jacket pockets.

"From who? People like you?" William countered, taking a step closer to L.J.

"This is Newark," L.J. shot back.

"Yeah, and you make them pay forever," William stared him down.

"He's gonna be rich," L.J. replied, shrugging his shoulders.

"What about those that don't make it?" William leaned in, pointing to one of L.J.'s thugs.

"What about you? I bet you were a player?" William continued.

Sleeper-Z looked away, uncomfortable with the direction the conversation had taken. L.J. advanced, getting in William's face.

"You can hurt me all you want. I'm asking you to leave Savior alone. He doesn't need you," William asserted.

L.J. stared at William for what seemed like an eternity.

"Let him go, L.J." Sleeper-Z shouted from across the court.

L.J. continued staring; then, he looked away.

"Get out of here before I change my mind," L.J. barked back at William.

"You're better than this, L.J. You got brains. Use them. Trust them," William nodded to him.

"Go home," L.J. answered, and watched William leave.

"I'm going home," one of L.J.'s thugs said, turning and leaving. L.J. stood and watched, as his crew dispersed, one by one.

Miles away in the quiet suburbs of Easton, life went on, oblivious to the urban blight and the street crime. Robin and Brandi sat on the living room couch watching "It's a Wonderful Life" on television.

"Don't we usually watch this at Christmas?" Brandi asked.

"That's right," Robin replied.

"Then why are we watching it now?" Brandi asked.

"Because it makes me feel good," Robin answered as she placed a bowl of fresh popcorn on the coffee table.

Brandi watched quietly, then turned to Robin.

"I like it when he remembers Zuzu's petals," she offered.

Robin brought Brandi closer to her, stroking her ponytails.

"Me too," Robin smiled back at Brandi.

William had one more task to complete before he left Newark. He sat in his car, parked on the street, staring straight ahead as he prepared himself. Then, he approached Lillian's front door. As he entered, Lillian displayed an ebullient mood. She playfully tossed William the keys. William, like a missile, turned straight to Savior, chilling out on the couch.

"Told you, I'm going to Easton," Savior pre-empts him.

"No you are not. There is no offer," William stares him down.

Savior jumped up from the couch, irritated.

"What did I do?" he asked.

"You did nothing wrong," William assured him.

"Savior isn't going to Easton," William turned to face Lillian, who appeared shocked.

"What? Did you tell him, Savior, I made my decision?" Lillian stammered.

"It's not your call. It's mine," William turned to face Lillian, who seemed confused and shaken.

"Wait, have something to drink," she responded, in a conciliatory tone.

"I need to go. I'm here to tell you Easton is not the place for your son. Go to Syracuse or Georgia Tech. Paul Hewitt is used to handling kids like Savior. He'll take care of him. Hell, he'll probably go number one," William responded.

"You said *you'd* take care of him," Lillian's voice quivered as she confronted William.

"He'd be a fish out of water at Easton. These kids learn to take care of money they already have," William replied.

"I'll have money one day," Savior offered.

"And you deserve whatever you can get. And listen to me. You be proud of who you are," William insisted.

Lillian, visibly upset, sank into the couch.

"If this is because of what happened today—" Savior interjected.

"No, it's not," William countered.

"Then tell me why. You owe her," Savior raised his voice, looking at Lillian, crying.

"Cause there's nothing left for me to do that she hasn't already done. Savior, you will always be in my life. You don't have to be my star player," William replied.

Savior looked over at Lillian, and then turned to William.

"This is bull…"

Savior slammed the door, leaving the house.

Lillian began to tear up, approaching William and tugged at his sleeve.

"You can still come to visit us, right?"

William slowly removed her hand and looked her in the eye.

"I already have a wife," he answered.

Lillian felt his words sting her and blocked his path.

"Whoa, whoa, what's changed?" she pressed him.

"I have. And so have you," William replied.

"I'm the same girl you've always known," Lillian insisted, wiping a tear with her finger.

William drew himself up to his full height and addressed her.

"That girl doesn't exist any more. That girl wanted to be a principal. This girl is a Vice-President."

"And I know a boy that wanted to be a pro and is now a coach and will be a hero to kids that need him," Lillian fired back at William.

Exasperated, William grabbed Lillian and confronted her, face to face.

"I'm a hero cause I left. You want me to come back? That's not a hero, that's a fool," he shot back.

"Then I guess I'm a fool," Lillian responded, crestfallen.

Her words hit him hard. William held Lillian at arm's length and confronted her once again.

"Listen to me. We are both heroes. You escaped Newark and found a way to stay here."

Waving his arms around her beautiful condo, he motioned as he spoke.

"Look at this place. How many people live like this? Now all you need is a family."

William steadied himself as he looked into Lillian's eyes, softening his voice.

"I have a family. And I'm going back to it. If they'll have me." Lillian held his gaze, doing all she could to keep back more tears.

"Do you want the truth about Savior? Will that make you stay?" she beseeched him.

"I already know the truth. Savior is your son," William replied.

"Willie Joe…" Lillian pleaded.

"My name is William," he answered, turned and headed for the door without looking back.

A certain knowing had washed over him—a wave of knowledge and insight that told him, even tugged at him. If Savior was his son, William needed to do what was best for Savior; that would ultimately be best for himself, as well. He made his connection with his son and that mattered most. The knowing told him that the caring for Savior would last. William searched the Newark skyline for the last time. If Savior had gone to Easton, Lillian would remain in his life. Torn between two worlds, he had to choose. He chose Robin and Brandi a long time ago. A man has to stick to his choices.

William fired up the noisy Subaru, wound around the street corners, never looking back as he left Newark behind him. This time he punched the buttons on the radio, listening to the newscast, skipping over the sportscast. He listened intently to the President's speech about the war dead. He could not support this team. This time the road seemed to glide past him. Miles of asphalt on Interstate 78 disappeared behind him. William felt elated. He was going home. He had no idea what would happen, but he knew he must.

Night had already fallen when William pulled into his driveway. He heard the faint sound of birds chirping in the distance, a dog barking and nothing else but his own footsteps after he closed the car door. He slipped the key in the door and walked across the threshold. Robin and Brandi stopped cleaning up the dinner dishes and waited for him. He entered the kitchen, looked at each of them and spoke.

"I've got a job to do here—not at Easton—*right here*. I will never see Newark again."

Robin covered her mouth to conceal her cry, but could not stop her tears from flowing. Brandi glanced over at Robin, ran to a flowerpot, plucked a few petals from the flower, ran to William and placed them in his pocket. William leaned over, hugged her and asked,

"What's this for?"

"You came home," Brandi replied.

All three of them embraced one another, and then ascended the stairs as Brandi recounted the events of her day, clutching William's hand. Robin leaned her head against William's shoulder as they reached the top of the staircase. William turned to face her.

"Thank you; thank you for just being you."

A man needs to know the real meaning of home. Sometimes he takes a wrong turn, but he still finds his way there. Getting lost is part of the journey. A woman who understands men knows this. For some, there are more wrong turns than for others. But most of us do find our way. William and Robin both slept soundly that night, knowing the real meaning of home. William dreamt. The old dreams came back, but they were different this time. He saw his mother in the hospital bed on the basketball court. But this time she smiled at him. He saw the circle of fatherless Black children surrounded by men. But this time Savior stepped out of the circle, began to play ball and the other children followed him. He saw Sarah the therapist naked on the beach, but he did not approach her. He turned away and found Robin waiting for him. William remembered years ago studying the ancient wisdom of the Hindu Bhagavad-Gita. He remembered the line that read, "All is as it should be." And the dreams evaporated.

After a full day on campus, the Easton team hit the court for one of their most crucial games. At half time, William entered the locker room to face his players. Several of them were sweat-soaked.

"Make sure you D-up, number 32. Remember; run high picks, look for back doors. They're lazy," he cautioned, then began slapping his hands together in rhythm. He went on to instruct them.

"Play like you asked the prettiest girl to dance and she said 'yes.' The hard part is over."

After the team filed out, Gordon and William slapped hands. Winning is about spirit, not about technique. William remembered the days when Coach taught him how to play his game in his head. It always worked better that way. He taught his players the same way. And it worked for them. There would be many more wins.

When there is a shift in the great consciousness, everyone feels it, everywhere. A favorite son had left Newark, but not until he left his mark on Newark. Even Tricks had felt the awakening and knew he would now find his calling. He gathered up the last of his discarded beer bottles and placed them into a large plastic garbage bag, dragging them out the back door of the Boys and Girls Club, to the dumpster, as the kids began to stream in to the gym. He turned to them.

"I'll be right there," he assures them.

After he returned, a deliveryman with a hand truck entered the gym with two huge corrugated cartons. Tricks signed for them as the kids circled around him, curious. Opening the boxes, Tricks stared inside, wide-eyed. The boxes were packed full of Nike sneakers and Easton shorts and tee shirts. The kids went wild. Tricks dropped to the bench, put his hands together and prayed, never taking his eyes off of the kids. Yes, there is a God and he lives wherever He is needed the most.

ABOUT THE AUTHORS...

Walter Townes, a native of Queens, NY, has proven himself in both the business and the sports worlds. This book—and the resulting future film, is his first effort into the literary world. Walter has led the charge in team building, serving as a college basketball coach for several prestigious schools. He has coached on all levels ranging from Big East St. Johns under legendary hall of famer Lou Carnesecca, to great academic institutions such as Dartmouth and Columbia University. Walter served as head coach at both Clarkson University and Drew University, also coaching at Rutgers University and College of the Holy Cross. He has recruited and coached numerous players who have gone on to the NBA and to Europe to play professionally.

In addition to his twenty-five years in collegiate athletics, Walt founded and ran community youth development programs and instituted alumni programs for student athletes, as well as developing new classes. He has turned around marginally performing teams that far exceeded their goals. Currently, he serves as Athletic Director fo the Knox School in St. James, New York, where he resides with his wife Kelly and their daughter Jordyn Elisabeth. Walter holds a Bachelor of Science Degree from Clark University, and has done graduate studies in Education Administration at St. Johns University. Although fictionalized, this book is semi-autobiographical in nature. Walt's message focuses on the importance of education—and rising above one's circumstances and humble beginnings.

Barry Cohen has devoted the last 32 years to a career in advertising and public relations. Born in Newark, NJ, he is a cum laude graduate in English from Kean University. He has addressed audiences at trade shows and conferences across the U.S., and contributed to several business and trade publications. Barry has been profiled in numerous publications and interviewed on several major radio stations. This collaboration is his third book. His previous titles include *10 Ways to Screw Up an Ad Campaign*, and *Startup Smarts; The Thinking Entrepreneur's Guide to Starting & Growing Your Business*, both published by Adams Media. In addition, Barry has edited five books for other authors.